THE LIBRARY
ST. MARY'S COLLEGE OF MARYLAND
ST. MARY'S CITY, MARYLAND 20686

Dutch Catholics long constituted by far the most cohesive political subculture in Western Europe. For nearly half a century virtually all Catholics in the Netherlands supported a single political party—the Catholic party—resisting appeals from both the left and the right. Then in the mid-1960s their allegiance began to crumble; by 1972 only a small minority of Dutch Catholics still voted for the party and a few years later it had ceased to exist. This book examines the role of the Dutch Catholic church, and especially of the bishops, in ensuring the solidarity of the Catholic subculture for so many years and, more remarkably, in promoting drastic social and political changes after Vatican II. This development transformed one of the most orthodox churches in Western Europe into the most radical and, as Professor Bakvis demonstrates, led to the decline and fall of the largest political party in the Netherlands. The author also discusses the recent formation of the Christian Democratic party and the impact of John Paul II's pontificate. He has drawn upon interviews with priests and politicians, as well as survey and ecological data, in his portrayal of life inside the Catholic subculture at both the grass-roots and the elite levels. The result is a substantial contribution to our understanding of the interaction of religion and politics in a plural society and the sources of party loyalty and subcultural cohesion.

Herman Bakvis, a Canadian born in the Netherlands, teaches political science and public administration at Dalhousie University.

Herman Bakvis

Catholic Power
in the Netherlands

McGill–Queen's University Press
Kingston and Montreal

© McGill-Queen's University Press 1981

ISBN 0-7735-0361-7

Legal deposit 3rd quarter 1981
Bibliothèque Nationale du Québec

This book has been published with the help
of a grant from the Social Science Federation
of Canada, using funds provided by the Social
Sciences and Humanities Research Council of
Canada.

Design by Naoto Kondo
Printed in Canada

Canadian Cataloguing in Publication Data

Bakvis, Herman, 1948 –
Catholic power in the Netherlands

Bibliography, p.
Includes index.
ISBN 0-7735-0361-7

1. Katholieke Volkspartij – History.   2. Catholics – Netherlands – Political activity – History – 20th century.   3. Christianity and politics – History – 20th century.   4. Netherlands – Politics and government – 1945 –   .   I. Title.
JN5985.C3B2   324.2492'08   C81-094872-9

For Julia

Contents

Tables	ix
Figures	x
Preface	xi

1 Introduction — 1

2 The Dutch Catholic Community: Ethnicity, Ideology, Organization, and Clientele — 10
   1. The Ethnic Dimension — 13
   2. Ideology — 19
   3. Organization — 28
   4. Clientele — 47
   5. Summary — 56

3 Dutch Catholic Politics — 58
   1. The Catholic Party — 59
   2. Mobilization — 78
   3. The Vote — 86
   4. Summary — 95

4 The Theological Revolt and Changes in the Catholic Community — 97
   1. Changes within the Church — 98
   2. Changes in the Clientele — 110
   3. Mobilization — 117

	4. Socio-Economic Organizations and Deconfessionalization	121
	5. Summary	131
5	**The Catholic Party: Decline and Fall, 1963–1980**	133
	1. Organizational Decline	133
	2. The Vote, 1963–1977	146
	3. Summary	172
6	**Conclusion: Political Change and the Future of Catholic Power**	174

Appendixes
| 1 | Interview Procedures | 187 |
| 2 | Aggregate Data and the Catholic Vote | 189 |

Notes	191
Bibliography	219
Index	233

Tables and Figures

Tables

1.1	Parliamentary Election Results, 1946–1977	3
1.2	Percentage of Catholics Preferring KVP by Age, 1970	7
2.1	Reading Preferences by Religion	17
2.2	Recreational Activities by Religion	18
2.3	Catholics per Priest by Country	35
2.4	University Degree Holders by Year by Religion	51
2.5	TV Program Recognition by Broadcasting Organizations	53
2.6	Easter Observance by Diocese, 1956	57
3.1	Type of Organization by Mass Attendance	87
3.2	KVP Vote by Birth Rate by Province, 1952	89
4.1	Position on Celibacy by Age Cohort	107
4.2	Clerical Defection and Recruitment, 1955–1975	109
4.3	Mass Attendance by Age	110
4.4	Attitudes of Dutch Catholics towards Birth Control, 1965 and 1968	115
4.5	Mass Attendance by Year, 1966–1979	117
4.6	Broadcasting Organizational Membership by Year	122
4.7	Trade Union Membership by Year	122
5.1	Vote by Deconfessionalization by Year	148
5.2	Voting Choice by Self-Assigned Social Class, 1970	154
5.3	Voting Choice by Occupational Level, 1970	156
5.4	Voting Choice by Organizational Membership, 1970	156
5.5	Voting Choice by Geographical Mobility, 1970	158
5.6	Voting Choice by Intergenerational Mobility, 1970	160

5.7	Vote by Age Cohort	161
5.8	% KVP Vote by Age by Urbanization	161
5.9	% KVP Vote by Age by North-South	162
5.10	% KVP by Age Cohort by Year	162
5.11	Voting Choice by Attitudes on Social Welfare, 1970	163
5.12	Voting Choice by Political Interest, 1970	164
5.13	Depillarization by Religion	166
5.14	Where Did the Ex-KVP Vote Go?	168
5.15	Where Did the KVP Vote Come From?	169
5.16	Vote in 1970, 1971, and 1972 of Catholics Who Voted KVP in 1967	173
6.1	Vote by Self-Assigned Social Class for Non-KVP/CDA Voting Catholics, 1970 and 1977	181

Figures

1.1	Map of the Netherlands	facing page 1
1.2	Percentage of Catholics Voting for European Catholic Parties	5
3.1	Percentage of Catholics Voting KVP by Context	94
4.1	Dutch Wages and Prices, 1946–1969	111
5.1	Percentage of Catholics Voting KVP by Urbanization	149
5.2	Percentage of Catholics Voting KVP by Region	150
5.3	Percentage of Catholics Voting KVP by Urbanization and Region	151
5.4	Percentage of Catholics Voting KVP by Catholic Concentration, Urbanization, and Region	152

front cover Opening of the Dutch Parliament
back cover Second Chamber of the Dutch Parliament

Preface

This book had its genesis neither in Canada nor in the Netherlands but in Scotland. In Glasgow, in the summer of 1973, while attending a workshop organized by Richard Rose at the University of Strathclyde, I was introduced to Jan Verhoef of Leiden University, who in turn introduced me to the subject of religious parties and political change in the Netherlands. I soon discovered that Dutch Catholics were distinctive not only in their theology but also in their politics. Dutch Catholic politics interested me to the extent that in the summer of 1975 I decided to embark on a full-scale study.

Over the next five years I incurred a great many debts to several individuals and institutions. I would like to acknowledge my obligations. While in the Netherlands, I used the facilities of the Department of Political Science at Leiden University as a base of operations. I am grateful to the chairman of the department, Hans Daalder, for providing me with work space and, more importantly, with invaluable advice. Jan Verhoef made me feel welcome to Leiden in 1976 and again in the spring of 1980. Arend Lijphart, Karl Dittrich, Galen Irwin, Ben Wempe, Rudy Andeweg, Joop van den Berg, and Sonia Hubée-Boonzaaijer also were generous with their help and advice.

Without the cooperation of several Catholic institutions and agencies in the Netherlands this study would not have been possible. The Catholic Social Research Institute (KASKI) in The Hague, under the directorship of B. J. M. Engbersen, let me have access to numerous reports and memoranda. H. van Zoelen of KASKI graciously guided me through the material. Extensive use was made of the archives of the Catholic Documentation Centre at the Catholic University in Nijmegen. The director of the centre, J. Roes, and J. M. G. Thurlings of the Sociology Department at the Catholic University, were most helpful. Executive officers of the major Catholic socio-economic organizations and the Catholic People's Party (KVP) gave several hours of their valuable time to answer my questions. So too did several members of the Dutch clergy.

I am also grateful to those in the Netherlands who aided in arranging interviews, obtaining hard-to-find documents, and searching out obscure newspaper articles and references. They include Frans Kuiper, Hanna Nieboer, Jan Knol, Nico de Voogd, Father van Laer, Father Merckx, Jan Fuchs, Leo de Bruyn of the KVP, and Dirk Kuiper. Paul Lucardie of the Centre for the Study of Dutch Political Parties at Groningen University provided unique insights into the nature of the Dutch New Left. For their valiant efforts in trying to bring my Dutch language skills up to a reasonable level I am indebted to Iete, Maarten, Liddeke, and Enneke Koens. The staffs of the Parliamentary Library in The Hague and the Dutch Central Bureau of Statistics were unfailing in their courtesy and efficiency.

The Workshop on the Low Countries, held at the University of Maryland in the spring of 1975, provided an excellent opportunity for developing and testing important concepts for the study. I would like to thank the organizers, Martin O. Heisler and Val Lorwin of the Universities of Maryland and Oregon respectively, for having invited me.

In the preliminary stages of the project several people helped by commenting on my prospectus and giving encouragement. Among them were Val Lorwin, Phil Goldman, and Bill Irvine of Queen's University, Lise Mounier of the University of Bordeaux, Stephen Milne, Lynda Erickson, Ian Slater, Alan Cairns, and Grace Skogstad, all at the University of British Columbia. Steven Wolinetz of Memorial University acted as an extremely useful critic throughout the research phase. Don Blake and Ken Carty at the University of British Columbia were unusually helpful not only in the early stages but also in providing detailed annotations on the entire first draft of the book. Also much appreciated were comments on later drafts received from Jean Laponce, William Nicholls, Arend Lijphart, Hans Daalder, and an anonymous reader for McGill-Queen's University Press. At the University of Saskatchewan Don Story, David Smith, Jeff Steeves, John Courtney, and Duff Spafford were kind enough to comment on individual chapters.

David J. Elkins, my mentor at the University of British Columbia, helped in numerous ways. His most important contribution was to persuade me at the outset to limit the scope of the study and later to tell me when I was finished. I am most grateful to him for his guidance.

My colleagues at Queen's and Dalhousie provided extensive moral support. For timely advice and encouragement I am especially obliged to Richard Simeon, Ed Black, James Eayrs, and Dale Poel. I owe a considerable debt to Murray Beck, professor emeritus at Dalhousie University, who took time from his own writing to read my manuscript from beginning to end. His detailed commentary was a godsend in helping with the final revisions.

The Political Science Department at Leiden kindly let me take back to Canada a copy of their ecological data file. Joe Houska of the University of California (Berkeley), for his own study, assembled a data set consisting of all Dutch election returns since 1946. I am deeply indebted to him for allowing me to have access to these data. The 1970 and 1971 Dutch election studies were made available through the Inter-University Consortium for Political Research, Ann Arbor, Michigan. The 1977 Dutch election study was made available by courtesy of the Steinmetz Archives, Amsterdam.

The map of the Netherlands (fig. 1.1) is reprinted by permission from *Delta: A Review of Arts, Life, and Thought in the Netherlands* 15, no. 1 (Spring 1972):117.

Lewis James at the University of British Columbia proved to be indispensable when it came to deciphering Dutch code books and merging data sets. Mike Burke assisted with the data analysis. The graphs were expertly drawn by Glen Grismer. Mrs. Mary-Ann Barr and Mrs. Leslie Adamson did an excellent job of typing the final draft. Special thanks are due to the staff of McGill-Queen's University Press, and to E. C. Beer, for their careful editorial work. Their help improved the quality of the book immeasurably.

Others were much less directly involved in the enterprise but played an important role nonetheless by providing aid, comfort, and support at crucial moments. I would like to thank Chris Angenent, Frank Langdon, David Winterford, Terry and Alice O'Hara, and, above all, Julia Eastman and my family on both sides of the Atlantic.

Finally, I would like to express my appreciation for the financial support given by three organizations. The original research was made possible by grants from the Canada Council. A grant from the Research and Development Committee at Dalhousie University enabled me to travel to the Netherlands in the spring of 1980. The book itself has been published with the help of a subvention from the Social Science Federation, using funds provided by the Social Sciences and Humanities Research Council of Canada.

None of the above acknowledgements should be interpreted in any way as an effort to apportion blame. I accept full responsibility for all errors of fact or interpretation.

FIGURE 1.1. Map of the Netherlands

Chapter 1   **Introduction**

The Catholic party* in the Netherlands is unique. From the end of World War I to the mid-1960s, it captured the votes of almost all eligible Catholics—a feat replicated by no other Catholic or Christian Democratic party in Europe.[1] Then a decline set in. By 1972 the party had lost the majority of its supporters. And in the autumn of 1980, the Catholic party—at one time the largest and most important party in the Netherlands, the key element in what Arend Lijphart has called the "politics of elite accommodation"[2]—formally ceased to exist.

How are we to account for this remarkable pattern of political cohesion and then sudden decline? In seeking an explanation one has to look at some of the unique characteristics of Dutch society. However, the specific questions we need to ask in the case of the Catholic party and its supporters are simultaneously universal ones, relevant to an inquiry into political parties and voting behaviour in any context. What role do elites—political, religious, and economic—play in sustaining a political party? Can their actions also lead to its demise? How do changes in social conditions, mass attitudes, or religious life affect voting behaviour? Political stability and change are universal phenomena

*The Catholic party has gone by various names: from 1904 to 1926 it was called the "League of Roman Catholic Electoral Associations" (BRKKV); from 1926 to 1940 (when the party was disbanded because of the German occupation), it was known as the "Roman Catholic State Party" (RKSP); and from 1946 to 1980 it was called the "Catholic People's Party" (KVP). Use of the term Catholic party refers to the party in its entirety. Use of a specific title (e.g., RKSP) means that the reference is only to a particular period.

of which the experience of Dutch Catholics constitutes a particularly interesting and indeed extreme case. For this very reason this study of the Catholic party and the Catholic community in the Netherlands highlights important relationships which may operate at a partially submerged level in countries like Canada, Germany, the United States, and elsewhere.

Let us consider the record of the Dutch Catholic party a little more closely. From 1918, when universal suffrage was introduced, up to and including 1963, the party enjoyed almost perfect electoral stability.[3] For a period of nearly half a century it consistently received between 29 and 32 per cent of the total popular vote. And in every election in this period at least 85 per cent of Catholics, drawn from all classes of Dutch society, voted for the Catholic party. At all times this party played a crucial role in the political life of the Netherlands, being represented in virtually every cabinet and mediating demands from the left and the right. Yet in 1967 the party experienced a sharp decline in support, dropping from 31.9 per cent of the popular vote to 26 per cent. In 1971 its vote fell to 21.9 and in 1972 to 17.7 per cent. Although in 1963 85 per cent of Dutch Catholics voted for the Catholic party, only 38 per cent did so in 1972. In 1976 the party entered into a federation with the two major Protestant parties. Although still maintaining separate organizations, they ran under a common Christian Democratic Party banner in the 1977 election; the Catholic party name no longer appeared on the ballot. In 1980 the three parties officially discarded their separate identities and organizations, and merged completely. This new party now carries the title "Christian Democratic Appeal" (CDA).

Within the Netherlands, the Catholic party is unusual. Table 1.1 (1946-77) indicates that the four other major parties which competed in the electoral arena, the Calvinist Anti-Revolutionary Party (ARP), the moderate Protestant Christian Historical Union (CHU), the Labour party (PVDA), and the Liberal party (VVD), although relatively stable, were not as consistent in their electoral support as the Catholic party (KVP) prior to 1967. During the 1967-72 period they did indeed lose ground along with the KVP. However, with the exception of the CHU, the smallest of the five, their decline was neither as spectacular nor as linear as that of the KVP. These parties managed either to stabilize their vote, to regain lost votes or, in the case of the VVD, to improve their overall position.

The duration and consistency of Catholic party support, and then its rapid decline, are also unique by West European standards. The 85 per cent-plus figure, representing the proportion of Dutch Catholics constantly voting for the party, is exceptional compared with Catholic

TABLE 1.1
Parliamentary Election Results, 1946–1977

Party	1946	1948	1952	1956	1959	1963	1967	1971	1972	1977
Major Parties:										
Catholic Peoples' Party (KVP)	30.8%	31.0%	28.7%	31.7%	31.6%	31.9%	26.5%	21.9%	17.7%	
Anti-Revolutionary Party (ARP)	12.9	13.2	11.3	9.9	9.4	8.7	9.9	8.6	8.8	
Christian Historical Union (CHU)	7.9	9.2	8.9	8.4	8.1	8.6	8.1	6.3	4.8	
Christian Democratic Appèl (CDA)										31.9%
Liberals (VVD)	6.4	8.0	8.8	8.8	12.2	10.3	10.7	10.4	14.4	17.9
Socialists (PvdA)	28.3	25.6	29.0	32.7	30.3	28.0	23.5	24.7	27.4	33.8
	86.3	87.0	86.7	91.5	91.6	87.5	78.7	71.9	73.1	83.6
Minor Parties:										
(Protestant)										
Political Reformed Party (SGP)	2.1	2.4	2.4	2.3	2.2	2.3	2.0	2.3	2.2	2.1
Reformed Political League (GPV)			.7	.6	.7	.8	.9	1.6	1.8	1.0
(Catholic)										
Catholic National Party (KNP)		1.3	2.7							
Roman Catholic Party (RKPN)									.9	.4
(Secular)										
Communists (CPN)	10.6	7.7	6.2	4.8	2.4	2.8	3.6	3.9	4.5	1.7
Pacifist Socialists (PSP)					1.8	3.0	2.9	1.4	1.5	.9
Farmers Party (BP)					.7	2.1	4.7	1.1	1.9	.8
Democrats '66 (D'66)							4.5	6.8	4.2	5.4
Democratic Socialists '70 (DS'70)								5.3	4.1	.7
Radical Party (PPR)								1.8	4.8	1.7
Middenstands (NMP)								1.5	.4	
Other Parties:	1.0	1.6	1.3	.8	.8	1.5	2.7	2.4	1.0	1.5
	13.7	13.0	13.3	8.5	8.4	12.5	21.3	28.1	26.9	16.4

Source: S. Wolinetz, "Electoral Change and Attempts to Build Catch-All Parties in the Netherlands," Paper presented at the Canadian Political Science Association Annual Meeting, 1973; Uitslagen Tweede Kamerverkiezingen, May 1977.

4 | Catholic Power in the Netherlands

parties in other West European countries or with Christian Democratic parties depending in large part upon Catholics for their electoral support.[4] The contrast between them is shown in figure 1.2. In Belgium and Italy one can see that support varied more from election to election than it did in Holland. However, for these parties support did not tail off as drastically in the last decade. Since both Belgium and Italy are countries where the entire populations are at least nominally Catholic, the percentage of people voting for church-supported parties may not be meaningful. In these countries it is difficult to sort out those individuals who have lost all contact with the church and those who have not.[5] However, it is interesting to note that of the Italians who attend mass regularly, 67 per cent voted DC, while in the Netherlands, according to 1956 survey data, 90 per cent of those who regularly attended mass voted KVP.[6]

Belgium and Italy are also less valid as cases for comparison insofar as the Catholics in the Netherlands are in a minority, constituting only 38 per cent of the population. Sixty-two per cent of the Dutch population is Protestant or non-religious. Much more significant for comparative purposes is the case of Switzerland. There the Catholic population, 40 per cent of the total population, is in a minority situation similar to that of Dutch Catholics.[7] The Swiss Catholic party has a record of stability which more or less matches that of the KVP in the period up to 1963, although no more than 50 per cent of Swiss Catholics voted for their party,[8] considerably less than the proportion in the Netherlands. However, the Swiss Catholic vote remained stable through 1971 while the vote for the KVP dropped off rapidly between 1967 and 1972.

Probably the best example with which to compare the Dutch Catholic vote is the Catholic vote for the German Catholic Centre party during the Weimar Republic (1918–33). Conditions were very similar to conditions in the Netherlands. There was a direct proportional electoral system and the ratio of Catholics to the rest of the population was virtually the same.[9] The Centre party was very stable in its voting support from 1920 up to the end of the Weimar Republic in 1933, obtaining from 11.2 to 12.2 per cent of the popular vote.[10] There was virtually no decline in its vote even during those fatal years of crisis in the early 1930s. Yet the Centre party never obtained more than 40 per cent of the Catholic vote, much lower than in the case of the Dutch Catholic party in both pre- and postwar times.[11]

By most standards the case of the Dutch Catholic party is unique. How does one go about explicating this particular pattern of voting stability and then sudden decline? Why did such a high proportion of

Introduction | 5

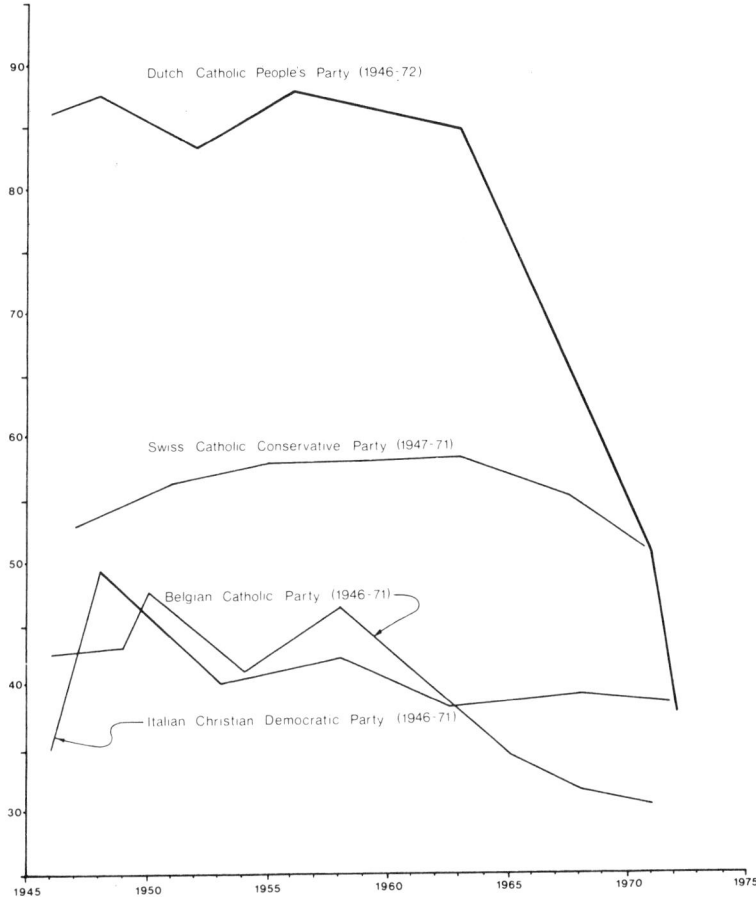

FIGURE 1.2. Percentage of Catholics Voting for European Catholic Parties
Source: *Annuaire Statique de la Suisse 1965*; Central Bureau of Statistics, The Netherlands, *Historical Statistics of the Netherlands, 1899–1974*; T. Mackie and R. Rose, *The International Almanac of Electoral History*.

6 | Catholic Power in the Netherlands

Dutch Catholics vote for the Catholic party? Why did the Catholic vote suddenly drop? In providing answers to these questions there are two competing explanatory frameworks available, the party identification and subcultural influence models.

Party Identification. Undoubtedly the most sophisticated and voluminous literature on electoral stability and change is concerned with what is generally referred to as "party identification." In the early 1950s at the University of Michigan, researchers were confronted by what appeared to be the unusual stability of American voters in their party preference. Some of the earlier voting studies by Lazarsfeld and others had assumed the existence of some sort of decision-making process on the part of voters in the few weeks before the election.[12] They were quickly disabused of this assumption when they discovered that few voters consciously arrived at a decision shortly before the election and only a small minority diverged from their party choice in the previous election.

To account for this stability in voting behaviour Campbell and others at the University of Michigan developed the social-psychological notion of "party-identification" or "partisanship."[13] According to this model individuals are socialized into this "identification" by their parents. There is a possibility that upon reaching voting age young adults may defect from their parental party identification. But once voters have settled down to a particular party choice over a number of elections, their loyalty to that party tends to harden. Once this stage is reached, party identification is considered to be a potent independent variable. On occasion voters may deviate and vote for another party but their party identification will tend to act as a homing device to draw them back in future elections.

The party identification model has been applied to countries other than the United States, largely in order to explain the stability or instability of party systems. According to researchers, the extent to which voters in a given population have developed loyalties to political parties determines how muted political change will be and whether or not "flash parties" will arise. Thus Dennis and McCrone claim: "Party system stability, in the sense of a persisting configuration of organized partisan competition, is a function of how widely rooted in mass public consciousness is the sense of identification with the parties."[14] Long-term party system stability, where it does exist, is accounted for not only by party loyalties on the part of current generations but also by the fact that these loyalties will be transmitted and imparted to future generations. Long-term electoral change is often explained as being due to the growth and decline of the different blocs

Introduction | 7

TABLE 1.2
Percentage of Catholics Preferring KVP by Age 1970

	Age					
	65+	50–64	35–49	25–34	21–24	Overall
KVP	76.1%	65.4%	59.8%	48.6%	31.0%	57.2%
N =	67	127	179	148	58	579

Source: 1970 Dutch election survey (provincial elections). Respondents were asked how they would vote if national election were held. Designation Catholic based on self-assignment by respondents.

of party identifiers because of different rates of fecundity, mortality, and socialization.

The best example of the party identification approach to change can be found in *Political Change in Britain* by David Butler and Donald Stokes.[15] They argue, for example, that the results of the 1964 British general election can be explained not by the defection of supporters from one party to another but by the growth of the working class, the majority of workers being Labour supporters, and the decline through natural causes of the proportionately older Conservative support base. Butler and Stokes allow that cataclysmic events, such as war or severe economic depression, may alter the basis of party alignment and lead to the development of new party loyalties among voters.[16] However, even in such instances, they claim, there is a very close connection between the renewal of the electorate, through the entrance of new voters and the death of older ones, and changes in party alignment. A voter is most susceptible to change when he is young while the older "partisan" voter is much less responsive to change when new grounds for party cleavage develop. Thus it may take many years before a change in alignment is fully reflected in party support.[17]

In the case of the Netherlands before 1967 the vote for the KVP was especially stable. Voters by consistently voting for the same party undoubtedly developed strong party loyalties. A number of students of Dutch politics state that a high proportion of strong party identifications provided a firm prop for the old party alignment during this period.[18] If so, the rapid dropping off of the KVP vote in the three elections subsequent to 1963 is somewhat surprising. During this period the size of the Catholic population, which formed the natural base of the KVP, declined only marginally. Table 1.2 shows Catholic support for the KVP among the differing age-groups.[19] Even if one assumes severe discontinuity in the transmission of KVP partisanship to younger

Catholics, it is obvious that many older Catholics must have abandoned their party loyalties, since in 1963 85 per cent of all Catholics voted KVP.

What evidence is there for the claim that the Netherlands, during the period of party system stability, enjoyed high levels of party identification? In the main, these high levels have been inferred on the basis of responses to a survey question asking what party the respondent supported.[20] Yet even if there had been a more direct measure of party identification, there is a problem of interpretation. For example, Campbell and Valen, in their examination of Norwegian voting behaviour, wonder whether party identification did have an independent effect: "The Norwegian labour union member who is a member of the Labour Party may display a strong party attachment, but one wonders if this does not merely express in different form his basic identification with the working-class."[21] On the whole, the party identification model is not very satisfactory. It does not provide an adequate framework for explaining electoral stability and decline among Dutch Catholics.

Subcultural Influence. In 1972 Phillips Shively raised doubts similar to those of Campbell and Valen about the party identification model.[22] However, he went one step further and developed an alternative framework, the subcultural influence model, to explain electoral stability and electoral change. He used the case of the Weimar Republic in the interwar period to test his model.

Shively argues that large blocs of voters, whom one would have expected to be unstable in their voting behaviour, for example, women who had only just obtained the right to vote in Weimar Germany, were in fact just as stable in their voting behaviour as those who would have had ample opportunity to develop party loyalties, for example, male Protestant voters. In the later Weimar period, 1928–33, when there was a surge of support for the Nazi party, he notes that "those groups which added disproportionately to the Nazi gains in the early 'thirties were the ones that had been relatively stable in the more 'normal' elections of the mid-'twenties."[23]

On the basis of his analysis of voting behaviour in Weimar Germany Shively states the following propositions:

> If the social or economic conflicts in which a voter is involved are sufficiently clear; and if the position of parties or groups of parties with regard to these conflicts is sufficiently clear; then there is no need for the voter to develop lasting ties to any party "per se" and he will not do so.
>
> ... [A] voter who is a member of a clear and distinct social or

economic group, for which he feels that some party or group of parties is the clear spokesman—a Catholic in the Weimar Republic, for instance, or a Welsh miner—may not need a further guide in voting. Since his social and economic position, coupled with the linkage of some party(ies) to that position, provides him with sufficient voting cues, he does not need to identify directly with a party.[24]

These propositions could be applied to party system stability in the Netherlands before 1967. In accordance with this model, one can see the Dutch KVP supporter as a conscientious Catholic who perceives the KVP as the only party which properly represents the interests of the Catholic subculture. The bond between the Catholic and his church would be quite strong while the bond between the Catholic and the KVP would be an instrumental one at best.

In general, Shively's model is quite attractive, although there are several points that need to be clarified. For example, from what source would a voter, as a member of a particular subculture, receive his cues to vote for a particular party? Would these cues derive from the voter's own evaluation of the situation, from neighbours, union leaders, religious authorities? The chief difficulty in Shively's model, however, stems from his explanation of electoral change. Applied to Weimar Germany, the model indicates that electoral change occurs when an alternative party moves in and successfully competes for the vote of a particular bloc. The new party is seen by voters as being able to represent better the interests of their subculture. The subcultural blocs themselves do not change. Unfortunately, Shively's model cannot really be used to explain party system instability in the Netherlands in the post-1963 period. In particular, it cannot be used to explain the decline in the KVP vote. In the case of the Catholic bloc or pillar[25] in the Netherlands no alternative Catholic party has successfully moved in.[26] Moreover, most commentators emphasize that the Catholic pillar in the Netherlands, with its "cradle to the grave" organizations, is undergoing a process of decay or "depillarization."[27]

For Shively's examination of voting in Weimar Germany, it was sufficient to assume subcultural cohesion. In this study, however, the cohesiveness of the Dutch Catholic community cannot be simply assumed. What needs to be explained is the unusual degree of cohesion on the part of Dutch Catholics. This requires a special focus on those factors making for subcultural cohesion. It will then be argued that it was a change in those factors which resulted in the transformation of the Dutch Catholic subculture into a much less cohesive body and thereby led to the decline of the KVP vote.

Chapter 2   **The Dutch Catholic Community**
Ethnicity, Ideology, Organization, and Clientele

Several writers on West European politics have stressed the importance of subcultures as factors in structuring political behaviour.[1] In what ways are subcultures important? How did they come to play such a role? In the Netherlands the authorities of the Roman Catholic church and lay Catholic leaders were largely responsible for the creation of a highly insular and cohesive miniature society involving virtually all Catholics residing within the Netherlands and imposing a high degree of conformity upon them. Prior to the changes within the church in the 1960s, Dutch Catholics rigorously followed prescribed norms of behaviour. Interfaith marriages were rare.[2] Catholics not only attended mass and confession regularly but also limited their reading to Catholic newspapers and periodicals, joined Catholic trade unions if they were workers, joined the Catholic employers' federation if they owned or operated large commercial enterprises, and joined the Catholic retailers' organization if they were shopkeepers or small businessmen.[3] And at election time the vast majority of Catholics voted for the Catholic party.

The Catholic subculture, however, has never been primarily political in nature. The main purpose in the insulation of Catholics from the rest of Dutch society prior to 1963 was to protect the core values of the Catholic community, values which were spiritual and social rather than political in nature. The spiritual and social cohesiveness of Dutch Catholics had political implications insofar as it greatly facilitated the mobilization of Catholics behind the Catholic party. And, as will be shown, the Catholic party did help in maintaining spiritual and social unity among Catholics. Nevertheless, it was the church which was mainly responsible for the maintenance of this unity, and its role will be the primary subject of this chapter.

Before beginning to probe the nature of the Dutch Catholic subculture one should ask, what is a subculture? What are the factors that make for subcultural cohesion? Unfortunately the term subculture has not been well defined, and different meanings have been attached to it. Nevertheless, it is possible to discern at least two and perhaps three basic conceptions of the term. Guenther Roth, in his study of the Social Democratic party in Imperial Germany, uses the organizational concept of subculture.[4] He refers to an entity called the Social Democratic subculture which for him was political in nature, consciously created by German labour leaders through organization. It encompassed a large proportion of the German working class, but it was not identical to that class as a whole. Rather, in terms of membership, it formed a subset of the working class. Individual choice by participants and organization are seen as the basic elements of such a subculture. Organization is also seen as the major factor making for subcultural cohesion.

A different notion of subculture is often used by those studying developing countries, for example, by J. S. Furnivall on Indonesia and M. G. Smith on the Caribbean.[5] These analysts focus mainly on characteristics common to a group of people, such as race, language, religion, or "primordial sentiments," which serve to impart a sense of identity to the members of the group and to demarcate them from other groups in society. In such a case the basis for subcultural cohesion is ethnicity, not organization.

Which conception of subculture is most appropriate for analysing the Dutch Catholic bloc? Val Lorwin, in his important article on segmental pluralism, argues that the notion of a subculture based upon race or caste is not appropriate for analysing most segments or "familles spirituelles" in Western Europe.[6] He points out that membership in such segments is, in theory at any rate, voluntary. People in Western Europe are not permanently marked by stigmata such as race or caste, and the lack of such stigmata makes opting out of a subculture easier than it would be in many developing societies. Lorwin admits that in countries like Austria or the Netherlands there are some conversion costs involved if an individual decides to switch from the Catholic to the socialist subculture, but such a conversion is not impossible. In a country such as Malaysia it would be virtually impossible for a Malay to drop his affiliation with the Malay community and become a member of the Chinese community. Lorwin's point is that a West European subculture such as the Catholic bloc in the Netherlands, based on organization, is qualitatively different from an ethnic bloc in a developing society. This is not in dispute. Nevertheless, there are instances in the West European context, and to some extent the North American context as well, where one does speak of a working-class subculture or a middle-class subculture. And in doing so one does not imply that such a subculture has a defined leadership or organization. At the same time, stigmata such as race are not necessarily present. Richard Hoggart and Richard Hamilton, for example, refer to the unique and distinctive cultural patterns of workers which help to set them apart from the rest of society.[7] Furthermore, they do not identify the working-class subculture as a whole with the organized working class. Phillips Shively also seems to use the concept of subculture in this sense. For him subcultural blocs in Weimar Germany consisted of aggregates of individuals who had certain characteristics in common. They were workers or Protestants or Catholics. He imputed to these blocs certain economic and cultural interests but not necessarily organization.[8]

The organizational structures developed by the Catholic church in the Netherlands were crucial in insulating Catholics from the rest of Dutch society. However, these organizations did not become fully developed until shortly after World War I; prior to 1853 the Dutch church did not even have an ecclesiastical hierarchy. Yet one can still speak of a Catholic subculture in the period of the mid-sixteenth century to the early twentieth century: Dutch Catholics formed a community and were conscious of having a unique identity. Basic stigmatic characteristics were of minimal importance in accounting for the cohesion of Dutch Catholics, but this does not mean that these characteristics were totally absent. And in the post-1963 period, when pressure from the church was relaxed, one can still talk of a Catholic culture which is distinct from one actively fostered through organization.

The term subculture or bloc will be used here in its wider sense, that is, it will refer to a group of people having certain characteristics in common, shared symbols, rituals, and the like, but not necessarily institutions. This facilitates comparison with other blocs both within and outside the Netherlands.[9] Thus, references to the Catholic bloc in Germany, the Netherlands, or Switzerland are to all individuals who are Catholic and not to a subset of Catholics who may be organized within particular institutions.

In the remainder of this chapter I will examine briefly the ethnic dimension of Dutch Catholicism, to see if racial, linguistic, or life-style characteristics have played a role in demarcating the Catholic bloc from the rest of Dutch society, and will then focus on the ideological and organizational dimensions and the socio-economic characteristics of the clientele. The emphasis will be on the period from 1918 to 1963, generally considered to be the zenith of the Dutch Catholic subculture in cohesiveness and cultural distinctiveness, although reference will be made to the development of ideology and the beginnings of organizational life in earlier eras.

1. The Ethnic Dimension

We often find that subcultures, especially those with ghetto-like qualities, possess distinctive characteristics derived from race, language, or religion. And often these characteristics reinforce each other to provide a basis for the division of societies into separate groups.[10] Such objective characteristics are usually highly interrelated and produce, or are associated with, a constellation of shared cultural elements. People belonging to such a subculture are usually said to have their own ethos and unique customs, habits, and rituals, comprising what is sometimes referred to as ethnicity. This is usually thought of as being subjective but it has the objective effect of further distinguishing a subculture from other subcultures or from the dominant culture. Ethnicity imparts to an individual a sense of identity, of belonging to a particular group.

To what extent was the Catholic subculture in the Netherlands based on or reinforced by factors such as race, language, or even territory? A review of some of the basic characteristics of the Dutch Catholic population suggests that racial, linguistic, and ethnic factors serve only in a limited way to help demarcate the Catholic subculture from the other blocs in Dutch society. Catholics have usually constituted from 35 to 40 per cent of the Dutch population. Approximately 45 per cent of them reside in the two southernmost provinces of North Brabant and Limburg (see fig. 1.1). Since the introduction of Christianity, both provinces have always been at least 95 per cent Catholic.[11] The southern part of the province of Gelderland, the province just above Limburg, is also largely Catholic. This part of Gelderland along with all of Limburg and North Brabant is usually referred to as "the area below the rivers."

Thus less than half the Catholic population resides in this homogeneous Catholic region. The rest are dispersed in the northern section of the Netherlands where, with the exception of several villages and a number of towns, Catholics are in a distinct minority position. For example, 23 per cent of the population of Amsterdam, 21 per cent of Rotterdam, and 29 per cent of The Hague are Catholic.[12] Within the cities and towns of this region there are virtually no areas which could be referred to as Catholic ghettos. Catholics in these places have always lived side by side with Protestants, socialists, and members of other groups. As will be shown, contextual factors such as the amount of Catholic concentration (i.e., whether Catholics are in a minority or majority in a given area), region, and urbanization do have some effect on the degree of loyalty to the subculture. However, it is worth noting that Catholics are by no means segregated within territorial limits.

There is no evidence that race is an important factor. Some attempts have been made to categorize Catholics from the south as being from alpinic stock while people in the north are said to be from nordic stock.[13] However, efforts to verify this have not been successful.[14] The same is true of theories which attempt to relate Catholicism to those of celtic stock. If these patterns had ever existed migration over the centuries would have blurred them considerably. This was especially true around the turn of the century when thousands of Catholics from North Brabant migrated to Rotterdam, many of them ceasing to regard themselves as Catholic. More importantly, there is no evidence that the Dutch people use physical stereotypes as a guide to pinpointing the religious persuasions of their fellow citizens.

Language is only of limited importance since the Netherlands is basically a unilingual nation. There is an ancient regional language called Frisian spoken mainly by people in the province of Friesland, but they constitute only a small proportion of the total population and among them are very few Catholics. There are a number of regional dialects which contrast somewhat with what is formally known as "Universal Civilized Dutch," the official Dutch taught in schools and based primarily on the Dutch spoken in the provinces of North and South Holland. People from the south can usually be identified by their speech; this is especially true of the inhabitants of the southern part of Limburg who have an intonation which is closely akin to German. And generally people from any part of the south can be identified by their pronunciation of the letter "g". In the northern part of the Netherlands it is made to sound quite harsh while in the south it is pronounced in a much softer, gentler fashion. However, this characteristic does not apply to Catholics living outside of the south and thus is not a general identifying characteristic of the majority of Catholics.[15]

Although Catholics are said to be prone to use certain types of greetings and idioms,[16] these are relatively minor variations on the Dutch language. The overall differences in language between Catholics and non-Catholics certainly would not act as an impediment to communication nor in themselves serve to demarcate and insulate the Catholic population from the rest of Dutch society.

The idea of a subculture often implies that its members have distinctive rituals and habits, and a unique musical and literary culture not directly related to the religious factor. To what extent is or was this true of the Dutch Catholic subculture? There is some evidence that there are differences between Catholics and their fellow Dutchmen in this regard. As noted, Catholics tend to use certain idiomatic expressions and ways of pronunciation. But this in itself would not have constituted a distinctive cultural style, although the Dutch historian I. Schöffer argues that before World War II these differences were more pronounced even for Catholics living outside of the south.[17]

In the early 1950s a team of researchers under the direction of I. Gadourek did an intensive case study of the village of Sassenheim in the province of South Holland.[18] They noted that in this village the rhymes and verses learned by Catholic children differed from those of Protestant children. In recreational activities they discovered that Catholics tended to favour pianos as opposed to the organs favoured by Protestants. It appears, however, that the citizens of Sassenheim were rather indiscriminate in their radio listening habits. Although radio broadcasting is divided along religious lines, and until 1965 it was officially forbidden for Catholics to listen to socialist radio programs, both Catholics and non-Catholics often ignored these divisions. Most preferred light music and would switch to the station offering it at the time, regardless of the religious affiliation of that station.

One expects any subculture to have its own distinctive literary tradition. For example, Richard Hoggart in *The Uses of Literacy* notes that this is the case of the British working class.[19] However, it is only partly true for the Dutch Catholic subculture. The period between the two world wars, an era in Dutch Catholic history referred to as the epoch of the "Rich Roman Life" (*Het Rijke Roomsche Leven*),[20] saw the production of a voluminous Catholic literature that fostered the sense of being Catholic and the Catholic ethos. However, some more talented Catholic poets and writers such as Anton van Duinkerken tended to offend the sensibilities of the church authorities and as a result the circulation of their work was curtailed.[21] More common fare for Catholics was a vast amount of pious literature of low quality extolling the virtues of sainthood. Although Catholics were inundated by this type of literature, how much was actually consumed is another question.[22]

During the interwar period the popular Catholic magazine *Catholic Illustrated* was filled with photographs of priests, nuns, and brothers

16 | Catholic Power in the Netherlands

celebrating their golden or diamond jubilees or standing on the deck of an ocean liner departing for distant lands to carry out their duties as missionaries. A regular feature was a large photograph of the "Roman family of the week" with captions such as "here we have the Jansen family with no fewer than 16 healthy children." Radio programs carried by the Catholic Broadcasting Organization (KRO) propounded similar themes. Generally, during the period of the "Rich Roman Life," Dutch Catholicism was most distinctive in terms of cultural spirit and élan. Against a background of processions, prayer sessions, retreats for young and old, most Catholics certainly felt themselves to be different from, and in fact superior to, non-Catholics.[23]

After World War II much of this overwrought piety disappeared, or at least the more public manifestations of it. Catholics were still exposed to large numbers of "approved" Catholic novels and magazines. However, Gadourek reports that in Sassenheim both Catholics and Protestants tended to read the same popular novels. Catholic and Protestant women also tended to share tastes in home-making magazines.[24] This finding is borne out by a 1956 nationwide survey carried out by the Dutch Central Bureau of Statistics.[25] The survey asked respondents, among other things, which radio program guide and newspaper they subscribed to and whether the novel they had last read was Catholic, Protestant, or neutral in orientation. The results are shown in table 2.1. Although the various groups are relatively segregated in their choice of newspapers and radio guides, these differences tend to disappear in the case of novel-reading.

In the Netherlands there are a number of popular images or stereotypes of the different religious groupings. Calvinists are thought to be much more serious and sober-minded than the fun-loving Catholics. For example, Dutch Catholics, especially in the south of the Netherlands, like their brethren in the latin countries, celebrate carnival, a week-long period of festivities in February. Gadourek discovered that the Catholics of Sassenheim indulged in card-playing and dancing more often than their Protestant counterparts.[26] These findings are again confirmed by the 1956 nationwide survey. Table 2.2 shows the responses to questions concerning recreational activities. A number of contrasts are evident, particularly in the attitudes of Catholics and Calvinists toward card-playing, chess, dancing, and watching sports events, which may indicate differences in life-styles. Nevertheless, Catholics do not differ drastically from the Dutch population as a whole. One cannot conclude from this table that Catholics have a radically different life-style.

It appears that in those basic characteristics determined by race, language, and ethnicity the Catholic population does not differ greatly

The Dutch Catholic Community | 17

TABLE 2.1
Reading Preferences by Religion

	Catholic	Moderate Protestant	Orthodox Calvinist	Other Church	No Church
	(%)	(%)	(%)	(%)	(%)
Radio Program Guide					
Catholic	89	1	—	—	2
Protestant	—	31	96	17	3
Neutral	10	68	4	81	93
Unspecified	1	1	—	2	1
	100				
N =	(823)	(797)	(235)	(97)	(509)
Daily Newspaper					
Catholic	79	1	1	1	1
Protestant	—	8	58	7	—
Neutral	13	87	26	87	96
R.C. + Protestant	—	—	2	—	—
R.C. + Neutral	7	1	—	1	1
Protestant + Neutral	—	2	13	4	2
N =	(1235)	(1146)	(300)	(151)	(712)
Novel Last Read					
Catholic	16	5	3	5	6
Protestant	5	19	31	17	8
Neutral	79	77	66	78	85
N =	(833)	(858)	(260)	(130)	(562)

Source: *Vrije-tijdsbesteding in Nederland winter 1955/56 Deel 9*, Centraal Bureau Voor de Statistiek, p. 19.

from the rest of Dutch society. And the differences that do exist would not by themselves support the development of a highly institutionalized subculture without the help of additional factors. With slight exaggeration one could say that the only obvious distinction between Catholics and non-Catholics has been, and still is, the fact that Catholics of both sexes wear their wedding ring on the left hand while other Dutch people wear theirs on the right hand.

Thus the ethnic dimension of Catholicism in the Netherlands is rather weak. It has been suggested, particularly by critics of the church, that many of the differences in culture and life-style between Catholics and others were the products of church influence rather than manifestations of racial, linguistic, or ethnic factors. It is the religious factor, in particular the Roman Catholic church as an organizational force, which was obviously a major, if not the major, factor in creating and maintaining subcultural cohesion.

The Catholic church with its hierarchical structure and emphasis on

TABLE 2.2
Recreational Activities by Religion
(*Percentages indicate proportion of respondents engaging in each activity*)

Recreation	(Men Only)					
	Catholics	Protestants	Calvinists	Other Church	No Church	Total
	(%)	(%)	(%)	(%)	(%)	(%)
Cards	71	51	21	33	65	57
Chess	15	16	24	20	21	18
Checkers	35	36	40	35	33	36
Dancing	33	20	5	9	28	24
Walking	6	7	8	8	6	7
Watching sports events	57	48	26	41	58	51
N =	(697)	(644)	(182)	(95)	(393)	(2016)

Source: *Vrije-tijdsbesteding in Nederland winter 1955/56 Deel 9*, Centraal Bureau Voor de Statistiek, p. 13.

the acceptance of centralized authority does appear to offer an ideal format for creating subcultural cohesion. The formal elements of the Catholic *Weltanschauung* include the beliefs that the church represents God on earth, that salvation can be obtained only through the church, and that papal authority is absolute. Before the second Vatican Council in the 1960s the chief characteristic of Roman Catholicism was that the beliefs and doctrines of the church were held to be absolutely true. For example, transubstantiation, the holy trinity, and the chastity of the Virgin Mary were believed to be literally true and seen not merely as symbols. Other important features of Catholicism have included the stress placed on the unitary nature of the church and the belief in the importance of absolution in order to be received by God in a state of grace.[27]

These basic features of Catholic doctrine have not always been accepted or fully understood by ordinary Catholics or by the clergy. Papal infallibility has come under attack both within and outside the church. And there have been a number of movements to transform the teachings of the church, the modernist movement in France and Germany at the turn of the century being one example.[28] However, in the past most questioning of church doctrine occurred within seminaries and universities. Rank-and-file Catholics, although not fully understanding or aware of many aspects of Catholic doctrine, nevertheless accepted the authority of the church. J. Poeisz, writing about Dutch Catholics in 1958, noted that the good Dutch Catholic "faithfully followed the directives for behaviour in Church and society laid down by the Church. He asked no questions but simply did what was expected of him. He had no specifically religious motives for his conduct. Normally his actions were motivated by an awareness that it was his duty to live in accordance with the Church's expectations."[29]

The church has available a number of sanctions to back up its directives. In extreme cases those Catholics breaking its rules can be threatened with excommunication, which involves not being allowed to take part in communion and being denied the holy sacraments. Moreover, the confessional can be used as a control mechanism. By being obliged to confess his sins to his parish priest, the Catholic is further subjected to the authority of the church. The priest in turn is subject to the control of his bishop and, through his bishop, of the pope.

In the Netherlands the authority and sanctions of the church were used by the ecclesiastical hierarchy to isolate Dutch Catholics socially and politically from the rest of Dutch society. Yet the Roman Catholic church is a universal church. Its organization does not differ drastically from country to country. Why was the strategy of the church so effective in the Netherlands? To answer this question one has to look at the ideology of Dutch Catholicism and the particular way in which the authority and sanctions of the church were used by Dutch bishops and clergy.

2. Ideology

Ideology has been defined as "a systematic set of ideas with action consequences serving the purpose of creating and using organization."[30] As we shall see, the ideology of Dutch Catholicism was neither systematic nor logically coherent; it was often contradictory. In particular there were tensions between ultramontane sentiments and the pragmatic attitudes which developed to ensure the physical survival of the Dutch Catholic minority within a society dominated by Protestants. Nor were these beliefs always used directly for purposes of creating and using organization. Nevertheless, particular ideas or strands of ideas can be identified which had important consequences for the behaviour of Dutch Catholics. And in the twentieth century these ideas became of paramount importance in the creation and use of organization.

The ideology peculiar to Dutch Catholicism is far from simple. Its various elements have different sources, yet at the same time are closely interrelated; there has been continuity, yet these elements have played a variable role in the history of Catholicism in the Netherlands.

They may be divided into three categories: (1) the isolationist mentality of the post-Reformation period when Dutch Catholics had to go underground in order to practise their religion; (2) the emancipation ideology dating from the time when Catholics were legally free to practise their religion and Rome had restored the Dutch hierarchy; and (3) the Calvinist penetration, concerned with the beliefs underlying the rigid adherence to the rules and regulations of the church by Dutch Catholics which has been ascribed to the influence of Calvinism.

A distinction is sometimes made between pure and practical ideology.[31] In the case of Dutch Catholicism it is possible to see beliefs in the Holy Trinity and the Virgin Mary as elements of pure ideology while the isolationist mentality, for example, can be seen as practical ideology intended to protect and further these elements. In practice pure and practical ideology are often interrelated and the distinction becomes difficult to maintain. In this analysis the different elements of ideology will be examined in terms of how they developed in relation to concrete historical circumstance.

The Isolationist Mentality. The reasons for the isolationist mentality of Dutch Catholics must be sought in their historical experience dating back to the time of the Reformation. In the sixteenth century the Netherlands did not become Protestant as a result of a fiat on the part of the government as in the case of Sweden and England. Rather the arrival of Protestantism in the Netherlands was intricately linked with the Eighty Years' War and the revolt of the Netherlands against Spanish rule. The church sided with Spain. Merchants in the larger centres and several members of the nobility who were influenced by the libertarian traditions of Erasmus feared the centralizing tendencies of the church, and they joined with sectarian Protestant groups in revolting against both Spanish rule and the church in 1566. Calvinism, which previously was restricted to lower and middle-class elements in Dutch society, proved to be increasingly attractive to the upper classes.[32]

Among the precipitating factors which led to the revolt were the poor economic conditions, the introduction of new taxes by the Spanish authorities, and the establishment of a new ecclesiastical hierarchy by the Catholic church. The Pacification of Ghent in 1576 marked the beginning of a united Netherlands. By this treaty the provinces of the Netherlands decided jointly to oust their Spanish rulers. At the same time they agreed to maintain the Catholic religion outside the provinces of Holland and Zeeland. Military successes in the north brought the cooperation of others previously inactive who, perceiving a change in the tide, joined the revolution. This led to the Union of Utrecht, a union of the northern provinces, in 1579.[33]

Only about 5 per cent of the population of the Netherlands belonged to the Reformed (Calvinist) Church before the revolts. However, Calvinism soon spread, mainly because the emerging economic and political elites found in it, rather than in Catholicism, a tolerant and pluralistic outlook which fitted in with their materialistic beliefs. It was at this stage that a more systematic attempt was made to convert Catholics in the northern provinces. The practice of the Catholic religion was officially banned and Catholics were barred from holding public office. Nevertheless large pockets of Catholicism remained. For example, in 1656 in what is now the province of North Holland 45 per cent of the population was still Catholic.[34] Why these substantial blocs of the population remained loyal to the Catholic church is a question on which there is considerable disagreement among historians.

One explanation has it that where there was a "worthy" priest, who could command respect and loyalty from his parishioners, the community remained loyal.[35] Other explanations place more stress on the apparatus of the church. Thus Jan Rogier notes that in those areas where the church had succeeded in reorganizing itself after the Reformation, the population remained Catholic. This, according to Rogier, would explain the "Catholic strip" along the coast of the current provinces of North and South Holland.[36]

Another important variable, stressed by Pieter Geyl, is that of force. In certain places the magistrate would summon the aid of armed troops to ensure the removal of the priest.[37] In one such community, for example, the priest was banished to foreign parts, yet succeeded in returning and re-establishing himself. He was again forcibly removed and again he succeeded in making his way back. The third time the magistrate finally was successful and the priest did not return. The villagers, left without spiritual care, succumbed gradually to Calvinism with the exception of one or two families. In other places force was not used and the authorities would either be indifferent or depend upon the local Calvinist minister and the parish council to ensure conformity.

Undoubtedly such variables as local leadership, church organization, and the use of force all played a role in determining where Catholicism would survive. The pockets in which the faith did survive remained in a tenuous position. Catholics had no civil rights and by law priests were subject to deportation. Catholic services were carried out in hidden locations, at first in private homes, later in more elaborate permanent structures built for this purpose. These were known as "underground churches" and the isolationist mentality of Catholics in the past has often been referred to as the "underground church mentality."[38]

Given the distribution of force in the northern provinces, neither priests nor lay Catholics were in a position to fight back or indulge in proselytizing activities. Instead they became highly introverted, nurturing a fervent hope that the church would be fully restored sometime in the future and the wayward fallen, namely the Calvinists, would return to the fold. "Their attitude was characterized by considerable anxiety concerning the dominant non-believers, paired with a high level of internal intolerance with regard to deviant tendencies among their fellow Catholics."[39]

In this atmosphere the church declined numerically, only the more fervent priests and their followers remaining faithful. Thus the Catholic population in all the provinces of the Netherlands fell from 47 per cent in 1656 to 34 per cent in 1726. Virtually all of this drop is accounted for by the northern provinces: in what is now the province of North Holland, for example, the percentage of Catholics dropped from 45 to 20 per cent in this period.[40]

After the revolt, Rome suspended the Catholic hierarchy in the Netherlands and the country reverted to the status of a mission ruled by a nuncio appointed by Rome. Leaders of the Dutch church such as Sasbout and Rovenius during the Eighty Years' War and Neerkassel in the second half of the seventeenth century did much to ensure the survival of Catholicism in the Netherlands. They reorganized the church according to the principles of the Counter-Reformation, yet at the same time steered a middle course when it came to dealing with the authorities of the republic. Unfortunately, although Dutch Catholics remained true to Rome to the best of their abilities, the papal authorities themselves did not always reciprocate. In 1702 Codde, the immediate successor of Neerkassel, was suspended by Rome following charges of heresy involving Jansenism.[41] Three-quarters of the secular priests (as opposed to those in religious orders) followed Codde and refused to recognize his successor De Cock. This led to the so-called Schism of Utrecht,[42] which in turn resulted in the founding of what is referred to in the Netherlands as the Old Catholic church, a sect which has survived to the present day.[43] However, since so much of the identity of the Dutch church was based upon the premise of loyalty to Rome, many priests who had followed Codde were caught in a crisis of conscience. By 1706 more than two-thirds of those priests who had left returned to the side of Rome.

The Schism of Utrecht helped reinforce the introverted nature of the Dutch church. In rather ironic fashion the Dutch clergy helped to maintain their belief in the church of the Counter-Reformation and their loyalty to Rome by becoming even more insular and independent not only of Dutch society but also of Rome itself. By keeping the influence of Rome at a distance, they could continue to believe that Rome was still the centre of spiritual authority on earth. Clashes which occurred between the Dutch church and Rome were blamed by Dutch clergy on faulty communication or on intermediaries who did not understand the intentions of the pope or misconstrued the true position of Dutch priests. The independence of the Dutch church was further reinforced by friction between secular priests and those in religious orders. The Dutch secular priests jealously guarded their autonomy and independence against what they felt were unwarranted intrusions by orders such as the Jesuits.[44]

Thus the survival of Roman Catholicism in the Netherlands in the early post-Reformation period did not depend upon the exercise of control from above. Local clergy took the initiative in organizing and protecting their own parishes with progressively less and less outside help. Moreover, they cooperated to some degree with the civil authorities. They paid extra taxes and permitted the civil authorities to perform marriage ceremonies. In return the civil authorities remained tolerant and, for example, allowed clergy to perform an additional marriage ceremony so that in the eyes of the church the marriage was a proper one. The commonly held belief was that this cooperation was a temporary necessity which would disappear when the Netherlands returned to the Roman Catholic fold. Through this means the clergy maintained a high degree of control over their flocks and were relatively free from outside control.[45]

All this was part and parcel of the isolationist mentality and could be observed in attitude and behaviour: a rigid emphasis on orthodoxy internally and a pronounced wariness, combined with pragmatic considerations, in communicating with the outside world. This curious posture on the part of the Dutch church was maintained well into the twentieth century. For example, in the late nineteenth century the priest Herman Schaepman, considered to be the father of the Catholic party in the Netherlands, had to defend himself from considerable criticism by both the bishops and conservative Catholics when he engaged in political activities. He was told his actions were endangering the position of Catholics in the Netherlands by arousing the ire of the non-Catholic majority. In 1904 the bishops ordered that an association of reform-minded priests and lay Catholics be disbanded on the grounds that priests and laymen could not consort with each other in a common society. The action of the bishops was in part motivated by puritanism (i.e., fear of the corruption of priests by socializing with laymen), but also by the fear that untoward demands made upon Dutch society by liberal-minded Catholics might disturb the social equilibrium.[46]

Another manifestation of the isolationist mentality occurred in 1954 when the bishops, in a well-publicized letter, reiterated the ban on belonging to non-Catholic organizations, listening to socialist radio programs, and reading non-Catholic newspapers, and ordered that communication with the non-Catholic majority occur only through official church-sanctioned agencies.[47] This again was in large part due to their belief that Catholics had to be insulated and protected from the influence of non-Catholic Dutch society.

The Emancipation Ideology. After the Reformation Catholics in the Netherlands were reduced to the rank of second-class citizens and shut out from all civil service functions. These positions were not only ones such as mayor but also minor posts such as lantern lighter and turf carrier. They were also kept out of the guilds, which aggravated their economically backward position. And as noted earlier there was always the threat of force on the part of civil authorities.

The church itself was harassed. Between 1703 and 1727 the papal internuncio was denied entry to the Netherlands.[48] In socio-economic terms Catholics tended to be located in the less well-off categories. As Jan Rogier has shown, in the parish of Saint Antonius in Delfshaven about 1829, not a single Catholic, aside from the pastor and his assistant, belonged to the intellectual and merchant class. In the categories of small businessmen, salesmen (e.g., fish wives), and workers, Catholics were over-represented in comparison with Protestants.[49] In the city of Den Bosch in 1786, a city which was 95 per cent Catholic, only four of the twenty registered lawyers and medical doctors were Catholic.[50] Much of this socio-economic imbalance was due to discrimination although some of it resulted from the rather narrow and restricted attitude of the church towards education.[51]

A number of better-off Catholics were certainly aware of the second-class position of Catholics in Dutch society. Yet in the seventeenth and eighteenth centuries this in itself did not lead to organized protest. One well-known Catholic writer even went so far as to suggest that there were distinct advantages in having civil service posts reserved for Protestants.[52] Most Catholics accepted their lot and focused on preserving what they had.

In 1795, with the establishment of the Batavian republic under French rule, Catholics were finally granted their full civil rights. This development, although generally welcomed, did not lead to great rejoicing. Objectively it led to improvement for Catholics in gaining access to civil service positions, though most did not take advantage of this. Some Catholics, however, did concern themselves with seeking an improvement in the status of their church. A number of priests and lay Catholics began agitating for the restoration of the Catholic hierarchy in the Netherlands, though according to Thurlings there was no consensus among Catholics on how this was to be achieved or even if it was a desirable goal.[53] Liberal non-Catholic politicians were ready to permit the return of the Catholic hierarchy but there was resistance from several quarters: from the Calvinists, from Rome, and not least from priests who valued their independence resulting from the lack of effective control by Rome.

In 1848 William II, under the influence of the liberal revolts then occurring all over Europe, instituted responsible government[54] with the result that liberal statesmen, like Thorbecke, who were tolerant, humanistic, and secular in outlook, were given a great deal of influence. The same group opened the way for the restoration of the ecclesiastical hierarchy, which occurred in 1853 when Rome finally overcame its hesitancy. This combination of secular statesmen and liberal-minded Catholics, referred to as the Papo-Thorbecke coalition, hoped for the integration of the Catholic church into Dutch society. Liberal Catholics placed great stress on openness as opposed to isolation and at the same time pressed for the emancipation of Catholics.[55] However, their influence soon faded. Directives from Rome in the form of the *Syllabus of Errors* and the encyclical *Quanta Cura* in 1864 warned the faithful of the dangers of liberalism and urged that children attend only Catholic schools. The "true to Rome" isolationist tendency in Dutch Catholicism reasserted itself but now combined with emancipationist feelings to produce a unique force—a new tendency in Dutch Catholics to be somewhat less cautious and to attempt to arrogate to themselves more influence over what they considered their own affairs.

Fortuitously the orthodox Calvinists under the leadership of Groen van Prinsterer and later Abraham Kuyper also began to press for educational rights as a defence against the liberal principles of the central authorities. Catholics and Calvinists joined in an electoral alliance and began pressing their case in parliament. Changes in the administration of the education act in 1888 and 1889 gave them partial victory. In 1917 what is known as the Pacification resulted in Catholics and Calvinists obtaining full state support for their school systems.[56]

The Pacification set a precedent for the meeting of further Catholic demands which were increasingly framed not in terms of the freedom and equality of Catholics as individuals but of the freedom of the church to set up its own organizations. Catholics took great pride in the institutional edifice that was developing. Emancipation came to mean more Catholic institutions. The outstanding examples were the Catholic University founded at Nijmegen in 1923 and the Catholic Broadcasting Organization (KRO) in 1926. In 1926 as well the political party known as the Roman Catholic State Party (RKSP) was founded (previously it had been simply entitled the Association of Catholic Electoral Associations). Many Catholics believed that since they now had the same institutional trappings as other groups, they were on an equal footing.

Catholics also began to see themselves as loyal Dutch citizens, a development which was reinforced by the events of 1918. The leader of the Social Democrats, Troelstra, who was under the influence of the revolutions that had occurred in Russia and Germany, advocated open revolt against the established order in the Netherlands. Although this resulted in only a minor crisis, since no one heeded Troelstra's call, the bishops and Catholic lay leaders threw their support behind the government and the throne, and for a time several of them were convinced that they and they alone were the saviours of the fatherland.[57]

In 1918 a Catholic became prime minister for the first time and during the 1920s the important post of minister of social welfare was given to a Catholic. All this was cause for rejoicing and aided in the development of a triumphalist spirit which characterized the period known as the "Rich Roman Life." But at the same time there was a feeling that Catholics were still being discriminated against since they continued to be underrepresented in the civil service and among those graduating from universities. This feeling persisted well into the 1950s and the early 1960s. In the early 1950s the leader of the Catholic party said that Catholics would only be truly emancipated when more than 50 per cent of the population was Catholic.[58] The *Mandement* of 1954, in addition to expressing isolationist sentiments, also reflected the perception of the bishops that discrimination against Catholics still existed in the Netherlands and that Catholic institutions were still necessary not only to protect but also to further the interests of Dutch Catholics.

The Calvinist Penetration. Calvinism is thought to be unusually severe and unyielding, stressing rigid adherence to the norms and values found in the Bible and laid down by the religious community. Catholicism, on the other hand, is generally considered to be more forgiving in matters involving the breaking of church laws, so long as the practising Catholic ultimately accepts the authority of the priest and the pope. However, the Dutch Catholic church, in contrast to the Catholic church elsewhere, was characterized by the extremely rigid manner in which it applied sanctions against Catholics who broke the rules and norms of the church. This rigorous approach to rule application by Dutch priests has been linked to the all-pervasive influence of Calvinism in the Netherlands.

The first apostolic vicar to the Dutch Roman Catholic mission, Sasbout Vosmeer, was extremely sparing in giving absolution or dispensation relating to fasting laws. In fact the dispute with Rome at the turn of the eighteenth century which led to the Schism of Utrecht was due to complaints brought to the pope of the rigorous behaviour of Dutch priests.[59] This behaviour has been ascribed to the influence of Jansenism, a highly moralistic stream of Roman Catholic thought which of all the intellectual movements within the church probably comes closest to Protestantism in spirit if not in form. Cornelius Jansenius, the spiritual father of this movement, taught at the University of Louvain and was bishop of Ypres (1585–1638).[60] Jansenist teachings tend to deprecate the authority of the church and to increase the emphasis on personal motivation. Holy communion can be received only under conditions of the utmost purity which requires intensive preparation. Absolution at confession can be received only after the priest is convinced that the parishioner is thoroughly repentant.

The sociologist F. van Heek suggests that Jansenism had an unusually strong influence on Dutch Catholicism,[61] citing the fact that during the seventeenth century many of the missionaries sent to the Netherlands received their education at Louvain. The evidence is not clear enough to suggest such a direct link. Nevertheless there is no doubt that the moralistic aspects of Jansenism had a ready market in the Netherlands. And it was received sympathetically, in part, because of a basic predisposition of the Dutch population as a whole to take matters of religion very seriously. J. M. G. Thurlings points out that both Protestants and Catholics in the Netherlands take religious rules and edicts in a much more literal fashion than is the case in Mediterranean countries like France and Italy.[62]

Secondly, there is evidence that the Catholic church in the Netherlands had taken over many attitudes and practices from the Calvinists. It was with the Calvinists, militant and well organized, that Catholics had the most social contact outside their own circle. And in defending themselves from Calvinist proselytizing the priests in particular, consciously or unconsciously, picked up many of the characteristics of Calvinism; they became distinctly more puritanical than Catholics in other countries. Rogier gives several examples of this. Observance of Sunday as a day of rest is minimal in most Catholic countries. In the Netherlands Catholics are much stricter in their Sunday observance.[63] The Carnival celebrations were banned in the Netherlands until 1815.

Afterwards, because of the Belgian influence, Carnival festivities penetrated into the two southern provinces adjacent to Belgium. When this occurred, however, Catholic priests did their utmost to discourage the festivities.[64]

This process of learning from the Calvinists was not restricted to the early post-Reformation period. In the late nineteenth century it was from the Calvinists under Abraham Kuyper that Dutch Catholics learned how to organize themselves politically in order to achieve their goal of state support for Catholic schools.[65] The norms of what was to be observed or adhered to are, of course, different for Calvinists and Catholics. Yet the spirit in which these norms were carried out has often been quite similar.

In summary, Dutch Catholicism, up to the early 1960s, placed considerable stress on physically insulating Catholics from the rest of the Dutch population. In the early post-Reformation period this was achieved through the means of the so-called underground churches; much later, organizations were developed to ensure that Catholics had no need to interact with non-Catholics in social and cultural spheres. The idea that Catholics were an oppressed minority who needed to be emancipated became an important element in the ideology. In the early part of the nineteenth century liberal Catholics hoped to achieve a degree of equality not only for the Catholic church but also for individual Catholics. In the latter part of the nineteenth century, however, largely because of the bishops, emancipation came to be defined in collectivist terms: Catholics needed to be emancipated as a group, not as individuals.

Throughout the years, Dutch Catholicism was marked by a zealous application of sanctions and stringent demands upon the individual. Church law, interpreted in a strictly literal form, represented a major element of control. The ideology which evolved had a significant impact upon the development and use of organization. The structures of the church and the subculture will now be examined with a view to highlighting the way in which the bishops, clergy, and lay Catholic leaders used organization to limit severely the range of individual behaviour.

3. Organization

Structure. The Dutch church province is divided into seven dioceses (before 1956 there were only five), each with a bishop.[66] The archbishop for the entire province is based at Utrecht. Each diocese is divided into *dekenaten* or deaneries and each deanery is further subdivided into parishes. There are a total of 129 deaneries and 1,800 parishes in the entire country and each parish contains anywhere from 800 to 10,000 parishioners. In the southern Netherlands, which is solidly Catholic, there might be two or more parishes in a single village or town. In the northeast, however, one parish might cover several villages.

Before changes in church organization and the clerical manpower crisis in the 1960s, each parish had at a minimum one pastor and usually one or more assistants. Their duties involved not only the preparation and performance of mass and the taking of confessions but also pastoral care, to which the largest part of the day's work was devoted.[67] Concretely it meant visiting parishioners in their homes on a regular basis, visiting them when they were ill, administering the sacraments, and tendering advice on the whole gamut of problems that might afflict a household. Systematic records based on a card index system were kept of each family in the parish.

Parish priests also held a number of "spiritual adviserships" in Catholic lay organizations operating in their parishes. A newly arriving pastor would be handed a list of such adviserships in organizations such as the local branch of the Catholic Farmers' Association, the Catholic Choral Society, and the Catholic Watch Makers' Association.

The numerous Catholic socio-economic organizations themselves were, and for the most part still are, organized on a diocesan basis by both priests and lay Catholics. Organizations such as the Catholic Health Care organization (the White and Yellow Cross) began on a diocesan basis under the aegis of diocesan approval. After a period of development organizations from the different dioceses usually decided to create a national organization on a federated basis or at least have a national coordinating office. The national organization would have a spiritual adviser appointed by the bishops. Catholic trade unions such as the woodworkers, printers, and painters also started off on a diocesan basis with chapters organized in terms of parish boundaries.[68] Later it became apparent that different arrangements were desirable, and industry and geography became the basis for more functional organization. This process of reorganization occurred not without considerable argument with the bishops.[69] Most Catholic bodies, however, even now tend to be organized in terms of ecclesiastical boundaries. As for the Catholic Broadcasting Organization (KRO) and the Catholic University, they were founded after first receiving approval from the bishops, have spiritual advisers sitting on the board of directors, and still have revisions in their statutes approved by the bishops.[70]

Given these organizational structures within the Catholic church and the Catholic subculture in the Netherlands, the next step is to see how they were used by the bishops, clergy, and lay Catholics to create cohesion among Catholics, and to look at the resolution of tensions and conflicts between different organizations.

The Bishops. The bishops have played the most active role in promoting the authority of the church, and in a manner quite different from that adopted by the hierarchy in other countries. In the Netherlands, particularly since the turn of the century, the bishops have tended to act collectively as a collegial body, speaking on behalf of all Catholics and issuing instructions or appeals to the faithful as a joint group. In doing so they in fact violate one of the principles of the Catholic church, namely the principle of territoriality which states that a bishop is the sole authority within his diocese.[71]

This collegiality means that pronouncements from the top carry the full weight of all the bishops. It also makes for a high degree of standardization and cohesion; decisions are valid not just for one particular diocese but for the entire province. It lessens the scope for leeway by individual bishops who might seek, for example, to disregard or considerably change some instruction from Rome. Thus in the Netherlands official letters to the faithful invariably carry the signature of all the bishops. In Belgium the exact opposite occurs. There only in exceptional cases do the bishops act in a collective fashion.[72]

The collegiality of the Dutch episcopate is due in part to the fact that the ecclesiastical hierarchy is a relatively new arrival in the Netherlands. Prior to 1853 there was no diocesan autonomy; thus diocesan territoriality was not institutionalized or given a chance to harden over time. The parishes themselves, however, were quite autonomous. Fairly strong collective action on the part of the bishops was needed to rejuvenate Catholic life at the time of the hierarchical restoration. Another major factor is the small number of bishops in the Netherlands. Ireland, for example, with a total population considerably lower than the Catholic population in the Netherlands (2.8 million versus 5 million) has twenty-six bishops while the Netherlands has only seven.[73] This circumstance greatly facilitated the reaching of common decisions and thereby enhanced centralized control in the period up to the early 1960s.

The chief interests of the bishops lay in ensuring that the faithful were suitably protected and sheltered from the non-Catholic world. Beyond the hope of obtaining Catholic schools, the hierarchy was not interested in institutional or subcultural development *per se*. Their attitude was one of conservatism and caution. They did not provide leadership in the sense of having a set of goals, a vision of the future which would lead to the transformation of the Catholic community in the Netherlands. Rather their role was to define the boundaries of the Catholic subculture, to decide what was acceptable or unacceptable behaviour. Initiatives for progress and change came not from the bishops but from progressive-minded priests and lay Catholics. The attitude of the bishops was that if Catholics were going to be involved in organizations those organizations had to be Catholic.[74]

This divergence in orientation between the bishops and some of the clergy is best illustrated by the case of Unitas at the turn of the century. Unitas was an interdenominational Christian union for textile workers based mainly in the eastern part of the Netherlands. Some members of the clergy, particularly those involved in helping to organize Unitas, favoured interdenominational organizations. Some members of the ecclesiastical hierarchy, however, were far from certain that they approved of any trade unions let alone interfaith ones. In 1906 the Dutch bishops collectively defined the official church position: Catholics should "unite and remain united in Catholic organizations."[75] It took two more pastoral letters over a six-year period before all vestiges of interconfessional trade unionism were eradicated. But at the end of this period the bishops had achieved their goal.

By the end of World War I the bishops had become convinced of the need for Catholic trade unions, particularly because of the fate of Catholic migrants from the south who came to work in the harbours of Amsterdam, Rotterdam, and their environs. Starting in 1800, a steady stream of poor Catholics from the rural areas of Zeeland, Brabant, and Limburg flowed into the northern cities, especially Rotterdam. Rogier estimates that the rise in the population of Rotterdam from 210,000 to 340,000 between 1890 and 1900 was due almost entirely to the influx of Catholics from the above-mentioned regions.[76] Unfortunately the clergy in the northern cities were unable to cope with this massive expansion of their flocks. The strongly conservative bishop of Haarlem, whose diocese encompassed Amsterdam and Rotterdam, remained blind to the needs of the Catholic migrants. Considerable work was done by a limited number of priests, mostly in the way of help for the destitute, but it was not sufficient. Many of the Catholic migrants found help from the socialists who were well organized, and in the process the migrants, removed from the influence of the church, lost their faith "by the tens of thousands."[77] It was not until 1910 that the bishop of Haarlem realized what was happening and called on the Capucin order for help in Amsterdam. They were not called into action in Rotterdam until 1918. When they grasped the magnitude of the disaster the bishops began to place stronger emphasis on organizing several aspects of Catholic life in order to ensure the spiritual protection of Catholics. In addition, the tendency towards collegiality among the bishops was reinforced even further.

Increasingly, Catholic institutions such as the Catholic Trade Union Federation, the Roman Catholic State Party (RKSP), the KRO, and the Catholic University were established on a national level. The bishops perceived that only on a collective basis could they maintain control of developments. Conferences and meetings between the bishops became more and more frequent. Officially an informal body, this council of bishops developed into the *de facto* governing body of the Dutch church. The image of the bishops as being jointly at the head of the Dutch church was deliberately cultivated by the bishops themselves.[78]

The bishops also proved to be far-sighted. In what was probably their most perceptive move in the twentieth century they condemned National Socialism, both in Germany and in the Netherlands, at a very early stage. In 1934, when the National Socialist party (NSB), the Dutch version of the German Nazi party, was first organized, it was immediately condemned by the bishops under the leadership of Cardinal de Jong. Any Catholic who gave "measurable support" to the NSB was not permitted to receive the holy sacraments.[79] In 1936 when it was evident that a number of Catholics, especially in Limburg, had voted for the NSB, the bishops repeated their warning and urged clergy and Catholic socio-economic organizations to make the utmost efforts to bring to the attention of Catholics the dangers of National Socialism.[80]

In 1940, when the Netherlands were occupied by German forces, the bishops became even more rigorous in their demands. Specific guidelines were issued prescribing appropriate behaviour for clergy and Catholics: members of the NSB could not be married in church or receive a church burial. Where there was any doubt about the relation of Catholics to the NSB, the clergy were required to refer the case to their bishop for a decision. In several instances Catholics were denied a church burial on the personal order of the bishops because of their links with the NSB.[81]

Even more significant were the lengths to which the bishops went in order to safeguard the autonomy of Catholic organizations. The German authorities had sought to ensure the integration and rationalization of organizational life in the Netherlands by permitting only one general or neutral organization for each sphere of activity whether it be trade unions or soccer clubs. The bishops ordered Catholic organizations not to cooperate with the German authorities. To prevent organizations from being forcibly taken over by the Germans the bishops simply ordered many Catholic organizations to disband.[82] Henceforth membership in such an organization served as the basis for excommunication. Thus the Catholic University and higher schools were promptly shut down. The KRO, the White-Yellow Cross, the Catholic Trade Union Federation, the Catholic Farmers' Association, and several other organizations were likewise disbanded, and their full-time officers were given relief payments from an emergency fund specially set up by the bishops.[83]

To the bishops the maintenance of subcultural unity, "our sacred unity" as they called it, was of prime importance. In the immediate postwar period the bishops again asserted their will. Cardinal de Jong announced that it was the wish of the bishops that all Catholic organizations, including the Catholic party, be revived.[84] Having proved that Catholic unity and solidarity had been an important force in resisting the German occupation, the bishops were confirmed in their belief that a highly insulated Catholic subculture would be invaluable in the future. They still perceived the outside world as uncertain and threatening, especially in the light of events in eastern Europe and the attempts made by the Communist-influenced Unity movement to dominate the trade union movement in the Netherlands in 1946 and 1947.

In the 1950s the bishops became convinced that the sacred unity of the Dutch church was being compromised. In 1952 the Labour party (PvdA) had made some inroads on Catholic party (KVP) support in the Catholic south;[85] the Catholic caucus in the PvdA had refused to heed earlier requests from various sources to leave the PvdA and come to terms with the KVP;[86] Catholics appeared still to be underrepresented in the civil service.[87] All this reinforced the basic belief of the bishops, especially that of Cardinal de Jong, in the importance of maintaining the isolation of Catholics. In 1953, at the time of the celebration of the one-hundredth anniversary of the reinstallation of the ecclesiastical hierarchy, Cardinal de Jong pleaded in a radio broadcast: "Dear fellow believers, we must remain one. Whatever we have accomplished in the past, particularly in public life, we owe to our unity in our dealings with the outside world. But as our emancipation progresses, that unity will be exposed to ever greater dangers. . . . Therefore, dear fellow believers of the Netherlands, stay one, one!"[88]

In 1954 the bishops issued a *Mandement* renewing the call for Catholic unity, warning of the dangers of socialism, and listing the penalties for indulging in inappropriate behaviour such as listening to the socialist radio station or joining a non-Catholic trade union.[89] The letter is interesting both for the insight it gives into the isolationist and emancipatory spirit of Dutch Catholicism and for the public support it received from all the bishops, even though in private some disagreed strongly.[90] Mgr. Alfrink, who succeeded Cardinal de Jong, continued to defend the document in the spirit of collegiality long after de Jong had died although he had opposed it in private when it was first discussed. In practice the penalties listed in the *Mandement* (denial of the sacraments) were rarely carried out. Nevertheless the bishops gave little public indication that they were willing to tolerate deviance. When asked to rule on specific cases, for example, a sports organization wanting permission to play with non-Catholics, they refused to give dispensation.[91]

Along with the emphasis on strong collective leadership in defining the boundaries of the Catholic subculture, the bishops adopted an unusually severe approach to issues only indirectly related to subcultural unity. Certainly they were much more literal and rigorous in the interpretations they placed on orders from Rome compared with bishops elsewhere.[92] For example, in 1929 Rome sent out a letter stating it was undesirable for clergy to be members or attend meetings of Rotary International. The tenor of the letter did not indicate a ban on membership in the case of Catholic laity. Within a year, however, the Dutch church hierarchy instituted a general ban on membership in the Rotary Club for both clergy and laity. In no other country did the church attempt to classify Rotary International as a banned organization.

In the matter of fasting the Dutch hierarchy was also considerably more severe. Because of World War II the canon law regarding fasting and abstention was suspended. In 1950 a new letter from the bishops listed fifty-six fasting days in the year. In Belgium, in contrast, only four days were classified as required fasting days.[93]

The Clergy. In the Catholic church, priests perform functions which we associate usually with "line" positions of organizational theory, translating orders into actual practice. They are the ones who in a concrete fashion represent God on earth. They actually carry out the tasks of celebrating the mass, administering the sacraments, and hearing confession. When Catholics have contact with the church it is usually with their local parish priest or pastor, who is responsible for the spiritual well-being of his parishioners. Before the theological changes of Vatican II, the priest primarily guarded the faith of his flock, and was directly responsible for applying sanctions against those who transgressed against the rules of the church. And in order that the tasks involved in spiritual care be properly carried out there had to be an ade-

TABLE 2.3
Catholics per Priest by Country

Country	Number	Country	Number
Switzerland	477	Italy	727
Netherlands	480	France	791
Luxembourg	495	Austria	910
Belgium	564	Spain	921
Ireland	636	West Germany	1,000
Britain	667	Portugal	1,635

Source: KASKI, "Het katholicisme in West-Europa," Memorandum No. 113, 1960, p. 18.

quate supply of manpower. Too high a ratio of parishioners to priests might have resulted in the lowering of standards. The church in the Netherlands has usually been fortunate in this regard, comparing favourably with the Catholic churches in other West European countries. In 1960, as one can see in table 2.3. only Switzerland with a ratio of 477:1 was marginally better than the Netherlands with a ratio of 480:1.

In most countries the local pastor was not only the authority on matters of spirituality but also an authority in most other fields. In the Netherlands the role of the pastor as a generalized authority figure lasted well into the 1950s. Especially in homogeneously Catholic villages in the rural areas, he was the prime carrier of the social and ethical traditions not only of the national and international church but also of the local group. He was the reflex element in the village collectivity. What the pastor believed, the village believed.[94] He carefully watched over the morals and orthodoxy of the village. He was *the* authority in matters such as marriage, the family, the upbringing of children, organizational life, and political life. Most agencies of social control were at his disposal. Well into the nineteenth century the local constabulary was frequently given the task of ensuring that parishioners attended mass and that the villagers observed the rules prescribing Sunday as a day of rest.[95]

The leadership of the priest was certainly authoritarian. In the popular literature he was usually depicted as being stern and unyielding but at the same time compassionate and helpful. Textbooks used by Catholic school children in the 1920s and 1930s frequently featured the pastor in challenging situations, for example, rescuing a postman who had imbibed too much and putting him back on the path of righteousness.[96] Along with the mayor and the school teacher the pastor was one of the few educated persons in the village or neighbourhood.

Therefore he was also the dispenser of advice on a whole range of subjects. He could help people fill out their income tax papers and could settle disputes between neighbours. He could also be helpful in a more material sense. A pastor in a village in the province of North Brabant noted in 1976: "You could say that until say ten to twelve years ago here in this village my pastorate served as a general social welfare agency. People would come here with every conceivable problem and very few of these problems had anything directly to do with religious questions" (Interview 23).

As spiritual adviser the pastor would be a member of the local school board, the Catholic Farmers' Association, Catholic Action, and so on. In this capacity his role extended far beyond that of merely commenting upon spiritual matters. At meetings he did not act merely as a chairman or arbiter but in fact dominated the meeting and his advice or suggestions were invariably followed. In the postwar period the role of spiritual adviser diminished somewhat in importance, especially in trade unions and in urbanized areas. In smaller centres, however, the pastor continued to be an important figure at meetings of Catholic organizations. And in a number of rural areas, especially those outside the Catholic south, the traditional conception of the role of spiritual adviser lingers to the present day. A pastor in a Catholic village in the eastern part of the Netherlands (outside the Catholic south) describes his role:

> When I first arrived as pastor in 1971 I was asked to be spiritual adviser for the various Catholic organizations. I said no. The time for such a role has passed. Besides I just do not have the time. . . . Now and then I do go to a meeting. . . . I suspect my word still carries a lot of weight, that people look up to me because I am the pastor. Usually I am asked to say a few words and I will say something on spiritual matters. Sometimes I am asked to give business advice at these meetings and I will do so because I may be the only one with sufficient education to give such advice. (Interview 12)

The authority of the priest was made apparent not only in church and at organizational meetings but also on a personal basis in at least two contexts: during regular visits to the homes of parishioners and in the confessional. These meetings were important not only because they meant close personal contact but also because occasionally they involved the application, or threat of application, of sanctions. As Mancur Olson has argued in the *Logic of Collective Action*, the use of incentives or sanctions in the case of individuals is an extremely powerful weapon in obtaining compliant behaviour on the part of a group as a whole.[97] Of the two contexts the home was much more important and was so viewed by priests. An 82-year-old priest, retired since 1972, stated: "House visits: I found that so important. . . . I would put it first on my list of duties as a priest. That was the way you maintained contact with the people. By seeing people in their homes you could sense immediately what the situation was like, if there were any problems" (Interview 17). Thus the prime function of house visits was control. The priest would ask about reading and listening habits, ensure that the trade union the person belonged to was Catholic, and check the "condition" of the marriage: "I would check the ages of the children and if there was a gap of three years between say the fifth and sixth-oldest children I would ask, 'What happened here?'" (Interview 8).

Parishioners who had erred in such things as reading habits would be told that they had committed a sin and their behaviour, if left unchecked, would profoundly affect their well-being in the hereafter. If their sins were sufficiently serious their names might be put on the black list so that they would not receive the sacraments at Easter time. Parishioners for their part would rarely argue with the pastor, but would meekly nod their assent and promise to mend their ways. Seldom did anyone openly disagree.[98]

Not all priests would use the threat of denial of the sacraments or the imperative mode of persuading parishioners to change their ways. One priest, of admittedly conservative persuasion, claimed to use a more liberal approach.

> When I visited a home I would keep my eyes open in order to evaluate the situation. If I saw a copy of the *Vrije Volk* [the socialist daily newspaper] I would not comment on this at all. I would avoid negative comments altogether. The important thing was to keep the conversation open, not to break off communication. . . . I would try to lure them out of the socialist camp. . . . I would never say "you must not" but try to set a personal example. For example I would say, "I read the *Katholieke Volkskrant*. It really is a very interesting newspaper." (Interview 12)

Although the techniques of control might vary, the object was the same: to ensure the maximum of compliance with the rules and norms of the church.

The confessional was never quite as useful as a means of control or source of information, although earlier it may have been more important. "Before the war [in Rotterdam] people came to confession quite often. I asked a lot of questions. . . . I had considerable influence in the confessional" (Interview 21). Yet in the main the evidence for the postwar period is that the confessional was not taken very seriously by either priests or rank-and-file Catholics. Often people would come to confession and rhyme off a verse that they had known since childhood. Several priests had anecdotes concerning older women who would confess, for instance, "'Last week I pestered my little brother and stole from the sugar pot.' [As clergy] we never really did much about this. . . . We more or less condoned this kind of routinization of an important aspect of being a Catholic. If we pushed too hard they might simply not have come at all. . . . It was not a healthy situation. We probably let it continue too long" (Interview 23).

The degeneration of confession into a rather perfunctory ritual made it somewhat more akin to superstition than a genuinely religious experience. Yet this element of superstition had its uses for reasons of social control. It was apparently needed by many people and this was reflected not only in their treatment of confession but in other practices as well. "In my first years as an assistant in a parish in The Hague [late 1940s, early 1950s] I remember the verger would go trundling around the neighbourhood with a cart selling bottles of holy water—a good business for the verger if I do say so myself—and the people would use it for everything. If there was a storm, for example, people would spray holy water around so that lightning would not strike their homes" (Interview 8). Priests did not fully approve of these practices but condoned them indirectly by catering in a limited way to the superstitions of their flock as a means of helping the church maintain contact with people.

In a large parish the pastor would have one or more assistants, who would often be assigned to particular neighbourhoods to carry out pastoral tasks. The data gathered from their house visits were put on file cards. After the evening meal the pastor would discuss their work and not infrequently check through some of the cards, thus controlling the work of his assistants and the state of his parish. There were other means by which the pastor maintained contact with his parish. Parishioners would frequently inform him of any unusual events or cases like the hospitalization of an individual. One pastor, who lived in a medium-sized city, had an arrangement with the milkman. If a new family moved into the parish the latter would ascertain whether or not the family was Catholic. If so, the pastor paid the newcomers a visit, thus ensuring continuity in their religious observance (Interview 8).

Control of the pastor himself came most directly in the form of visits from the local dean. Two or three times a year he would drop in for tea and a chat. Visits could also be expected from the administrative officials of the diocese, who would check the financial records, the condition of the buildings, the furnishings, and the gold and silver. Authority was also exercised by the bishops in the form of letters and missives, documents which often had to be read to the parish at mass. Priests could be shifted from their posts at very short notice. Orders to move to another parish would come from the diocese; appealing such a decision was unthinkable. In those parishes under the control of religious orders, decisions governing the posting of members might be made by authorities as far away as Rome. The behaviour of priests towards the community, female servants, and in other contexts was governed by canon law.[99]

On the whole there was very little in the way of direct personal control of the behaviour of parish priests by higher authorities within the church. It was not really needed; provision of a set of rules and expectations appears to have been sufficient. Although many priests were not always happy with the rules of the church, for the most part they obediently carried out their duties. When asked if they ever tried to experiment with the mass or to challenge the authority of the church, most priests responded in a negative fashion. "No, that was something you just did not attempt." "You could think about it, but actually doing it? No, you would never dare!" "If you did ever try to do anything they [the bishops] would soon find out about it and you would be sure of getting rapped across the knuckles" (Interviews 8, 21, and 23 respectively). The urge to conform resulted not only from the knowledge that retribution would follow any attempt to deviate from the norm but also from an acute awareness of the minority position of Catholics in the Netherlands. Many priests undoubtedly believed that unfailing devotion was necessary for the church's survival.

> Question: Did you ever think of disregarding an order of the bishop, of bucking the system?
>
> Answer: Oh heavens no, you couldn't begin to think of anything like that. . . . But that was all for the best. Unity had to be safeguarded. You couldn't start experimenting. Where would it end? It would have been much too dangerous. (Interview 17)

The manner in which the clergy were recruited and educated contributed to their loyal and rigorous behaviour. Before 1795 candidates for the priesthood received their training outside the Netherlands, mostly in Belgium and Germany; thereafter the diocesan priests had their own seminaries. Clerical refugees from Bismarck's *Kulturkampf* in Germany organized several new seminaries in the Netherlands in the late nineteenth century. But it was not until the twentieth century that large-scale expansion took place. In 1910 there were fifty-two seminaries; in 1952, 139.[100] None was connected with any of the universities. Even in the 1950s in the diocese of Haarlem seminary students were forbidden to have any contact with the universities of Amsterdam and Leiden.[101] The aim of the seminary, according to Cardinal de Jong, was to cure students of the habit of thinking critically.[102]

A disproportionately large number of students were the sons of farmers and shopkeepers.[103] The usual route for the aspiring priest began at about the age of twelve and went via the so-called small seminary, located well away from urban areas. Selection procedures were designed to admit only those who had a good chance of completing the several years of study necessary to become a priest. In the interwar period many seminaries began to use the services of psychologists to weed out unsuitable candidates.[104] At the seminary there was little contact with the outside world. While on holiday breaks with their families student priests were encouraged and in many cases required to report to their local pastor for advice, guidance, and protection.

The seminary system was responsible for a continuing supply of manpower for the priesthood and for ensuring that Dutch clergy received an education which stressed loyalty to the goals of the church. It should not be thought, however, that qualities of loyalty and obedience were coupled with low intelligence and lack of common sense. The Dutch clergy for the most part were highly capable people. Up to the late 1950s the priesthood was considered not only an important profession but also a prestigious one. The brightest, most capable students, particularly those with a talent for leadership, were considered to be obvious candidates for the priesthood, which in turn was highly prized as a means of becoming upwardly mobile, especially for the families of small farmers and shopkeepers.

In summary, the attitude of priests toward their parishioners was authoritarian and highly paternalistic: "You had to do everything for them"; "they were much too undeveloped to think for themselves." They were very strict when it came to enforcing the rules of the church, especially with regard to birth control and mixed marriages. Yet there were limits. Many priests now will confess to having given a church burial to a socialist prior to 1965. In the case of divorce or remarriage a number of priests were willing to bend the rules. Furthermore, most priests had a reasonably well-developed social conscience.

In fact, it was the lower clergy, many with an acute awareness of the social problems of their day, who were mainly responsible for setting up several of the socio-economic organizations in the late nineteenth and early twentieth centuries.

Socio-economic Organizations. The bishops largely concerned themselves with maintaining the boundaries of and keeping alive the ultramontane tendencies within the church. It was the lower clergy who were deeply concerned with social questions and who provided the leadership which considerably changed the character of the Dutch Catholic subculture. It was they who were chiefly responsible for the vast increase in the number and size of Catholic institutions in the twentieth century.

Most of the early Catholic trade unions were started by priests. Even before the beginnings of a rudimentary trade union organization a number of priests were active in caring for workers, protecting them from undue exploitation, and using their influence to prevent the worst excesses involved in the use of child labour.[105] Many Catholic organizations received their start in this era. The Catholic Goat Breeders' Association—later to become the source of many jokes—was started by a priest, Father van der Noort, whose aim was to provide some help for poor farmers. Since the keeping of goats was the common denominator among these people, he decided to use this as a basis for organization.[106]

Father Ariëns in the eastern part of the Netherlands played an important role in organizing workers in the developing textile industry in 1889. At approximately the same time in the province of North Brabant, Father Mutsaers helped organize Saint Raphaël, a union for railway and streetcar workers. Other priests were also involved in this type of organizational work, mostly in the eastern and southern parts of the Netherlands.[107] The diocese of Haarlem was an exception. Although some social work was performed, the bishop was unsympathetic and gave little support.

A number of priests, and progressively minded lay Catholics such as P. J. M. Aalberse of Leiden, were keenly interested in what was generally referred to as the social question. In 1891 this movement received a boost in the form of an encyclical by Pope Leo XIII, *Rerum Novarum*, which declared that it was the task of the church to help the downtrodden and to confront the evils of industrialism. It recognized the right of workers to organize in order to alleviate their conditions. By 1901 Aalberse and his compatriots had founded Catholic Social Action, an organization intended to help fulfil the promises contained in *Rerum Novarum*.[108]

None of this, however, was intended to promote class conflict. One of the purposes of founding the Federation of Roman Catholic Trade Unions in 1888 was to help reconcile the interests of the different classes. The emphasis was on harmony. Clergy and Catholic lay leaders explicitly disavowed the notion of class conflict, but in the years following *Rerum Novarum* the needs of the less well-off received increasing attention. By the early 1900s many Catholic businessmen were referring to Catholic Social Action as Catholic socialism.[109] Nevertheless in 1903 Catholic and Protestant workers refused to join other workers during a strike against the railway system.[110] They were praised for their loyalty and at the same time lay Catholic leaders such as Aalberse increased their efforts to improve conditions which had originally led to the strike.

The outstanding example of a far-sighted priest who managed to organize a large bloc of Catholic workers was Dr. H. A. Poels in the mining district of South Limburg. Nowhere in Western Europe but the Netherlands did the church maintain its hold over mining communities. All other coal mining districts, such as those in Belgium (contiguous to those in the Netherlands), France, and Germany, became strongholds of socialism and anticlericalism.[111]

The mining industry in Limburg expanded rapidly at the turn of the century, South Limburg being quickly transformed from a mainly agricultural region to one in which mining was the chief source of employment. At the same time the size of several towns and villages quintupled. The population grew from 69,736 in 1900 to 242,444 by 1935.[112] For the most part this increase was due to a vast influx of outside workers not only from other parts of the Netherlands but also from countries like Germany, Hungary, Poland, and Yugoslavia. By 1927 native Limburgers working in the mines were in a minority.[113]

The rapid industrialization of South Limburg had potentially grave social consequences. Well before World War I the crime rate and incidence of immorality were much higher than elsewhere in the Netherlands. In 1910 Poels was appointed as full-time chaplain to the miners, most of whom were Catholic, and for the next twenty years he was instrumental in shaping the nature of social and economic life in South Limburg. The Catholic Miners' Union was strengthened by financial and moral help from the bishop, and cooperatives for food and clothing were organized. One of Poels's aims was to avoid the growth of large urban conglomerates. Through the housing society he ensured that at every mine there would be a sufficient number of homes for the workers. At the centre of each small community would be the parish church.[114] Considerable effort was made to ensure the spiritual and material welfare of miners. Dutch priests were sent to countries like Hungary and Poland to learn the languages of those countries in order to be able to communicate better with foreign migrants.[115] Socialism and liberalism were condemned in no uncertain terms by Poels and his co-workers, and the proponents of those ideologies found it extremely difficult to penetrate the bulwark created by the church in Limburg.

Before World War I the social question was an important, if not the most important factor impelling many clergy and lay Catholics to set up Catholic socio-economic organizations. After the war the emphasis shifted. It was felt that many of the organizations, particularly the trade unions, had achieved their goals of obtaining social justice and that their protective role was now the most important. Catholics were urged by the ecclesiastical hierarchy to safeguard what had been achieved and to maintain their sacred unity. Subsequent organizational developments were frequently a result of copying the other blocs. The Catholic University (1923) and the KRO (1926) are good examples of this. These two institutions were seen as the jewels of the whole gigantic organizational edifice. Catholic organizational life came to be seen as a testimonial, a monument to the Roman Catholic church. Nowhere else in the Western world had Catholics managed to achieve all this and it was a source of immense pride.

Spiritual advisers were still very important in the interwar period. The papal encyclical *Quadragesimo Anno* (1931) expounded further on themes first broached in *Rerum Novarum*: the benefits of capitalism should be distributed more widely; there should be greater cooperation between the classes; owners should be prepared to let workers and consumers help in the management of their enterprises. These themes were picked up and propagated by a number of Catholic clergy and Catholic intellectuals.[116] Retreats were organized by parishes and socio-economic organizations. The people at a retreat would all be of one social group, comprising, for example, housewives, students, butchers, or metal workers, and each group would be lectured on its particular obligations to society. Catholic tobacconists would receive not only religious instruction but would also be told about the evils of unfair competition, price-cutting, and similar practices. These instructions would be based directly on *Rerum Novarum* or *Quadragesimo Anno*.[117]

With the revival of Catholic organizations after World War II, the climate changed once again. Much of the religious élan of the interwar period had disappeared. Many organizations became more bureaucratized, routinely carrying out their functions. Many spiritual advisers of the more important socio-economic organizations, such as the trade unions and the employer federation, deliberately cut back the scope of their role or at least recognized that the lay leadership in these organizations was sufficiently well developd that they could function without continual guidance. In addition, they recognized that these organizations might no longer be willing to tolerate their interference.

In most trade unions at the national level during the postwar period spiritual advisers sat in on meetings but took little or no part in the proceedings, other than to say a special prayer or officiate at burials. On the other hand, in the Catholic Farmers' Association, spiritual advisers continued to play a strong role. For example, the spiritual adviser to the Catholic Farmers' Association in Limburg from 1946 to 1962 had a degree in agricultural engineering and virtually ran the organization single-handedly. Catholic organizations which were organized on a largely diocesan basis were more prone to control by the church, perhaps chiefly as the result of a vacuum. If a pastor perceived a need for a Catholic harmonica club, in response to the appearance of a non-Catholic harmonica club, more often than not he might have little choice but to organize and run one himself.

What effect did socio-economic organizations have in influencing Catholics to act as they might not have done without the presence of these organizations? William Petersen has drawn attention to an interesting case involving Catholic lay organizations and the high value that the Dutch church placed on large families. Shortly after World War II the boundary between Germany and the Netherlands was slightly redrawn. As a result a parish which had previously been in German territory became part of the Netherlands and henceforth came under the influence of Catholic lay organizations although the pastor remained under the control of his German diocese. From 1949 to 1959 the birth rate among Catholics in this community rose from 19.5 per 1,000 to 25.0 per 1,000. The birth rate among Catholics in the adjoining territory in Germany fell from 16.3 to 12.9 in the same period. Petersen attributes most of this increase to the activities of Catholic welfare organizations such as the White-Yellow Cross.[118]

Catholic organizations undoubtedly played a role in insulating Catholics from the rest of society by limiting their interaction with non-Catholics. Yet the proselytizing or pastoral functions of these organizations should not be overestimated. In many organizations, even including Catholic Action, there was very little of this.[119] One of the most important characteristics of Catholic organizations was, and to a large extent still is, that the services and benefits offered were virtually identical to those of the socialist, liberal, and Protestant organizations.

With the exception of the educational system, most Catholic organizations were social or economic rather than religious in orientation. This was most evident in the area of trade unions. By the early 1950s the Protestant, Catholic, and socialist trade union centrals had set up a joint council, a forum where joint programs, proposals and positions on wages, taxes, and the like were hammered out and presented jointly to the government and employers. Dues and membership benefits such as insurance, legal aid, and other services were virtually identical for the three trade union centrals.[120]

The Catholic Trade Union Federation (KAB/NKV) based its appeal to potential members on the useful work it had done, particularly in providing services and benefits. In 1954, after the bishops released their *Mandement*, Catholic trade union leaders hastened to inform the leaders of the socialist trade union federation (NVV) that this document would not be used by the KAB in membership drives.[121] In most spheres of socio-economic life in the 1950s there was mutual toleration among the different blocs. Protestants thought it perfectly natural that Catholics would want their own organizations and did not think of competing for clients among Catholics.[122] To a lesser extent this was also true of religiously neutral organizations, both socialist and liberal.

Catholic organizations in areas like sports, culture, and services, for example, Catholic soccer leagues, music federations, and health insurance associations, met an acknowledged need of Catholics and were under little pressure.[123] The performance of their specific role was rarely questioned, particularly if it did not bring them into conflict with other Catholic organizations. In certain areas, however, conflict was inevitable. The four major groupings in Catholic society whose special interests did conflict were, of course, the Catholic Trade Union Federation (KAB/NKV), the Catholic Employers' Federation (NKWV), the Catholic Retailers' Organization (NKOV), and the Catholic Farmers' Association (KNBTB). Over the years a number of structures were set up to reconcile the differing economic interests of these organizations or at least to mitigate the consequences of conflicting positions taken by them. For example, in 1919, largely as a result of the climate created by Troelstra's abortive attempt at revolution, Catholic workers and employers in four different industrial sectors announced the creation of the Roman Catholic Central Council of Corporate Organization.[124] The goal of this council was to implement an elementary form of workers' participation at the level of the different branches of industry (but not at the individual plant level) to deal with the determination of wages and hours. This experiment in cooperation collapsed, however, during the recession of 1922, when the largest industries walked out of the council.

In 1945, as part of postwar reconstruction, Dutch government planners hoped to set up a corporatist society involving the participation of every relevant socio-economic grouping, including consumers, at all levels of industrial enterprise.[125] This concept was known as "Publicly Ordered Enterprises" (PBO) and was influenced by Catholic thought as derived from *Rerum Novarum* and *Quadragesimo Anno* and by social democratic thinking of the 1930s. It was also strongly favoured by Catholic political leaders in the late 1940s. Unfortunately the PBO scheme, which was supposed to cover virtually every type of commercial activity, was unsuccessful except in certain agricultural sectors. Nevertheless it illustrated the willingness on the part of many groups in the Netherlands, especially Catholics, to find schemes which would reconcile the different economic interests in one harmonious whole.

Within the Catholic subculture one institution which did enjoy some success after World War II was the Catholic Council of Discussion (*Raad van Overleg*), consisting of the leaders of the four major Catholic socio-economic organizations.[126] However, it was not a decision-making body: during meetings agreements were never arrived at nor were possible solutions to problems likely to be discussed. The major purpose of these meetings was to provide the leaders of the four organizations with a mutual understanding of their differing positions. The council met no more than two or three times a year and the meetings stopped in the early 1970s.[127]

A mutual understanding of their respective positions may have helped leaders in the development of compromises in major socio-economic issues in arenas outside the Catholic bloc. One important forum in which decisions were often arrived at was the Social Economic Council (SER),[128] created in the postwar reconstruction period and still in being today. All major interest groups in Dutch society are represented in this council, which is responsible for providing the Dutch government with concrete advice and proposals on socio--economic questions. Up to the late 1960s it was the single most important economic policy-making body in the Netherlands. At meetings of the SER in the 1950s and 1960s, Catholic employers and labour leaders tended to support their Protestant, socialist, or liberal counterparts rather than their co-religionists.[129]

There were other conflict-reducing bodies and coordinating agencies within the Catholic subculture. There was (and still is) a committee to provide some coordination among Catholic organizations active in social welfare, youth work, care for senior citizens, and so on.[130] The KRO draws its twenty-six directors from the different sectors of the Catholic subculture. This policy of ensuring that its board represents a cross-section of the Catholic population is enshrined in the KRO statutes.[131] The Catholic party, as we shall see in the next chapter, did try, in a more informal fashion, to ensure that major sectors within the Catholic subculture were represented within the parliamentary party.

At the top of the Catholic organizations there were cases of overlapping memberships. For example, a top executive of the Catholic Retailers' Organization, W. Perquin, was simultaneously a member of the board of the KRO and chairman of the Catholic party. J. van der Campen was active in several social welfare organizations such as the Catholic Emigration Bureau, the Catholic Bureau for Internal Migration, and the Catholic Council for Social Welfare.[132] Yet even these leaders operated within a limited circle. Rarely indeed was a leader involved in Catholic education, cultural organizations, socio-economic organizations, and the Catholic party. Rather they operated within restricted areas such as economic life or cultural life, and might meet each other only within organizations such as the KRO or the Catholic party.

On the whole little attempt was made to coordinate the activities of the Catholic organizations or to enforce a uniform standard. The common denominator was that these organizations were Catholic. Their statutes were all approved by the bishops. Before World War II the bishops were quite stringent in their assessment of new organizations and occasionally applications would be rejected. In the 1950s, however, approval by the bishops became a more routine matter. The statutes of virtually every Catholic organization still contain the preamble that the organization is based upon Catholic principles and the Catholic vision of society and that the goal of the organization is to implement these principles in everyday life.[133] Yet after receiving approval the organization, particularly in socio-economic and service areas, would proceed to operate in a manner very similar to that of liberal, socialist, or Protestant organizations. There was very little about them that was distinctively Catholic.

4. Clientele

Without doubt the bishops, clergy, and lay Catholic leaders invested a great deal of energy in ensuring the cohesion of the Catholic subculture. Yet in focusing on the leadership and the role of organizations one should not neglect the other factor in the equation making for subcultural cohesion, namely the clientele. Why did ordinary Catholics willingly follow the instructions of the bishop and the clergy for so many years? This question raises a second one relating to the unusual composition of the clientele: insofar as the Catholic population represents a cross-section of Dutch society containing Catholic nobility, Catholic manufacturers and businessmen as well as Catholic workers, how did they reconcile their class or group interests with membership in the Catholic subculture?

To answer these questions one first has to examine the general social and economic conditions which enabled the church to mobilize and encapsulate the Catholic population. Throughout most of the nineteenth century the Dutch economy was largely stagnant. Based primarily on agriculture, trade, and commerce, it had only a low level of industrialization. Generally the Netherlands had not changed much since the golden years of the seventeenth century.[134] In the nineteenth century the country became urbanized to some degree but it has never developed large urban centres like Manchester or Glasgow. Rotterdam is the only city which comes at all close to this model.[135] It is even possible to talk of a process of de-urbanization in the eighteenth and early nineteenth centuries. The population of Amsterdam fell from 241,000 in 1748 to 180,000 in 1815. Cities like Leiden and Haarlem saw their population drop by almost half.[136] Poor crops and lack of industrial activity resulted in conditions which, according to William Petersen, were just as bad as, if not worse than, those in Ireland. Perhaps because of this the Dutch working class throughout the nineteenth century has usually been characterized as docile, grateful to receive work of any kind. The Dutch economic historian Brugmans writes that the Dutch worker was "one dully resigned to his miserable existence, lacking the physical and spiritual strength to rouse himself, with too limited a development to make even the possibility of an improvement in his situation conceivable."[137]

Employers were often seen as father figures, "philanthropists who gave work to the poor."[138] This was true of both Catholic and non-Catholic workers. Many of the early trade unions were first conceived of as mutual aid societies and were decidedly non-militant. Their statutes often contained a preamble denying the notion of class-conflict or noting that their aim of improving the lot of the working class was consistent with all due respect for the different classes in society. In 1872 a local of the cigar makers' union in Rotterdam (non-Catholic), in a collective letter to their employer thanking him for a raise, noted that "workers themselves and not necessarily society were largely to blame for their poverty."[139] In the second half of the nineteenth century a number of commentators remarked upon the harmonious relations existing between employers and employees in the Netherlands compared with the situation in countries like France.[140]

When industrialization did begin in the late nineteenth century, it was not as rapid or explosive as had been the case in Germany. Many of the Catholic clergy who had seen at first hand the consequences of industrialization in other countries tried to forestall them in the Netherlands by organizing workers. The work of Father Poels in the mining district of Limburg has already been described. In so doing the priests discovered that many workers were uncooperative and lacking in interest. Father Ariëns, in setting up a trade union for textile workers, complained that he often could not entice workers to come to organizational meetings with a view to improving their condition unless alcoholic refreshments and entertainment were provided.[141]

While the working class in the Netherlands was generally less militant than in other West European countries, the religious workers were particularly quiescent. Catholic and Protestant workers refrained from participating in the railway strike of 1903.[142] The attitude of the Catholic workers can best be described as uncritical, and this was largely due to the influence of the church and the Catholic educational system. Catholics were taught to accept the authority and guidance of the church without question. Many Catholic priests thought that acquiring skills beyond elementary reading and arithmetic was their prerogative alone. If ordinary Catholics received any further education it was in a trade school (boys) or a household school (girls).

On an aggregate basis Catholics were less well educated than other blocs in Dutch society. For example, in table 2.4 one can see that Catholics are significantly underrepresented among those holding university degrees. Thus in 1947, although Catholics constituted 38.5 per cent of the total population, only 18 per cent of those holding degrees were Catholic. In recent years Catholics have been catching up with the rest of the population in educational achievement, though as of 1971 they still lagged behind.[143]

According to the Catholic sociologist M. Matthijsen, the low level of educational achievement in the past can largely be explained by the lack of an extensive Catholic secondary school system. Before 1917 there were virtually no Catholic secondary schools in the Netherlands and Catholic students were discouraged from attending non-Catholic secondary schools.[144] In the 1920s, when the Catholic emancipation movement was at its strongest, a program of building schools was begun which continued right up to the 1970s. By 1930 18 per cent of all secondary students attended Catholic schools (Catholic population 35 per cent of total). In 1947 the proportion was 26 per cent and in 1964 38 per cent (Catholics 38.5 and 40.4 per cent of the total population in 1947 and 1960 respectively).[145] Despite this dramatic increase, before the 1960s Catholics were generally less well educated than the rest of Dutch society. This helps to explain why Catholics were less critical than non-Catholics and more open to suggestion, and also why the clergy spent a great deal of time protecting their flocks from wayward influences. It should not be thought, however, that Catholics were completely undemanding or docile when faced by pressures from within or outside their subculture. One can think of the Catholic population as a market for services delivered by the church and one of the reasons for the viability of the church in the Netherlands was the fact that it delivered goods in a satisfactory manner.

Employing the market analogy, one can begin by asking to what degree the Dutch Catholic spirit of Jansenism, so characteristic of the ecclesiastical hierarchy and the clergy, was evident in the Catholic population at large. Was there a market for the rigorous control exercised by the bishops?

In the years following the Reformation, when the practice of Catholicism was forbidden in the northern part of the Netherlands, it took a high degree of motivation for Catholics to overcome their fears and practise their religion by attending mass at the so-called secret churches. Over the years the less motivated ceased to be Catholics; only the more strong-willed persisted.[146] In doing so they willingly accepted the tenets of the Catholic faith and acted upon them. In a study made in 1951 of the attitudes of young women of different faiths concerning the number of their future offspring,[147] A. E. Diels found that both Catholic and Calvinist women wanted a significantly larger number of children than other groups. Instructive are some of the responses given by Catholic women when asked how many children they would like:

No occupation (aged 27): As many as our dear Lord finds suitable.

Household servant (21): As many as God sees fit to send me and I am not afraid of ten.

Nurse (32): No limit, the more, the better, in the hope that God will bless me with a large number of children.

Cleaner (23): Even if there would be twenty, each child brings its blessing and every child is a new wonder. I find it beautiful to work with God in the creation of a child; that is why they would

TABLE 2.4
University Degree Holders by Year by Religion (per 10,000)

Year	Catholic	Protestant	Calvinist	Lutheran	Remonstrants (small Protestant sect)	No Church	Total Population
1930	28	40	27	244	618	172	62
1947	51	73	52	371	982	174	92
1960	74	88	87	446	1157	204	116

Source: P. van Hooijdonk, "Intellectuele emancipatie van de Nederlandse Katholieken in de laatsen jaren," *Sociale Wetenschappen* 8 (1965): 219 (reprinted by permission).
Note: Population consists of everyone over age 30.

all be welcome. God will help us whatever the circumstances. I enter into my marriage filled with joy.[148]

The church catered to religious needs which to a large extent were genuinely felt. To go to mass, to partake of communion, and to receive absolution provided comfort and peace of mind for many Catholics. Although this market for religious needs was in large part created by the church through early socialization, it nevertheless did exist and would not have immediately disappeared if the church had suddenly ceased to exercise its mechanisms of social control.

What about the market for services less directly linked to religious needs? The question arises whether Catholics joined Catholic sports organizations or signed up with Catholic health insurance programs merely because they were told to do so by their pastors. The influence of the church did indeed tend to limit freedom of choice, but for the most part this did not involve any unusual sacrifice on the part of Catholics. Or to put it another way: there was no particular incentive for Catholics *not* to join or partake of a service offered by the relevant Catholic organization. As mentioned earlier, many Catholic organizations provided services that were identical to or at least competitive with the services offered by their Protestant and neutral counterparts.[149] This was particularly true of trade unions in the postwar period, but also to a large extent of broadcasting, newspapers, health services, and the like, where there were no marked differences in the quality of the services rendered. In fact there is evidence that ordinary

Catholics may have felt that the services offered by some of their own institutions were superior in quality even by non-religious standards. In 1960 the KRO undertook some marketing research to discover which programs Catholics recognized. The names of both KRO programs and those of the other broadcasting organizations were included in the survey (see table 2.5). Respondents were asked whether they recognized the program rather than whether they actually watched it. Nevertheless it is reasonably safe to infer that a high rate of recognition indicates that people watch the program as well. Interestingly, four out of the five top-ranked programs were those broadcast by the KRO. These programs can best be described as for the most part popular light entertainment, which suggests that Catholics watched them not for religious reasons but because they wanted to be entertained. It appears that the KRO was highly successful in catering to those tastes.

In the course of Dutch trade union development, the Catholic unions won a number of crucial economic battles. Father Poels was highly successful in playing upon the sentiments of Catholic workers, exploiting latent anti-north Holland feelings of the miners by pointing out that the socialists had their base there. He led protests against mine management by complaining that virtually all the higher executives of Dutch State Mines (the mines were operated by a state-owned enterprise) were non-Catholic. Yet he was also able to exact decent wages from management. In 1915 the socialist mineworkers went on strike, demanding a 10 per cent increase. They were joined by the Catholic unions. When mine management proved to be unyielding, leaders of both Catholic and socialist unions asked Poels to intervene on their behalf. Poels talked to management and succeeded in obtaining the full 10 per cent raise, and according to Th. Wöltgens the influence of the socialist mineworkers' union diminished considerably thereafter.[150]

On a European-wide basis the success of the Dutch church in not alienating Catholic workers has already been noted. This leads to the further question of how the Dutch church also succeeded in not alienating middle- and upper middle-class Catholics, whose interests were not infrequently in conflict with those of Catholic workers. Broadly speaking, the Catholic church, and the Catholic subculture as a whole, were sufficiently flexible and differentiated to provide a role and status for all Catholics.

During the interwar period and to some extent in the 1940s and 1950s the parish church would organize retreats for the different classes, ensuring that a group on a retreat was homogeneous in terms of socio-economic status. In the parish church itself people could, and did, pay for specially reserved places, at a rate which varied according

TABLE 2.5
TV Program Recognition by Broadcasting Organizations

Program	AVRO (Liberal) %	Rank	KRO (Catholic) %	Rank	NCRV (Protestant) %	Rank	VARA (Socialist) %	Rank
Attention (religious)					21.2	17		
Father Knows Best			22.2	14	26.6	8		
TV Dance Program			43.2	2				
Piste (cabaret)							39.3	4
St. Germain des Prés (cabaret)			33.2	6				
Brandpunt (news program)	20.5	18						
Rooster (news program)			52.2	1				
Saturday Evening Accords (religious)			21.3	16				
Monthly Concert Hour			21.7	15				
From Our Sports Editor			26.0	9				
Flipje the Sorcerer's Apprentice			23.5	11	22.2	13		
The Bennett Sisters			38.7	5				
Dutch Evening Lecture							30.7	7
Quiz Show								
Ivanhoe							22.3	12
Top or Flop			39.8	3	24.3	10		
Hitchcock (film series)								
Memo								

Source: KASKI, "De betekenis van het sociaal onderzoek van radio en televisie. Voorstel voor een onderzoek ten behoeve van de KRO," Memorandum No. 130 (1961), p. 18.

to the distance from the altar. Weddings and funerals could be arranged on a scale ranging from the austere to the grandiose, again priced accordingly. There were, and still are, several organizations catering to the recreational, professional, and economic interests of non-working-class Catholics. In the south the prevailing anti-north sentiments helped reinforce the loyalty of Catholic businessmen and entrepreneurs to Catholic socio-economic organizations. For those in sectors such as the pottery and porcelain industries, which were predominantly located in the south and in Catholic hands, a Catholic-based organization was a natural choice.[151]

At the organizational level there was always a degree of tension between Catholic employers and Catholic trade unions and this tension did at times threaten to damage the "beautiful unity" of the subculture wrought by the church. Yet generally the Catholic middle classes played an important role in helping to maintain the cohesion and viability of that subculture. Denied entrance to the civil service and many professional activities like the practice of medicine, first by law and later by covert and sometimes not so covert discrimination, many Catholics went into commerce and light manufacturing such as the pottery industry, gin making, and the making of cigars. Many Catholic entrepreneurs of the early nineteenth century were newly arrived immigrants from Germany who played an important role in revitalizing the rather stagnant condition of Catholic life at that time. Later Bismarck's *Kulturkampf* brought more Catholic businessmen and entrepreneurs.[152] Most of the major department store chains in the Netherlands were started by such immigrants and are still in the hands of their descendants.

These and other firms owned by Catholics often provided employment for Catholics, thus helping to create an environment suitable for insulating Catholics from potentially damaging influences. The church actively encouraged the development of such enterprises, particularly in northern areas where Catholics were in a minority.[153]

The existence of a middle and upper middle class within the Catholic subculture, albeit relatively smaller than those of the other blocs, provided avenues for upward mobility. Although vertical mobility among Catholics has been quite low,[154] it did mean that those aspiring to higher goals could for the most part attempt to reach those goals without denying their Catholicism or having to move outside the subculture.

Generally speaking, in the twentieth century the range of Catholic organizations and institutions was sufficiently extensive to cater to the needs of Catholics whether they were plumbers or sculptors. There was always some tension between working and non-working-class elements, and between the church and certain cultural organizations such as those for artists and writers. However, few Catholics rejected their faith because of conflicts of this sort, which were usually contained within the subculture.

A further aspect of the clientele is related to the question of social control—a notion which usually implies control from above. Thus in the case of the Catholic church control emanates from the top, filtering down through the clergy to the laity. Social control, however, can also be horizontal, that is, control by one's peers. One characteristic of Dutch society is the high degree of social conformity, a characteristic often thought to be related to the influence of Calvinism. Dutch citizens appear to want to show both God and their neighbours that they are good citizens, that they have nothing to hide.[155] For example, in the evening on a typical street one is able to observe through large picture windows, the curtains deliberately left undrawn, families going about their ordinary business. The practice suggests that Dutch people, both Catholic and non-Catholic, are very sensitive as to what the neighbours might think of their behaviour. Many Catholics in the past undoubtedly conformed to the precepts of the church for this reason and not only because of what the pastor might do or say. Particularly in the Catholic south, and in largely homogeneous Catholic villages and towns in the north, absence from mass could lead to a good deal of speculation among the absentee's acquaintances. In more urbanized areas, particularly in cities like Rotterdam, pressure from one's peers as well as from the church may have been easier to avoid.

Before the mid-1960s no data on attendance at mass were gathered, at least not on a systematic and reliable basis.[156] There are data, however, on the rate of Easter observance for the year 1956. Table 2.6 indicates the variation in Easter observance within the Netherlands. The highest rate of observance occurred in the dioceses of Breda, Den Bosch, and Roermond, which basically cover the Catholic south. The dioceses of Groningen and Utrecht cover the east and northeast, which is less populated and urbanized than the western part. In these two dioceses the rate of Easter observance is almost as high as in the south. The rate is lowest in the dioceses of Haarlem and Rotterdam, which encompass major cities like Amsterdam, Haarlem, Rotterdam, The Hague, and Leiden. The willingness of Dutch Catholics to follow the dictates of the church compare favourably with that of Catholics in other countries. In 1954 53.7 per cent of West German Catholics attended mass at Easter. In Austria the figure was 42 per cent for the year 1955.[157] In contrast the rate in the Netherlands was 87.9 per cent for the year 1956.

Rates of Easter observance and even of mass attendance are not the best measures of religious loyalty. It is difficult to identify the different influences or to judge how much sacrifice is involved in going to Easter mass. The most reliable evidence of the loyalty of Dutch Catholics is their behaviour under circumstances of stress. A number of times the allegiance of Catholics was severely tested, yet in all cases they ended up by obediently following the orders of the bishops. There was never a crisis in which a substantial number of Catholics revolted against the authority of the church nor did there ever develop a strong anticlericalism based upon a pool of disaffected Catholics such as in France, Belgium, Italy, or Austria.

The example of the textile workers' union, Unitas, cited earlier, is worth describing in greater detail. In 1912, in all the churches of the eastern Netherlands, priests read from the pulpit a letter from the bishops to the effect that textile workers were forbidden to remain as members of this interconfessional union. Father Ariëns, one of the founders of the union, was personally most upset by the decision of the bishops and feared the alienation of the workers from the church. Nevertheless he proceeded to help carry out the order. The Catholic workers did give up their membership in Unitas but stubbornly refused to join the new Catholic union, Saint Lambertus. For the next four years the clergy worked to implement the changeover to the new union. Upon the completion of this task Father Ariëns breathed a sigh of relief and noted gratefully "that not a single soul has been lost as a result of the Unitas conflict."[158]

5. Summary

Several elements of the Catholic subculture accounted for its cohesion over a long period. Of particular importance was an ideology, dating from the time of the Reformation, which emphasized rigorous orthodoxy and minimal contact with the rest of Dutch society. Following the reinstallation of the ecclesiastical hierarchy in 1853 several generations of bishops perceived Dutch society as threatening and anti-Catholic. At the same time they fostered ultramontane sentiments, hoping that one day all of the Netherlands would once again be Roman Catholic. While pragmatically pursuing a course of peaceful coexistence with the rest of Dutch society, they also attempted to insulate Catholics from that society. The bishops were aided in this by a willing clergy, a willing lay leadership, and a willing clientele.

Social control and coercion on the part of the church were important in ensuring the loyalty of rank-and-file Catholics. But it should be stressed that loyalty to the church did not involve an unusual de-

TABLE 2.6
Easter Observance by Diocese, 1956

Location	Percentage
Groningen	92.6
Utrecht	90.1
Haarlem	78.0
Rotterdam	72.5
Breda	94.5
Den Bosch	95.4
Roermond	94.9
Total	87.9

Source: KASKI, Memorandum No. 113 (1960), table 20, p. 16.

gree of self-sacrifice or voluntarism. There was a strong element of self-interest involved in the behaviour of Catholics. First of all, the individual Catholic's spiritual needs and comforts were catered to by the church. Secondly, the services rendered by Catholic organizations in secular areas were of sufficient quality that a working-class Catholic, for example, did not need to join a socialist trade union. The clergy played an important role in obtaining social justice for workers, poor farmers, and less well-off groups during the period of industrialization. After World War II, when the predominant motive was the insulation of Catholics from the rest of society through Catholic organizations, the latter nevertheless remained competitive in quality with other organizations and offered services which were often identical to those of their neutral and Protestant counterparts.

It is also worthy of note that the Catholic subculture became highly differentiated over the years. There came into existence several highly specialized organizations which had little in common with one another, and in some cases operated quite autonomously. This was a factor contributing to the strength of the Catholic subculture; the flowering and institutionalization of many interests allowed the Catholic population to operate as a miniature society within a larger society. We will now turn to the examination of one major Catholic organization—the Catholic party—which although primarily a product of the subculture, nevertheless contributed to the well-being of the Catholic community by acting as a bridge between these numerous interests, and by representing Catholic interests to the outside world.

Chapter 3 **Dutch Catholic Politics**

One obvious answer to the question of why the vast majority of Dutch Catholics voted for the Catholic party up to and including 1963 is that the institutionalized elements of the Catholic subculture such as the church hierarchy, the clergy, and various lay organizations maintained a high degree of control over the behaviour of Catholics, thereby ensuring a solid basis of support for the party. Yet such an interpretation by itself would be inadequate. The Catholic party, like the Catholic Broadcasting Organization (KRO) and Catholic trade unions, could not rely solely on the authority of the church. There had to be some minimal return, some justification for its existence beyond the assertion of the bishops that a Catholic party was necessary for the cohesion of the Catholic subculture.

Even assuming that the Catholic population in the Netherlands before 1960 voted simply on the basis of clerical guidance, a further question remains: how did Dutch Catholics manage to field a party in election after election, participate in virtually every government coalition from 1917 onwards, and at the same time maintain a semblance of unity at the parliamentary level well into the 1960s? There were conflicting political, social, and economic interests within the Catholic subculture which needed to be reconciled. Furthermore, the Catholic party could not simply absolve itself of responsibility for the actions of Catholic cabinet ministers and for the behaviour of Catholic party members in the Second Chamber (which contains the elected members of the bicameral Dutch legislature). If the actions or policies of the Catholic party had been unsatisfactory for or detrimental to the interests of Catholic labour, farmers, or employers, the result might have been splits within the party, defections, or withdrawal of support. If such incidents had occurred on a sufficiently large scale it would have been difficult to preserve a viable and cohesive Catholic party. The electorate might have been faced with two or more competing Catholic parties.

In the following pages, therefore, this study will be concerned with how the Catholic party came into existence, how it maintained a semblance of unity and reconciled differing interests, and the nature of the role it played in the Dutch political arena. Was the party engaged in advancing the interests of the Catholic community, or was its role primarily a defensive one? Furthermore, what kind of load was placed upon the party in carrying out its responsibilities? The role of the ecclesiastical hierarchy in maintaining the unity of the party, and in ensuring that the number of defections and breakaway factions were kept to a minimum, will also be examined.

I propose to look at the means by which the Catholic party and the church were able to deliver the Catholic vote, the agencies involved and the techniques used, and the changes which occurred in these processes over the years. How much energy was expended by the party, the church, and other institutions? Was the use made of the church's authority direct or indirect? Finally, the manner in which the Catholic population responded to these mobilization techniques, and reacted to appeals to remain true to the party, will be discussed.

1. The Catholic Party

It might be supposed that the Dutch Catholic party was an efficient and disciplined political organization with a well-defined program, energetically and systematically seeking to advance and implement the goals of the Catholic subculture.[1] However, in most respects the picture that emerges from a close examination of the party is the exact opposite; as a parliamentary party it bordered on being a loose coalition of individual and group interests even at the best of times. In terms of policy the party's major role was the defence of the subculture's position vis-à-vis Dutch society. The behaviour of the Catholic party towards the other parties was marked by definite feelings of inferiority. Furthermore, there was often a wide gulf between Catholic ministers in the cabinet and members of the parliamentary party and between the parliamentary party and adherents at the grass-roots level.

The parliamentary party, from the late nineteenth century on, was frequently blessed with the presence of a strong leader. This leader was usually in close touch with, and highly dependent upon, the ecclesiastical hierarchy in maintaining the unity of the party, and in minimizing the damage that breakaway factions could inflict upon the party. All these characteristics in turn reflect elements of Dutch Catholic ideology described in the preceding chapter. The significance of these characteristics will be discussed after a historical overview.

Origins. Attempts to establish a Catholic political presence can be traced back to the efforts of Le Sage ten Broek in 1813, shortly after Catholics had been given full citizenship rights. His efforts were aimed not so much at political organization as political education. Through his newspaper, *De Ultramontaan*, he tried "to awaken even the most primitive feelings of political confidence among Catholics."[2]

In 1848 King William II granted limited responsible government under which there were to be direct elections for municipal councils, provincial legislatures, and the Second Chamber.[3] The elections for the Second Chamber were to be based on the district system. In that year Dommer van Poldersveldt proposed an "electoral organization for Catholics."[4] A central coordinating committee came into being but after a short period it was disbanded by the organizers themselves. The reason given was that "awareness by the general public of the existence of a Catholic electoral organization would place our fellow Catholics in physical jeopardy."[5] This fear of non-Catholics and their reactions was to continue into the twentieth century.

After 1848 Dutch electoral organizations of all kinds began to develop at the district level (the number of districts varied from sixty-eight to eighty-two between 1848 and 1888), usually dominated by local notables. Along with the various liberal and conservative organizations there was a handful of Catholic ones. Many Catholics, however, tended to support the secular Liberals, especially in the provinces of North and South Holland. These Catholics, mainly young intellectuals centred around the Amsterdam newspaper, *De Tijd*, saw their support for liberalism as a means of securing their religious institutions. Specifically, they hoped it might serve their cause of reestablishing the Roman Catholic ecclesiastical hierarchy.[6] They managed to obtain the support of the clergy in the south, who were important in mobilizing the vote,[7] and as a result many of the Catholics elected in the south were liberal in orientation. Aside from helping to mobilize the vote the clergy as a whole remained aloof from politics.[8]

There was no Catholic party as such although Catholic politicians did tend to coalesce on certain issues such as those concerning parochial schools. One Catholic politician, Nuyens, writing in 1857, noted: "If one understands the word 'party' to mean a certain number of men, who share the same principles, and who defend similar interests then indeed there does exist a Catholic party. However, if one understands this word to mean an association, organized with the aim of obtaining certain objectives, disciplined and led by a recognised leadership . . . no! then there exists in our group no such party."[9]

In 1853 the Catholic-Liberal Papo-Thorbecke coalition, was successful in reestablishing the Catholic hierarchy. However, the Liberals had not been so favourably disposed towards parochial education as had first been hoped. Moreover, many secular Liberals were rather snobbish and that tended to offend Catholics. In 1864 the papal encyclical *Quanta Cura* demanded that all Catholics do their utmost to ensure that their children received a Catholic education and warned against the dangers of liberalism. In 1868 the Dutch bishops reaffirmed the intent of *Quanta Cura*,[10] and this contributed to a falling out between the Catholics and the Liberals.

In 1870 the Roman Catholic Electoral Association of North Brabant, organized under the leadership of J. B. van Son, attacked the Liberal-Catholic coalition, thereby obtaining the support of local clergy who were strongly influenced by *Quanta Cura*. It had immediate electoral success, taking virtually all the seats in that province.[11] This marked the shift away from the Papo-Thorbecke coalition of the 1840s, 1850s, and 1860s, a shift which occurred largely at the urging of the clergy in the two southern provinces. In addition, manufacturers in North Brabant began to oppose the Liberals for economic reasons, namely the tariff law of 1862 which had placed them at a disadvantage.[12] However, there was still no national organization or federation of Catholic electoral associations.

It was the example of the Calvinists under the leadership of Groen van Prinsterer and Abraham Kuyper that gave the Catholics impetus towards developing some sort of party organization. Just as the Catholics were rebelling against the Liberals, the orthodox Calvinists were rebelling against the Conservative party. Appealing to the "small people" (*Kleyne Luyden*) with the claim that government institutions and schools were no longer sufficiently Protestant in character, Van Prinsterer and Kuyper began organizing the Anti-School Law League in 1872.[13] In the same year they also started the daily newspaper, *De Standaard*. In 1879 the league, having enjoyed phenomenal growth, transformed itself into the Anti-Revolutionary Party (ARP) ("revolution" here signifying the centralizing and secular principles of the French Revolution).[14]

In 1880 Father Herman Schaepman was elected to the Second Chamber and during the next twenty-three years came to play a crucial role in nurturing a nascent Catholic party. He perceived that there was a common cause to be made between Catholics and Anti-Revolutionaries on the schools issue; both groups wanted control of their own educational systems. Inspired by the proposed Anti-Revolutionary Program of 1878, he designed a similar document for Catholics and in 1883 introduced "The Catholic Party: A Proposed Program."[15] Although Schaepman was an extremely energetic and imposing figure, his efforts produced only large-scale criticism. A number of Catholic politicians felt that the needs of Catholics were best served by supporting the Conservative party. Indeed, within the Second Chamber during the early 1890s there were actually two Catholic factions: a conservative one led by Bahlmann from North Brabant and a democratic one led by Schaepman.[16] The two factions had meals in separate sections of the parliamentary dining-room; there was little interaction between them. What divided them was not so much their differing views on Catholic interests with regard to schools, for example, as it was their views on the extension of the franchise and the question of Catholic aggressiveness in pursuing this and other goals. Conservative Catholics, who tended to reflect the interests of Catholic businessmen, felt that Catholics should maintain a low profile in politics. Schaepman, in contrast, had connections with the already developing Catholic trade union movement and was quite willing to use political means to achieve his aims.

It was during this period that Schaepman engineered the alliance with the Anti-Revolutionaries. In an electoral system based on district representation Catholics were at a disadvantage in districts outside the south. Schaepman persuaded a number of Catholic electoral associations and clergy to support ARP candidates, thus ensuring the election of several ARP members where they normally would not have won. This meant that Anti-Revolutionaries tended to be over-represented in the Second Chamber compared with the Catholics.[17] Moreover, since the ARP was better organized and more militant, it tended to take a leading role in the battle for confessional schools. In 1889 and 1891 important concessions were obtained, giving partial state support to confessional schools. This success was due to the fact that the Catholic-ARP coalition had obtained an absolute majority within the Second Chamber in the election of 1888, largely as a result of the lowering of the franchise qualifications in 1887. Most of the new voters turned out to be anti-Liberal.

In 1896 the franchise was extended once again. Schaepman's growing influence was apparent in the 1897 election,[18] in which he was helped considerably by the progressive papal encyclical *Rerum No-*

varum. The Catholic members of the Second Chamber who gathered in the city of Utrecht in 1896 had promised to accept faithfully all papal encyclicals in the formulation of their programs and in particular to use *Rerum Novarum* as the basis for their program on social questions.[19]

The acceptance of a common program by Catholic members of the Second Chamber did not imply the development of a national party organization. That did not begin until 1904—one year after Schaepman's death—when the General League of Roman Catholic Electoral Associations came into being. It consisted of a central office and, co-equal with it, all Roman Catholic electoral associations. In spite of attempts to provide as much autonomy as possible for individual associations, the North Brabant association refused to join the league.[20] At this point the bishops were still ambivalent about Catholic participation in politics and thus made no effort to ensure a cohesive Catholic party. The league held annual meetings attended by representatives from the individual associations. For the most part it remained a purely electoral organization. In the Second Chamber Catholic members were not a cohesive group, but highly undisciplined when it came to voting on different bills.[21]

In 1917 the joint efforts of the ARP and Catholics came to fruition with the so-called Pacification. This agreement, the result of a bargain among the Liberals, ARP, and Catholics, with the Social Democratic Party (SDAP) playing a supporting role, resolved three outstanding issues, introducing not only full state support for confessional schools but also full suffrage for all males over twenty-five (women received the vote in 1919) and a direct proportional electoral system.[22]

The new electoral arrangement had two effects on the cohesiveness of the Catholic party. For one, the use of candidate lists, as required by the proportional electoral system, meant that a greater degree of centralization and coordination was necessary on the part of the league in order to present connected lists in the eighteen electoral districts.[23] On the other hand, the possibility of a unified party was threatened by the ease with which Catholic splinter groups could enter parliament by virtue of the extremely low threshold requirement. The league was helped, however, by the church hierarchy. The bishops in 1918 forbade Catholic social organizations to participate in politics and ruled that the R. C. League was the only appropriate political organization for Catholics. Smaller Catholic parties which did compete in the electoral arena were effectively cut off from such significant bases of direct support as the Catholic trade unions and the clergy.[24]

The most powerful competitor of the Catholic party in the early

1920s was the Saint Michäel's League, a left-wing Catholic political movement attracting the support of many young Catholics and Catholic workers. It did not actually run in elections but threatened to do so and proved to be a demoralizing force for the Catholic party. At the request of the bishops, negotiations were begun between the R.C. and Saint Michäel's leagues, and in 1923 an agreement was reached. Saint Michäel would be incorporated into the main R. C. League on the understanding that the latter would transform itself from a mere league to a genuine democratic national Catholic party. An organizing committee was named and the Roman Catholic State Party (RKSP) was born in 1926.[25] The reorganization involved a central party council, individual memberships, and greater supervision of the eighteen district associations. A research bureau was set up which was responsible for drafting election programs and consulting Catholic social organizations as to their interests and demands.

This did not end centrifugal tendencies within the party or the rise of competing Catholic political organizations. However, the Catholic party from then on demonstrated a remarkable capacity to contain and resolve conflict within the organization and to absorb or co-opt the competition. These central features of the Catholic party endured well into the late 1960s when significant elements of the party withdrew, never to be reabsorbed.

The Instrumentality of the Catholic Party. The unusual capacity of the Catholic party to contain and absorb conflict resulted in part from the practice of not requiring rigid adherence to a set of principles and rules on the part of the membership. The bishops merely said that there should be only one Catholic party. This allowed a great deal of flexibility which was enhanced by the fact that most people viewed the party, and the need for a party, in instrumental terms.

Much of the literature on political parties and political processes focuses not only on the concrete functions they perform but also on their affective or symbolic roles.[26] Not only the general public but also elite members of a society tend to develop loyalties and emotional ties to their party. This was true of Dutch Catholics and their party, yet at the same time a common denominator among many Catholic political leaders, as well as the bishops, was their ambivalence about the very need for a Catholic party. The primary emotional significance of the party lay in its contribution to the unity of the Catholic subculture.

Schaepman himself, usually seen as the father of the Catholic party, had originally favoured an interconfessional party, hoping that cooperation with the ARP would lead to the development of such an organization.[27] For him, a Catholic party was necessary only insofar as there

Dutch Catholic Politics | 65

was no alternative. In his view Catholic interests needed political representation and goals such as state support for confessional schools could only be obtained through political action. For these functions, a centre party with an interconfessional basis was sufficient and therefore preferable. But since the ARP was unwilling to join in such a venture a strong Catholic party remained necessary. Schaepman's feelings were not unique. The position of most Catholic politicians during the nineteenth and early twentieth centuries was to look to existing parties as vehicles for promoting both Catholic interests and their own socio-economic interests as well as those of the special interest groups to which they belonged. Thus we have Catholic political leaders first supporting the Liberals; then flirting with the Conservatives; and then supporting the ARP.

In the years immediately following the introduction of a proportional electoral system in 1918 the proposal for a more centralized Catholic party received considerable opposition from certain Catholic political leaders. P. J. M. Aalberse, one of the outstanding figures in Dutch Catholic history, protested this development as unnecessary and even dangerous. A Catholic political party, he pointed out, would have to take at least some responsibility for unpopular government measures. Blame might thereby fall on the church, doing irreparable damage to its position in Dutch society and possibly evoking retaliatory measures by non-Catholics against Catholics.[28] Aalberse was one of the most active, intelligent, and socially progressive of Catholic leaders. Furthermore, he was an avowed Catholic and proud of it. As a student at the University of Leiden he was instrumental in organizing the Catholic Student Society as a reaction against the secular, liberal-oriented Leiden Student Corps. He was a strong proponent of national Catholic trade unions and had been an adviser to, and a supporter of, the bishops in their decision to order Catholic workers to abandon the textile workers union, Unitas. Yet when it came to defining the Catholic position vis-à-vis the political world, Aalberse stopped short. In part his views were based on perceptive analysis but they were also influenced by the isolationist tendencies of Dutch Catholicism and the collective inferiority complex from which the Dutch Catholic subculture suffered.

Generally the Catholic party lagged behind other Catholic organizations in institutional development. When it did achieve formal existence in 1926 it tended to be overshadowed in importance by the newly formed KRO and the Catholic University. These institutions, during the interwar period, were much more likely to stir feelings of pride in the hearts of Dutch Catholics. And Catholic trade unions and employer associations were much more successful in obtaining approval and support from the bishops.[29]

The period immediately following World War II is also illustrative of the party's development. The German occupation had brought together many people from different blocs, especially within the resistance movement. And it was during this time that some Catholics decided that the pillarized structures in Dutch society were unnecessary and wasteful. The postwar Labour party (PvdA, based on the prewar SDAP) made a point of guaranteeing freedom of religion and religious institutions. Several left-wing Catholics joined the Labour party.[30] The Catholic hierarchy, however, led by Cardinal de Jong, made known its wish to see resurrected not only Catholic social institutions but also the Catholic party. This process of rebuilding Catholic institutions received a head start from the fact that the southern Catholic part of the Netherlands, where many Catholic leaders were based, was liberated first by the Allies and was thus a fertile area for the reestablishment of these institutions.[31] Left-wing Catholics who were committed to *not* resurrecting the Catholic party were for the most part located in the northern part of the country and unaware of what was happening in the south. One of the more prominent leaders of the postwar Catholic party described what happened:

> During the war I was active in the *Nederlandse Volksbeweging* [a resistance movement]. . . . I intended to become a member of the PvdA. . . . On thinking back I remember being quite upset when I saw all these Catholic party bureaucrats from before the war come down from Tilburg and Den Bosch [cities in the south], setting up shop in The Hague as if absolutely nothing had changed. I asked, "Where did you guys come from? I haven't seen you for years!" In the end I became involved with the Catholic party [KVP] because after all I was Catholic. I was a rather unwilling recruit, however. (Interview 4)

Commitment to the Catholic party before the war was low. Among some Catholics at the end of the war, this commitment had been lowered even further, largely because of the experience of cooperating with non-Catholics during the German occupation. Most politically active Catholics, however, did rejoin the new Catholic party. In part the leverage used by Catholic party leaders was emotional. They cited the moral reasons given by the bishops, namely to safeguard the Catholic religion and ward off the evils of communism. However, the three important Catholic leaders who did the actual work of resurrecting the party—Romme, Stokman, and Witteman—also stressed pragmatic aspects. They were successful in recruiting not only older Catholics but also a number of young Catholic intellectuals by emphasizing the proposed socially progressive orientation of the new Catholic party. The party name was changed from the Roman Catholic State Party to the Catholic People's Party (KVP). The party's research bureau was given a new label and a nonpartisan air.[32] One such new recruit, hired to work in the research institute, noted: "For me the programmatic aspects were extremely important. I had to be convinced that the new party would be socially progressive, that it would cooperate to the utmost with the PVDA. . . . My commitment was to the program not really to the party" (Interview 16).

There were other practical aspects as well. The ARP had firmly reestablished itself as had the Christian Historical Union (CHU). The situation was uncertain and the safest prediction one could make in the early postwar period was that the prewar social and political structures would reassert themselves. For many politically active Catholics it seemed best to rejoin the Catholic party.

A commitment to the Catholic party that was both pragmatic and based on a strong loyalty to the church meant that no unusual loads were placed upon the party—at least for the time being. There were no rigid principles to be upheld or to define beyond a commitment to uphold the integrity of the church. This resulted in a high degree of flexibility and the ability to co-opt people of diverse political tendencies.

Policy and Programs. The Catholic party's flexibility with regard to political attitudes among the membership is also reflected in its policies and orientations towards the other parties. The major stimulus which originally brought Catholics together in the political arena was the schools issue. The agreement which resolved the demands involved in that issue, the Pacification of 1917, served as a template for the resolution of similar problems. Broadcasting was organized on socio-religious lines and state funds for health-care were channelled to socio-religious health-care agencies. These were issues which could in some sense be defined as Catholic. Since the major goals had been achieved in 1917 the tactics subsequently employed can best be described as defensive ones aimed at safeguarding what had been won. For example, at various times attempts were made (mostly by the Liberals) to do away with the pillarized nature of broadcasting and to substitute an organization based on the model offered by the British Broadcasting Corporation.[33] Each time this topic was broached, the Catholic party, as well as the other confessional parties, made it known that they strongly opposed such a change. In 1965 a government which included Liberal ministers fell after failing to reach agreement on a proposal for revamping the broadcasting system.

The interwar period is usually referred to as the heyday of the confessional parties. At election time the three parties (ARP, CHU, and RKSP) polled between them 50 to 60 per cent of the vote. They dominated the cabinet, usually taking the most important portfolios. Yet the Catholic party was never successful in attaining even modest goals directly concerning the church such as the repeal of the ordinance against religious parades in the north. In part, this was because the confessional parties were largely concerned with the problems of running a government. Especially during the depression years the RKSP was preoccupied with the debate about how to deal with the overwhelming economic problems of the day. There were battles within the Catholic party between the left and the right wings on what policies to support. The flexibility of Catholic party ideology, however, permitted the party to flow with the general tide of opinion, as set by the ARP. During the 1930s the RKSP supported, with two exceptions, fairly conservative fiscal policies aimed at balancing the books and maintaining the value of the guilder.[34] Religious issues remained in the background.

In the postwar period Catholic party policy, again demonstrating a high degree of flexibility, supported the Labour party. In the beginning, the emphasis was on cooperation, the rebuilding of the economy, and a high degree of social justice so that people would never have to suffer again as in the depression of the 1930s. In this atmosphere a series of coalition cabinets were formed in which the PvdA and the KVP were the major partners. The KVP stressed bread and butter issues such as increasing the supply of housing and family allowances. They noted that the resulting government policies were policies for the household, a theme which dovetailed nicely with Roman Catholic beliefs concerning the sanctity of the family. The only action by the KVP which was directly related to religious beliefs was their veto of a proposal to give a government grant to the humanist association, allegedly a group of atheists whom the KVP felt were determined to undermine the Christian basis of Dutch society.[35]

It was in their relations with other parties that the uncertainty and general lack of self-confidence of the Catholic subculture becomes evident. It was the ARP which had taken the initiative in fighting for full state support for confessional schools. According to I. Schöffer, in examining relations between Catholic and Protestant leaders in the interwar period, it is plain to see who were the leaders and who were the led.[36] The fact that in 1918 Ruys de Beerenbrouck became the first Catholic prime minister had a certain symbolic value, but he was generally conceded to be a rather weak figure, a kindly diplomatic person without strong leadership qualities. The ARP political leader, Colijn, who later became prime minister, was considered a much stronger, even obstinate figure.[37] Not that the Catholic parliamentary party lacked strong figures. P. J. M. Aalberse, a centrist and not part of the RKSP's left wing, did outstanding work in his cabinet portfolio of social affairs, pushing through much needed social welfare legislation in the 1920s. Yet his one-term cabinet appointment was not renewed though it was known he would have continued in that post if it had been offered to him again. Furthermore, he was never seriously pushed by the RKSP as a candidate for the prime ministership.[38]

On the other hand, the Catholic party was represented in every cabinet but one between 1918 and 1977, a record equalled by no other party. The one exception occurred in 1939 in a government that lasted only fifteen days, demonstrating that a cabinet without Catholic representation was not likely to have a very long life expectancy. As Hans Daalder has pointed out, it became axiomatic that Dutch cabinets could not be built without the Catholic party.[39]

The refusal to take a strong position in government, and the fear of being left in opposition, indicated both the Catholics' lack of self-confidence and their pragmatic, cautious approach. The behaviour of Catholic political leaders was also indicative of the difficulties involved in balancing the different socio-economic interests within the Catholic subculture. By taking responsibility for controversial decisions there was a considerable chance of alienating one or more of the factions within the party. And during the 1930s the Catholic Trade Union Movement did in fact withdraw its support from the Catholic party. The constant Catholic presence in cabinet was frequently cited by Catholic party leaders as a reason why different interests should support the party: they would always have some voice in and connection with government. Thus, although the Liberals or SDAP/PvdA may have appeared to be more in tune with their interests, Catholics were told that those parties or any new Catholic splinter parties could do little for them if they were in opposition.

Leadership. If the Catholic party had the reputation of producing weak and vacillating cabinet members the exact opposite was true of the parliamentary leadership. After 1880, when Schaepman first entered the Second Chamber, the Catholic party always had a strong, authoritarian leader who stood head and shoulders above his colleagues in parliament. He played a crucial role in damping conflict within the Catholic party, in putting together coalition cabinets with leaders of the other parties, and in leading and controlling the Catholic party caucus in parliament. The three major Catholic party leaders, who between them controlled the parliamentary party for well over sixty years, were stern, even unattractive figures; Schaepman, Nolens, and Romme were not well liked by their fellow Catholics. Yet they were effective. For example, a member of the Catholic parliamentary caucus during the 1950s noted: "Yes, at times there was a great deal of discussion and argument. But usually at a certain point Romme would stand up, everyone would become still, and he would say, 'We are going to do so and so . . .' and that would be it. No one would dare cross swords with Romme. . . . If he did he would pay for it dearly" (Interview 16).[40]

A corollary of the unwritten rule that no cabinet could be formed without Catholic representation was that the Catholic party's parliamentary leader never entered a cabinet.[41] At first it was a general perception among Catholics, probably an accurate one, that non-Catholic Dutch society would never be able to accept a priest as a cabinet minister. Both Schaepman and his successor, Nolens, were priests. This tradition of remaining outside the cabinet was maintained by the non-clerical Catholic leaders who followed them. Undoubtedly their strong leadership was needed to help maintain some semblance of control within the Catholic party caucus. However, the role of the Catholic party leader was also indicative of the ambivalence of the Catholic subculture towards the rest of Dutch society: a subculture remaining isolated, communicating with the non-Catholic world through a leadership which remained aloof, never fully participating in the affairs of state.

Relations between the Cabinet and the Parliamentary Party. As in other democracies, one of the features of the Dutch political system is responsible government. However, the relationship between the parliamentary party and the cabinet is much more muted in the Netherlands. This has the consequence of helping parliamentary parties, in particular the Catholic party, to avoid major rifts or splits since they are to some degree absolved of responsibility for the cabinet's behaviour. All Dutch governments have been coalitions usually incorporating from three to five parties. Parties are rarely regarded as responsible for policies collectively decided upon by cabinets, although individually they have occasionally been seen as responsible for the fall of governments. That there is little or no sign of a party's platform or program in government policies can be explained away by references to compromises that had to be made upon entering a coalition. Cabinet-building in the Netherlands is usually a long and arduous process often lasting for several months after an election. Not infrequently the previous government, in a caretaker capacity, will continue to govern the country while the cabinet-building process takes its course. And often a party's justification for entering a government is that it does so in the national interest as a means of resolving a deadlock.

Another feature of the Dutch political system is the rather nonpartisan position which the cabinet occupies, in contrast to its role in the British and Canadian systems. In order to enter the cabinet a member of parliament must resign his seat in the Second Chamber and give up his membership in the party caucus. A cabinet position is seen in very statesmanlike terms, as a role that must be performed in a proper, dignified, and at the same time business-like fashion. Some cabinet members remove themselves almost entirely from party affairs.[42] In a somewhat different way Daalder has described these attitudes and values as the "regents' mentality" in government and cites tendencies toward rejection of criticism, secrecy, and an inflated sense of self-importance as evidence of this.[43] The parliamentary caucuses in turn tend to assume a fairly critical, often ideological stance in parliament, even when their party is participating in the government.[44] But they are usually reliable in their support of government bills. Withdrawal of support by a participating party is extremely rare.

The fact that the Catholic party was never dominant within cabinet aided in damping conflict and maintaining cohesion. In a different situation, where, for example, the Catholic party had a majority of seats and full control over cabinet appointments, the demands and expectations within and outside the party would have been too great a burden. As it was, the ability of the party to disclaim responsibility for many of the affairs of state helped considerably to placate the widely divergent interests it contained. At the same time the Catholic party during elections usually claimed credit for the performance of its own cabinet members, particularly those in the portfolios of housing and education often held by the party.

Relations between the Parliamentary and Non-Parliamentary Party. Another potential source of strain within any political party lies in the linkage between the party leadership, particularly in parliament, and the grass-roots organization. Rank-and-file members and local party officials often have particular local or regional concerns and they may want to ensure that these receive preferential treatment. Disaffection in the ranks or in supporting organizations may result in a withdrawal of support which could seriously affect a political party at election time.

The Dutch Catholic party in the period up to the mid-1960s never lost the support of its local organizations. Yet the gulf between the leaders and the rank-and-file was extremely wide. I. Schöffer, writing on the confessional parties of the interwar period, claims: "Inside the Roman Catholic State Party there was a broad and virtually unbridgeable gap between the party leadership which was then more or less in the hands of Catholic nobility and proper middle-class citizens from 'above the rivers', and the Catholic population consisting of fairly simple people in large part living 'south of the rivers'."[45] In the postwar period the party leadership was more representative in terms of social origins. Greater efforts were made to place representatives of labour on the executive and in parliament. But there was still a large gap between leaders and led.[46] Indeed, the relationship between lower-echelon party officials and the leadership can best be described as deferential. The latter was more or less left with a free hand, having to meet very few demands from the bottom.

Nationally the Catholic party was organized in terms of the eighteen national electoral districts, in each of which essentially the same candidate list was presented. Each electoral district (*kieskring*) had a separate organization with an executive. That organization was subdivided into smaller units (*statenkringen*) and these in turn were subdivided into local organizations often using parish boundaries as a basis, particularly in the south.[47]

The chairmen of the *kieskringen* wielded considerable power since they more or less ran the election campaigns. Collectively they were responsible in the postwar period for putting together approximately half the election list, hence determining in large part who would get into parliament (central party headquarters was responsible for the remainder of the list). Although they always tried to obtain some regional representation, the main emphasis was on quality. Potential candidates were those who had done outstanding work either at universities or in community affairs. Although the KVP had primaries of sorts (the only party to have them) there was little overt competition; rather, potential candidates would be asked by the chairman of a *statenkring* or *kieskring* if they were willing to let themselves be considered for a position on the list. It was considered in very poor taste to let it be known that you were willing to be a candidate or worse still, that you wanted to be a candidate.

A fair amount of competition existed for places on lists for municipal and provincial elections, especially in the south where the KVP was the only party, but this did not occur for places on the Second Chamber lists. "There were only one or two places on the list [for each *kieskring*] and everyone in the district realized who would be the best qualified" (Interview 43). Statesmanlike qualities were preferred; those who could fill a cabinet position if need be or act as a responsible critic of a particular portfolio would be seen as good candidates. In addition to regional representation there was also a demand for specialist or expert qualifications, and if both regional and expert criteria could be met in the same person so much the better. Specialists would be, for example, a high-ranking military officer for defence matters, and university professors specializing in such areas as agriculture, social welfare, or economics. This penchant for expertise has not been restricted to the Catholic party, and all parties continue to place a high value on expertise in specific areas.

After the candidates had been selected, the list was finalized (through joint bargaining between the *kieskring* chairman and party headquarters) and submitted to the electorate. Subsequently, those candidates who became members of the legislature were more or less left to their own devices. They were rarely called upon to fulfil obligations to *kieskring* chairmen or others. The *kieskring* chairmen were mostly volunteers with full-time occupations outside politics (many of them school teachers) and were involved in organizing not only national elections but local and provincial elections as well. To have influence over local party affairs with little outside interference may have been a sufficient reward in itself for *kieskring* chairmen. The expectation in the Catholic party was that members of the Second Chamber would defend Catholic institutions when the relevant issues came up, but would be equally concerned to help administer the affairs of state in the interest of the country as a whole. This ethos helped to reduce the pressures placed upon the parliamentary party. They were neither expected to advance militantly the ideological interests of Catholics nor to deal constantly with particular interests of Catholic individuals or groups.

The Party and Pressure Groups. In 1918 the bishops expressly forbade Catholic social organizations to participate in politics or even to nominate candidates formally to the Catholic party. The party, however, did develop the principle that all interests within the Catholic subculture had to be consulted in the drawing up of party programs and in the selection of candidates for the Second Chamber. This consultative process came to mean that specific people from the socio-economic organizations would be asked to become members of the party executive or candidates on the Second Chamber electoral list. Efforts would always be made to ensure that two or more candidates would be from each of the major socio-economic organizations, as well as from military, banking, educational, and other circles.[48] These people would usually be referred to not as representatives but, again, as specialists. Thus Father Stokman, a priest and a member of the parliamentary party in the postwar period, was always referred to as the KVP's specialist on religious affairs, "in case any questions arose in the house on religious matters."[49]

The socio-economic organizations closest to the Catholic party were always the Catholic Retailers' Organization and the Catholic Farmers' Association. W. Perquin, for example, was for several years chairman of both the Catholic Retailers' Organization and the KVP. Officers of the former group were often seconded to the campaign committee of the KVP and the organization served as an important conduit for election funds. The Catholic Farmers' Association was also tightly linked to the KVP, supplying many members of the executive and the First and Second chambers. Of all the organizations it was considered the Catholic party's strongest supporter. The Catholic Employers' Association was also a loyal supporter although it did not have as many direct links with the party.

The weakest link was always between the party and Catholic labour. In 1934 the Catholic Workers' Movement (RKWV) actually withdrew its support from the RKSP because of the government's policies during the depression.[50] In the postwar era relations between Catholic labour (KAB, later NKV) and the KVP were distant if not cool, even during the "Roman-Red" (KVP-PVDA) coalition period. The KVP always had trouble in obtaining enthusiastic representatives from Catholic labour, especially in later years. In 1966 the NKV became the first and only major Catholic socio-economic organization to break with the Catholic party. One strong KVP supporter, formerly of the NKV and later a member of the Second Chamber for the KVP, notes that he had always advised his colleagues in Catholic trade unions that they could have much more influence within the KVP if only they participated more in its activities (Interview 32).

Nevertheless, although Catholic labour as a whole tended to be aloof from the Catholic party, representatives from Catholic labour in the Second Chamber were usually committed to the party and got along well with their party colleagues. Catholic labour leaders both within and outside the party frequently received appointments to the First Chamber (roughly the equivalent of the Canadian Senate) or occasionally were put on the election list for a provincial legislature. Perhaps because those in the Catholic trade unions less favourably disposed to the Catholic party did not in fact enter it, centrifugal pressures within the party were minimized. From 1946 to 1958 the KAB/

NKV supported the KVP in part because of loyalty to the church and in part because the KVP was represented in a series of coalition cabinets with the PVDA. The interval from 1958 to 1965, when the Catholic party ruled in conjunction with the Liberals and the other confessional parties, was a period of economic growth (stimulated by the discovery of natural gas in the North Sea in 1959) which saw the removal of rigid wage controls much to the benefit of Dutch labour as a whole.[51] Even though the PVDA was then in opposition the KAB/NKV was reasonably satisfied with government policies and economic conditions. Furthermore, in 1958 Romme, the KVP parliamentary leader, stressed that he was not ruling out any future coalitions with the PVDA.[52]

Thus the picture that emerges is one in which demands placed upon the Catholic party by its regional and other lower-level organizations were limited. In large part this was because the deferential ethos led to an emphasis upon giving the central leadership a free hand in conducting the affairs of the nation and because central leaders, in turn, gave a free hand to local leaders in municipal and provincial affairs. The emphasis on statesmanlike qualities, the transformation of interest representation into the giving of expert opinions by specialists, all helped to maintain the cohesion and stability of the parliamentary party. Special interest groups like the farmers, the self-employed middle class, and the industrialists were solidly entrenched within the party and were reasonably satisfied with the way their demands were handled. Communications between these groups and their specialists in the Second Chamber were good. Conflict among such special interests was minimal.[53] And even though the links were not as strong, Catholic labour by and large supported the party.

The Church and the Catholic Party. The above factors were all important in helping to impose a degree of stability and cohesion upon the parliamentary party. Yet these factors in themselves would have been insufficient. It was the influence of the church hierarchy which ensured that the Catholic party was not rent asunder. According to Schöffer it would have been virtually impossible for the RKSP to have stayed in one piece during the interwar period if it had not been for the official blessing and support of the church hierarchy.[54] As well as making public statements on the need to preserve unity in the political arena the bishops also operated on a less public level to try to ensure that their wishes were implemented. In the 1920s they were important in bringing the Saint Michäel League and the League of R.C. Electoral Associations together, a reconciliation of which the RKSP was the result.

In 1922 a dissident left-wing Catholic party calling itself the Roman

Catholic People's Party made its appearance. It was publicly condemned by the bishops and never obtained more than 1.19 per cent of the total popular vote.[55] In 1926 the leaders of this party tried to obtain if not approval then at least the tolerance of the hierarchy. The reply from Mgr. Callier of the diocese of Haarlem, writing on behalf of the bishops, was blunt: "The R.C. People's Party is located outside the RKSP. As such it causes a division among Catholics. We cannot comprehend how a good Catholic could even possibly think of helping to foster such a division let alone be the cause of it."[56]

The RKSP leaders frequently consulted the bishops on various political issues. Furthermore, Father Nolens, parliamentary leader of the RKSP, and Father Stokman, KVP member in the postwar period, would as priests certainly have known what constituted appropriate behaviour. Through these channels the bishops undoubtedly made their feelings known. In all likelihood, however, they did not often intervene directly on a personal level. Usually it was a case of the bishops responding to a particular request for dispensation or some sort of action rather than acting on their own initiative. Initiatives would invariably be of the more general, public kind, such as a statement indicating their wishes and hopes. Thus in 1944–45 the bishops expressed a fervent desire to see the various Catholic socio-economic organizations and the Catholic party resurrected but did not issue specific directions to particular individuals.[57]

In the early 1950s the bishops, in particular Cardinal de Jong, were disturbed at a number of developments. The Catholic caucus in the PVDA, which had helped found the PVDA in 1946, had up to that time refused overtures by the KVP to return to the fold. Secondly, in 1948 a prewar Catholic party minister of colonial affairs, Ch. Welter, left the KVP and founded the Catholic National Party because of dissatisfaction with the KVP's decolonization policy (carried out in conjunction with the PVDA).[58] In 1948 the KNP received 1.26 per cent of the vote and in 1952 a little more than 2 per cent. Moreover, in 1952 it appeared that the PVDA had increased its vote somewhat in the solidly Catholic south.[59]

All these developments caused consternation within Catholic circles. In January 1953 the KVP set up a special commission, the Van der Grinten commission, to study the possibilities of political unity among Catholics.[60] A few months later the commission submitted a report which concluded that political unity among Catholics was indeed both desirable and necessary and that the KVP was the appropriate vehicle. In May 1953 Cardinal de Jong, on the occasion of the centennial of the reestablishment of the episcopal hierarchy, launched an appeal for the political unity of all Catholics. In July of that year the KVP invited Welter of the KNP and Ruijgers of the Catholic PVDA caucus to a meeting to discuss the cardinal's declaration and the contents of the Van der Grinten commission report. Discussions continued throughout that year and into the next. On May 1, 1954, the bishops came out with the *Mandement* which again explicitly stated the church's wish for political unity among Catholics. The Catholic caucus of the PVDA, after studying the consequences of the *Mandement* for some time, rejected the idea of entering the KVP. The KNP, however, announced that in view of the wishes of the bishops they would be willing to rejoin the KVP.[61]

These public calls of the bishops were the most direct forms of political intervention. They were not direct orders but attempts to delineate guidelines, to define what was appropriate and inappropriate behaviour without necessarily calling specific individuals to task.

In the postwar period the KVP tried to develop into a programmatic rather than a purely religious party, to sell itself on the basis of its platforms rather than relying on the exhortations of the bishops. Romme, leader from 1946 to 1958, publicly defended such calls as the 1954 *Mandement*, but personally was reported to have been made most unhappy by these interventions. Yet without the urging of the bishops it is doubtful whether the Catholic party would have been revived in 1946, the work of many lay Catholics notwithstanding. And without the continuing support of the bishops, the KNP splinter party might have been a prelude to further defections. For example, during the 1950s, in addition to the Welter group, another element in the party, the Steenberghe group, publicly announced that the KVP was going too far to the left and was neglecting the interests of large business in the Netherlands. In reaction to the Steenberghe group the De Bruyn group, centred around the KAB representative De Bruyn, threatened to leave the KVP and form a Catholic labour party. Protracted negotiations with the two groups finally resulted in the promise that the interests of the Steenberghe group would be given greater attention but that the partnership with the PVDA would not be broken off in the foreseeable future. Throughout these negotiations KVP leaders made continual references to the expressed wishes of the bishops.[62]

At the same time there is evidence that the church was quietly beginning to extricate itself from political affairs after the death of Cardinal de Jong in 1955. For example, in 1961 Father Stokman retired from the KVP and the Second Chamber, and the KVP requested the church to appoint another priest to replace him. The bishops refused to do so, implying that the party could easily find a lay person to handle the chores of a KVP religious specialist in the Second Chamber. The ecclesiastical hierarchy did not, however, begin publicly redefining the nature of authority or the basic parameters upon which the KVP depended until much later.

Obedience to the concept of political unity among Catholics as outlined by the bishops was one reason why potential splinter groups remained within the Catholic party and those that had left returned to it. The idea of being Catholic imparted a sense of common purpose. One Catholic party politician during the 1960s noted that when discussions within the KVP became protracted, "there was always the thought 'Well, we're all Catholic, thus we have to come to some sort of solution'. And we usually did" (Interview 4).

One additional factor undoubtedly preyed upon the minds of those who considered setting up a competing party: Catholic splinter parties in the past had enjoyed remarkably little success. Even if Catholic leaders did not heed it, the call for the maintenance of political unity was usually much more successful among the Catholic populace at large. This raises the question of how the authority of the church was used in the mobilization of the Catholic vote.

2. Mobilization

It can be stated with reasonable confidence that the authority of the church was the most important force in impelling Catholics to vote for the Catholic party. Yet one has to be careful in specifying the manner in which this authority was used and the paths along which it travelled. As in the case of the Catholic parliamentary party, the authority of the church was not always used directly.

The Interwar Period and Church Mobilization. It was during the interwar period, the time of the "Rich Roman Life," that the church intervened most forcefully. At election time the bishops would issue a pastoral letter warning Catholics to remember their duty, to remain one in order to safeguard their sacred unity. This message would be read from the pulpit by the pastor at mass, during national, provincial, and local elections. Warnings would also be directed against the evils of socialism (i.e., the SDAP), the Communists, and in the 1930s the National Socialist Party. The result was a constant stream of directives from the clergy on the need to remain within the fold and to keep other political parties or movements at arm's length.

In many cases the clergy did far more than merely preach from the pulpit. S. Vellenga reports that in Limburg before World War II the RKSP asked the local clergy directly for help in mobilizing voters. Pastors and their assistants responded by holding special classes for their parishioners, many of whom were only semi-literate, on how to fill out election ballots (which identified parties by numbers, altered from election to election).[63] The parish newspapers contained considerable political propaganda for the Roman Catholic cause. Father Poels, the major force behind the Catholic mineworkers' union, was highly active at election time. He urged his fellow priests to participate, saying that he had no use for "supra-naturalists," those priests who put their trust in God but did no practical work.[64]

Postwar Period and Church Mobilization. Messages from the bishops were read from the pulpit before the elections of 1946 and 1948. Thus on May 4, 1946, the Dutch bishops declared: "It belongs to the authority of the Church to explain to the faithful the moral obligations which result from the right to vote." The message went on to say that it was a Catholic's duty to elect persons who were guided by the norms of Christianity. The bishops never actually said "vote KVP" but advised Catholics to maintain unity and indicated that the KVP offered the best guarantee for this.[65] In 1948 they made stronger statements on behalf of the party, directly urging Catholics to support it. This was the last time that the bishops made such statements during an election campaign.[66] In 1953, a non-election year, Cardinal de Jong urged the Catholic population to "remain one" socially and politically and this appeal was made again in greater detail in the *Mandement* of 1954. The KVP used these instructions and documents in their propaganda material. But after 1948 the pulpit was no longer used by the bishops as a direct means of influencing Catholics at election time.

More importantly, little or no evidence exists that the rank-and-file clergy were as involved in mobilizing Catholics as was the case before the war. A chairman of a KVP local, who had been active in his village in the eastern part of the Netherlands since 1947, noted that his local never had a spiritual adviser. Furthermore, the respondent claimed that the pastor never said anything about politics from the pulpit. "It was not necessary" (Interview 34). After World War II, in fact, virtually no KVP local had a spiritual adviser. Although pastors were always very active in organizations such as the local Catholic Farmers' Association, they rarely intervened in the operations of the KVP.

Another KVP activist described a meeting he chaired just after World War II in Rotterdam.

> At one point during the meeting the local dean came in and sat down. . . . I didn't say anything. After the meeting a number of people came up to me and said that I had shown Father ——— a

discourtesy in not introducing or welcoming him and in not having invited him to say a few words. I disagreed with them for several reasons. . . . A few days later I saw the dean again and he told me I had done the proper thing; that he was to be treated like everyone else. He felt the KVP had to stand on its own two feet. (Interview 29)

An 82-year-old priest, who had retired in 1972, and who had had parishes in various towns and villages in the northeast, noted that he treated political matters differently.

To tell people squarely that they had to vote KVP—that I did not dare do. . . . With politics you had to be a little more careful. Just after the war, from the pulpit once or twice I said "support our party". . . . Until perhaps 1960 I would tell people to vote KVP if they asked for advice. . . . But people never asked much. People were not so political. They were much less developed. . . . Fifty years ago, of course, you could do everything. (Interview 17)

No direct pressure was applied by priests in part because of diffidence, that is, a reluctance to become involved in political matters, and in part because of the belief it was not necessary. Parishioners rarely asked how they should vote, and if they did they knew what the answer would be. These expectations of support for the KVP were not actively fostered, at least not by the clergy, but they were there nevertheless and nothing was done by priests to relieve parishioners of the implied obligation. With two exceptions, all fifteen priests interviewed believed that the *Mandement* of 1954 had specified that voting for a party other than the KVP could lead to the denial of the sacraments.[67]

The Catholic Party and Mobilization. What role did the RKSP/KVP play in mobilizing voters, in ensuring that the vast majority of Catholics voted for the one and only Catholic party? It should be remembered that their work was greatly facilitated by the compulsory voting law that existed in the Netherlands up to 1970.[68] The task of actually getting voters to the polls was in large part resolved. Furthermore, their dependence upon the church, especially before World War II, also lightened their labours.

Before the war the running of election campaigns was the responsibility of the eighteen *kieskring* associations. They restricted themselves to pamphleteering, the painting of slogans, and the organization of election rallies. Since parades and processions were forbidden

Dutch Catholic Politics | 81

by law, bicycle rallies at election time were very popular. Large numbers of Catholic youths—their bicycles festooned with streamers, flags, and slogans in Catholic party colours (yellow and white)—would pedal furiously through town and country. Catholic party leaders would talk over the radio and address special meetings. The strongest language was reserved for attacking not their major opponents such as the SDAP but Catholic splinter parties such as the New Catholic Party and the Roman Catholic People's Party, those parties which would "dare to damage our beautiful unity."[69]

The postwar KVP took over much of the RKSP machinery. The eighteen *kieskring* organizations were reactivated and the prewar weekly party newspaper, *De Opmars*, was revived under the same name. Between national elections the machinery of the KVP was kept ticking over, particularly during provincial and municipal elections. The KRO provided ample broadcasting time. According to an official of the KRO, "You could say that up to the early 1960s the KRO was more or less the mouthpiece of the KVP" (Interview 14). Romme, leader of the KVP, had a bi-weekly radio program at prime time on Friday evenings until 1955. From 1956 to 1961 the KVP presented a program entitled "Are you also a member of the party?"[70] Romme was also political editor of the largest Catholic daily newspaper, *De Volkskrant*.

The party frequently held membership drives and at one time membership totalled over 400,000.[71] The vast majority of these people, however, were members in name only, although theoretically they were eligible to participate in meetings and to vote in primaries to help determine the order of candidates on election lists. Memberships were sold on a door-to-door basis or in blitzes in shopping areas. They were marketed much like other Catholic items, for example, calendars for missionary work. "To tell you the truth most people probably did not know the difference. To them it was all for the 'Roman business'" (Interview 44). In the 1940s and 1950s some rural party officials claimed to have enrolled virtually every adult in their locality. These claims were probably not too far-fetched in that there were instances of villages where the number of KVP members tallied perfectly with the number of votes cast for the party.[72] Memberships were a prime source of funds for the KVP and those who took out a membership were referred to as *betalers*, which means,· literally translated, "those who pay."

For each election campaign a special national "Propaganda Council" was set up, drawing upon expertise outside the full-time members of the party organization. Thus, for example, J. van Schaveren, parliamentary reporter for *De Volkskrant*, and Dr. W. J. J. Kusters of the

Catholic Social Research Institute (KASKI) were both members. Fulltime members of the central party office compiled a special blue book denoting various speaking engagements, placement and timing of advertisements, and related matters. Several months before the election appeals would be made for contributions in the party newspaper, *De Opmars*. Up to 1952 party workers would actually stand outside the church to solicit parishioners for funds. Contributions were also received from Catholic firms, particularly the large department store chains. The Catholic Retailers' Organization was usually heavily involved in fund-raising as well as acting as a funnel for funds generally.

The organizers of KVP election campaigns characterized their own efforts as amateurish. Until the 1960s public relations firms were not consulted. The party was heavily dependent upon volunteer labour and much of the responsibility for the campaign fell upon the shoulders of the *kieskring* organizations. Every *kring* would have a propaganda committee which formulated the party program in its particular electoral district and helped to draw up the candidate list. These committees were given a large proportion of the available election funds to spend. The *kieskring* program was usually based upon documents and guidelines sent out from party headquarters. Thus party programs would not vary much from region to region. Decisions on the spending of funds involved such questions as what sort of give-away items to buy, e.g., ballpoint pens, balloons; how much to spend on placards and pamphlets; and whether or not to invest in a sky-writing plane. After 1956 more and more emphasis was placed on the frills of electioneering, including campaign buses, pompon girls, flowers, and illustrated folders.

During the 1950s the party was reasonably successful in mobilizing volunteers to distribute handbills and pamphlets, placards for display in windows, and the like. In 1952 the KVP claimed to have at least 10,000 hardcore activists.[73] In the smaller villages virtually every Catholic would be assured of receiving something in the mailbox from the KVP. In larger cities the Catholic Action would often be utilized for this sort of work. The KVP was reasonably successful in attracting substantial crowds to meetings which featured speakers and films. At first these meetings were mostly local affairs, but in the late 1950s and early 1960s, probably because of American influences, much more emphasis was placed on large-scale meetings drawing up to two or three thousand people.

Yet curiously enough there was not much personal contact. The KVP, like most other political parties in the Netherlands, did no doorknocking or canvassing in order to get out the vote and left the experimenting to the PVDA.[74] The closest thing to this style of electioneering by the KVP was the small pamphlet entitled "A morning greeting" put in mailboxes on the day of the election. Even in small villages very little direct pressure was put upon people to vote KVP. But then as one party official said, "It was not really needed" (Interview 34).

The KVP depended heavily upon the media to influence Catholics in their voting behaviour, by means of talks on the KRO by the "top" candidates on the KVP election list and Romme, and reminders to Catholics of their duty in the latter's newspaper column in *De Volkskrant* and on his radio talk show. Publications of such groups as the Catholic Retailers' Organization and the Catholic Farmers' Association urged members to vote for the KVP and gave personal reminders at meetings. The KAB/NKV was much less enthusiastic in mobilizing support but nevertheless suggested that its membership vote KVP. Statements appeared in trade union publications to the effect that the chairman had approved the KVP program, but little was done beyond this. "To tell you the truth the climate in which to do that sort of thing [telling Catholic workers to vote KVP] was lacking. They would have resented it. . . . There were a number of study days for NKV members on political matters to the effect that one was a citizen and should vote. But the implication of these sessions was that the choice of party was a member's own responsibility" (Interview 32).

To what extent did the KVP appeal to the voters on strictly religious or ideological grounds and exploit their Catholic identity? In the early postwar period *De Opmars* made several references to the need for cohesion, evoking images of dikes, walls, and fortresses. The chairman of the KVP wrote that "The KVP stands there as the political bulwark of Catholic might, a stable might which gives strength to the Dutch nation."[75] Just before the election of 1948 *De Opmars* warned of evil outside forces "against which we have to form a front, in which no breach can be formed, on which all attacks will fail."[76] In the mid-1950s at election time the same newspaper contained statements that the emancipation of Catholics was not yet complete and that a great deal of work remained to be done. However, the Catholic voter was not inundated with electioneering propaganda which made direct references to discrimination against Catholics. Rather the programmatic aspects were stressed, often by outlining the records of KVP cabinet ministers. The positive aspects of the diverse socio-economic base of the KVP were emphasized; it was depicted as the only genuinely balanced political party because its support base represented a virtual mirror image of Dutch society in terms of class and region.[77]

This does not mean that appeals based on the Dutch Catholic identity were lacking, for between elections the KVP often did play upon the fears and religiosity of Catholics. *De Opmars* contains several references to the alleged second-class citizenship status of Catholics and to the belief that the KVP was the one and only party for Catholics. Parallels were drawn between battles of the past and contemporary conflicts. Thus on 18 March 1956 *De Opmars* headlined an article criticizing a non-Catholic cabinet minister for refusing funds for a second Catholic hospital in Amsterdam as follows: "After the struggle for schools, the struggle for hospitals." On 24 September 1954 the newspaper published an article on the KRO which stated boldly that the existence of the KRO was conditional upon the existence of the KVP. "Without the KVP there would be no KRO." An article in the issue of 21 January 1955 alleged that Catholics were deliberately being discriminated against in civil service appointments in the province of Gelderland. In the October 1957 issue an entire page was devoted to the theme that the Dutch Catholic was still a second-class citizen and that strong anti-Catholic sentiments still existed. As an example, it was pointed out that in the laying of the first stone of a new church the ceremony had taken place behind a screen, allegedly for fear of evoking the wrath of non-Catholic Holland if it were held in the open.

Much was made of the Catholic connection. Reports on party congresses usually included detailed descriptions and illustrations of the special masses held for the participants. On 20 January 1956 *De Opmars* published a number of photographs of Cardinal Alfrink with various leaders of the KVP at a special banquet commemorating the party's tenth anniversary. A gigantic motorized bicycle rally, organized by the KVP just before the election of 1956, ended in the city of Assen with an open-air mass.[78] Members of the church hierarchy were often cited on political matters. In the 4 March 1955 issue of *De Opmars* Mgr. Hanssen is quoted as saying that although the socialism of the PVDA had become "more moderate it was still unacceptable." The religious bond between Catholics was used as a direct justification for political unity, as when Romme noted in *De Volkskrant* (2 December 1955) that "The individual members of the different classes do not sit together only on Sundays within the same room. It is also in daily life that they are obliged to remain conscious of their Christian unity."

The persistent use by the KVP of religious and ideological issues can in part be explained by the intervention of the ecclesiastical hierarchy. The party had to provide some sort of reaction to the public statements of the bishops such as the *Mandement* of 1954. In contrast to Catholic organizations such as the KAB, which paid little attention to this document and downplayed its importance, the KVP vigorously defended the *Mandement*. Since they were in a sense "the ministry of external affairs"[79] for the Dutch Catholic bloc, KVP leaders undoubtedly felt it was their responsibility to defend the document. However, their uncritical and enthusiastic acceptance of it indicates that many of the leaders genuinely did believe that they were still second-class citizens and that it was their duty, and the duty of all Catholics, to follow faithfully the directions of the church hierarchy. Party propaganda undoubtedly articulated the feelings of many Catholics and at the same time reinforced those feelings. *De Opmars* (11 June 1954) heralded the *Mandement* in large type:

> Catholic Holland can, with a great deal of justification, feel enriched. It is a genuine Catholic gift given to us by men who are deeply conscious of their great responsibility of carrying out their pastoral role. Those . . . who do not understand that Catholics accept this *Mandement* as among the most beautiful of all possible gifts and those who complain about the infringement of liberty, do not know what it means to be Catholic and even less what true liberty is for a Catholic.

Professor J. Gielen, the minister of education (KVP) at the time, in interpreting the *Mandement* stated that as Catholics, "We cannot entertain thoughts which in large measure go against the wishes of the bishops."[80] And even before its appearance Romme asked rhetorically in *De Volkskrant* (19 July 1953) if one could still talk about freedom of choice if Catholics were morally obliged to vote KVP. "Yes, certainly, because one is not compelled to be Catholic, that is to say, one has the freedom to leave the Church if one wants."

Whatever the personal feelings of KVP leaders, the 1954 *Mandement* undoubtedly had the effect of stimulating greater activity within the party. Jean Beaufays has demonstrated that KVP membership had gradually dropped from 409,084 in 1948 to 269,376 in 1954. In 1955 the number jumped to 429,939, the highest ever reached. From this point membership started to drop again, falling to 218,374 in 1965.[81] Since most memberships were sold on a door-to-door basis the sudden increase probably indicated greater energy on the party of KVP activists in a more receptive market. Although the party had suffered some losses in 1952 it was not until 1955, after the appearance of the *Mandement*, that the KVP did further spade-work to ensure that the party was in better shape for the election in 1956.[82]

Thus in the postwar period the KVP was still highly dependent upon the authority of the church both in providing a basis for mobilizing support and in giving the party a necessary jolt at appropriate times to keep party workers active, and thereby help to ensure electoral success.

3. The Vote

Specific propositions can be put forward concerning the behaviour of Catholic voters up to 1963. It has been shown that the influence of the church had made most Catholics highly dependent upon it for guidance. The first proposition, therefore, is that Catholics tended to view voting for the Catholic party as being little different from going to mass, attending Catholic schools, and reading Catholic newspapers. More specifically, the expectation was that Catholics behaving in an appropriately confessional manner would also vote for the Catholic party. They would tend to fuse all this behaviour under one rubric, making little or no distinction between different modes of behaviour, and hence were unlikely to choose a Catholic organization in one context and a non-Catholic organization in another context. Secondly, they undoubtedly had the feeling that they were receiving some minimal return for their support. There was a pragmatic or rational element in their behaviour, and all the more so because their loyalty to the Catholic cause, including the policies of the Catholic party, did not undermine their economic or social interests.

The church attempted to make its influence felt throughout the Netherlands. Yet there were a number of factors which made such social control much more effective in some areas than in others, as illustrated by the regional differences in observance of Easter mass (see table 2.6). The following propositions concern these factors: Catholics were more likely to vote KVP in the Catholic south where the high concentration of Catholics provided an additional means of social control; Catholics living in non-urbanized or less urbanized areas outside the Catholic south were also more likely to support the KVP; Catholics living in major urban areas, where conditions for social control were less favourable and exposure to non-Catholic influences greater, were less likely to do so.

In testing these propositions some reference will be made to the RKSP of the interwar period. However, the availability of data will restrict much of the discussion to the postwar period, particularly in treating the last three propositions.

Religiosity, Associational Life, and Voting. High-quality measures of religiosity are lacking, but the evidence exists that Catholics who regularly attended mass generally participated in Catholic organizational

TABLE 3.1
Type of Organization by Mass Attendance

	Attend Mass	Do Not Attend Mass
Member of R.C. organization only	73.5%	3.7%
Member of both R.C. and non-R.C.	10.6	3.7
Member of non-R.C. only	15.9	92.5
Total:	100.0%	100.0%
	(N = 94)	(N = 27)

Source: KASKI, Report No. 293 (1963), p. 64.

life or were at least members of Catholic organizations. They also tended to vote KVP, as studies made at the national and local levels indicate. One done in Amsterdam in 1963 of young parishioners between the ages of thirteen and nineteen noted that those who "fell out," that is, stopped going to mass, quickly lost all contact with Catholic organizational life. Those who continued to attend mass regularly remained loyal. Table 3.1 illustrates the degree of difference between the two groups. Mass attenders remained largely insulated within Catholic organizations; the others were almost completely cut off from Catholic organizational life. Since this sample is drawn from Catholic youth in Amsterdam only, it is not representative of the entire population. Nevertheless, a 1955 national survey found that 69 per cent of all practising Catholic males belonged to Roman Catholic organizations only, while the proportion was only 9 per cent for those who did not attend mass regularly.[83] Another study of a medium-sized northeastern city in 1960 reported that 77 per cent of all Catholics in that city were "organized," each having an average of 1.42 memberships.[84]

Although no studies or surveys of that era combine information on religious practice and organizational membership with data on voting behaviour, there is evidence that those Catholics who attended mass regularly also voted KVP. Wolinetz, analysing a 1956 national public opinion poll originally used by Lijphart, found that 90 per cent of Catholics who attended mass regularly voted KVP (N = 346), contrasted with 41 per cent of Catholics who went to mass irregularly (N = 41).[85] Since nearly 90 per cent of Catholics were practising members of their church, it follows that 85 per cent of all Catholics in the sample voted KVP.[86]

Other evidence likewise indicates that voting behaviour and religious orthodoxy among Catholics were closely linked. It was noted in chapter 2 that the Dutch church placed a very high value on those marriages which produced several offspring and that parish priests visiting homes would inquire into the number and ages of children. One would expect, therefore, that in areas where the birth rate among Catholics was very high the KVP vote would also be high. In table 3.2 the degrees of political orthodoxy of municipal districts in the largely Catholic provinces of Limburg and North Brabant are shown to have a definite relationship to the annual birth rate.

Perhaps the best evidence that confessional loyalty, organizational membership, and voting behaviour were highly interrelated is that the church itself used voting statistics as a measure of loyalty. For the church a low level of political orthodoxy among Catholics in any area was cause for anxiety. Not only was the threat to political unity a matter of concern but, more importantly, the spiritual and social well-being of the Catholics within such areas would be open to question.

The Catholic Social Research Institute in The Hague (KASKI) was frequently called upon by dioceses to undertake studies of problem areas afflicted by high levels of unemployment, crime, and immorality among Catholics. A detailed analysis would first be made of voting patterns, often on a poll by poll basis, pinpointing the areas where support for the KVP among Catholics was low.[87] Using this technique it was possible to identify neighbourhoods or pockets where social conditions were likely to be particularly bad. These data would be collated with reports from parish priests, social workers, data on unemployment, disease, and so on, and the findings would lead to recommendations such as for increased welfare services or the encouragement of Catholic enterprises, both to provide jobs for unemployed Catholics and to insulate Catholics from secular influences. Thus, for the church, examining the voting behaviour of its flock was a way of checking the pulse rate, a way of keeping an eye on the spiritual as well as the social and economic well-being of the Catholic population.

As noted in chapter 2, most Catholics did not join Catholic organizations for purely spiritual reasons. Nor did these bodies perform or attempt to perform any spiritual or apostolic function and this was true even of those such as Catholic Action. Catholics joined such organizations because it was expected of them—it defined the essence of being Catholic. Most Catholics accepted this duty uncritically and apparently their attitude towards the Catholic party was the same. I. Gadourek reports that Catholics residing in the village of Sassenheim displayed a level of knowledge concerning political affairs that was lower than that of Protestants and those having no religion.[88] A

Dutch Catholic Politics | 89

TABLE 3.2
KVP Vote by Birth Rate by Province, 1952
(Number of births per 1,000 population)

% KVP Vote among Catholics	North Brabant	Limburg
95% +	22.0	20.1
89-94	20.4	19.6
93-88	19.3	18.9
77-82	17.1	17.7
70-76	15.5	15.5
69 and less	14.2	13.9

Source: KASKI, Report No. 171, p. 60.

1958 in-depth study by KASKI of the political beliefs and attitudes of Catholic workers revealed that these workers were barely, if at all, acquainted with the KVP party program, even though this document was widely distributed at election time and publicized in the Catholic and KVP press. A little more than half the sample of 105 knew of the existence of a party program but were unaware of the contents. The remainder of the sample knew nothing of a KVP program.[89]

The evidence is that Catholics did not really perceive politics and support for the KVP as a distinct form of behaviour. Gadourek notes that for Catholics in Sassenheim it was very difficult to distinguish political activities from other church, social, and cultural activities. "The lack of differentiation between the sphere of religion and that of politics was thus repeatedly affirmed by our research."[90]

The Catholic Vote and Rationality. Catholics, it has been shown, voted for the Catholic party in large part because of their uncritical acceptance of strong church pressures; they tended to be over-represented in the less well-off sectors of Dutch society; they were not as interested in or as well informed about politics as non-Catholics were. On the basis of this evidence it might be argued that in voting for the Catholic party Catholics were behaving in a less than rational fashion, that is to say, voting against their own economic interests.

In the case of the Catholic working class, the highly conservative fiscal policies of confessional cabinets during the 1930s were in part responsible for keeping unemployment at a very high level, causing hardship for both manual and non-manual workers.[91] Catholic workers might have been better off if they had given their support to the SDAP, which had policies and programs with strong Keynesian overtones designed by economists of the calibre of Jan Tinbergen. Yet it must be remembered that the events of 1918, the year in which the SDAP leader Troelstra made a call for revolution, were still strongly imprinted on the memories of both Catholics and non-Catholics. Furthermore, even though the SDAP had quickly changed its position and become more moderate and responsible, many Catholics may not necessarily have perceived the election of an SDAP government as leading to an improvement of their objective conditions. In view of developments in France (e.g., the election of the Popular Front government of Léon Blum and the resulting economic instability), and the conservative policies of the National government in Britain, such a view of social democracy had some basis in fact.[92] Also, even if the Catholic working-class had decided *en masse* to support the SDAP, it would not necessarily have meant electoral victory for that party.[93] However, the entry of the SDAP into a coalition in 1939, for the first time in Dutch history, occurred largely at the instigation of the RKSP which had to overcome strong resistance from the other confessional parties.

It is impossible to reconstruct the mental processes of Catholic workers at that time. Certainly the church was worried that the SDAP, as well as the National Socialists, would be making inroads into Catholic support, particularly in the mining areas and large cities like Rotterdam. However, given the effective work done on behalf of Catholic workers by their political and social leaders, many workers may well have concluded that their fate was at least as secure in the hands of Catholic politicians.

In the postwar period the KVP and the PVDA were the two major participants in a series of coalition cabinets lasting from 1946 to 1958. The two parties are usually considered the major architects of postwar economic recovery programs which involved rigid wage and price controls. The KVP presented itself as the "social party" that was strongly attuned to the needs and wishes of Catholic workers. The 1958 KASKI study of the political beliefs of Catholic workers noted that both KVP and non-KVP voters were highly suspicious of the government's wage and price control policy. They voiced the opinion that unspecified "powerful groups in society" were being given undue advantages.[94] Yet at the same time both KVP and non-KVP voters were in favour of the Roman-Red coalition and were strongly against the coalition breaking up. The KVP voters in the sample maintained that their support was in part contingent upon the continuation of the Roman-Red coalition.[95]

During this period the KVP also emphasized that it represented all classes. Since the only nonconfessional business-oriented party, the Liberal party, was in opposition for a large part of the time, the KVP could claim with some validity that it was a highly suitable conduit for Catholic business interests seeking to communicate with government and have some influence on government policy. This argument was credible since the Catholic party was represented in virtually every cabinet in the period from 1918 to 1972. On an aggregate basis it received a larger number of cabinet positions in proportion to its numerical support than any other party.[96]

In 1958 the Roman-Red coalition ended largely as a result of the hardening of party lines, especially within the PvdA which underwent a change in leadership. For the next seven years the KVP held office in a coalition with the Liberals and the two other main confessional parties (ARP and CHU). During this period large reserves of natural gas were discovered in the North Sea and were successfully exploited to the benefit of the Dutch economy. Real income rose, particularly after 1963, when price and wage controls were finally phased out.[97] At the same time KVP leaders emphasized that they would not rule out future coalitions with the PvdA and in 1965 the KVP once again participated in such a coalition.

In short, the position of the Catholic party was usually competitive vis-à-vis the other parties. In the postwar period the natural inclination on economic grounds of Catholic workers might have been to support the PvdA and that of the middle classes to support the Liberals. Yet their support for the KVP, resulting from their loyalty to the church, involved no sacrifices: they could vote for the party without necessarily harming their economic interests. Like the KRO, Catholic trade unions, and other Catholic institutions and organizations, Catholics had no incentive to switch their support to an alternative political party in order to gain significantly better conditions. Conversely, there were no losses involved in obeying the wishes of the church and supporting the Catholic party.

Homogeneity, Urbanization, and Church Influence. Two basic sets of factors, boundary maintenance and pressure by the church, and the provision of adequate services by the socio-economic institutions of the Catholic subculture, were important in ensuring that the vast majority of Catholics voted for the Catholic party. The operation of each set was governed to some extent by certain basic structural characteristics.

Some leakage from the Catholic subculture occurred as was evidenced by the gradual decline over the years in the proportion of Catholics who voted KVP. Thus in 1948 89 per cent of all Catholics voted for the party. By 1963 this percentage had gradually dropped to 84.8.[98] This was clearly not a major decline, nor is there any evidence that the KVP paid much attention to it or was even aware of it. During this period the Catholic proportion of the total population grew from 38.5 per cent (1947 census) to 40.4 per cent (1960 census).[99] So although the percentage of Catholics voting KVP slowly declined the percentage of the total popular vote for the party remained relatively constant.

The nature of this leakage, however, is informative about the conditions which facilitated or hindered the effectiveness of the church and the institutions of the Catholic subculture. Two variables in particular, urbanization and the degree of Catholic concentration, are especially worthy of consideration.[100] In chapter 2 data were presented on the rate of Easter observance by Catholics in each diocese. Unfortunately a broad category like diocese fails to take account of important variations such as the degree of urbanization. For the period 1946 to 1963, however, there are available data at the municipal district level concerning urbanization, proportion of the population which is Catholic, and the voting returns for the different parties.[101] These data allow one to test propositions concerning urbanization and Catholic concentration in some detail.

The rural-urban distinction is especially important in the area above the rivers, particularly in the large urban centres like Rotterdam where the socialists made a considerable effort to wean Catholics away from the church. Moreover, modern, cosmopolitan influences made it easier for those who were less than enthusiastic about the church to escape its social control mechanisms and the influence of friends and family. In non-urban areas outside the south one might well expect the KVP vote to have been higher than in urban areas (e.g., in terms of orthodoxy of Catholics). In villages and towns where life tends to be traditional the church was well entrenched and there was less likelihood of escaping its control. As W. Goddijn has noted, much was done to ensure that Catholics outside the south, especially in the so-called diaspora areas where there were few Catholics, would remain within the fold.[102]

The rural-urban difference is also of relevance within the Catholic south, where a great deal of urbanization took place during the interwar and postwar periods.[103] For example, the multinational Philips Corporation, which began life in the late nineteenth century in the North Brabant town of Eindhoven with a handful of employees, employed 19,500 people in 1937 and 56,000 in 1955. Its rapid expansion had a significant impact on the province, drawing scores of Catholics from the rural hinterland to the city of Eindhoven.[104]

The second factor is that of Catholic concentration. A higher proportion of Catholics within a given area offered an additional means of social control. Fear of gossip, pressure from neighbours and friends, and similar influences could persuade people to be good Catholics or at least give the impression of being good Catholics and this could carry over to the ballot box. This factor was especially important in the solidly Catholic areas below the rivers, and also in those pockets of Catholicism above the rivers.

One way of measuring the effects of urbanization and Catholic concentration is to look at the political orthodoxy, over time, of Catholics located within the categories resulting from combinations of the two variables. The data are shown in graph form in figure 3.1, which demonstrates that the greatest difference results from the rural-urban cleavage (categories 1, 2, and 3 versus 7 and 8). Catholics residing in non-urban areas were much more likely to support the KVP even outside the Catholic south. Thus it appears that church control was much more effective in non-urban areas. On the whole, Catholics residing in the area below the rivers, the Catholic south, gave more support to the KVP than those residing above the rivers (compare category 4 with category 6). In the south the mutual reinforcement of fellow-Catholics, along with church influence, probably helped to ensure a high vote for the KVP. Breaking down the data further, however, reveals some interesting differences. Catholics most likely to vote KVP were those residing in non-urban areas in the north where the majority of the population within a village or town was at least 60 per cent Catholic.[105] In northern communities of this type, where the Calvinist penetration and the isolationist mentality were much more important, the vigilance of the clergy and the weight of tradition, combined with mutual support among local Catholics, probably account for the very high vote for the KVP among Catholics.

Within some of the above-listed categories, however, there is also considerable variation. Thus the Catholic vote in Rotterdam (60 per cent) was much lower than that in Amsterdam (74 per cent). The Catholic vote in the mining areas of Limburg was also somewhat lower than in other areas in the south. Strong local historical traditions appear to be at work in these cases. It was in Rotterdam at the turn of the century that the church was least effective in handling the problems of an industrializing society involving large-scale migration of workers. The consequences of those failures appear to have been carried well into the post-World War II period.

Thus structural variables such as the rural-urban cleavage and the degree of Catholic concentration do appear to have had an effect on the KVP vote, as instanced by a spread of more than 20 percentage

94 | Catholic Power in the Netherlands

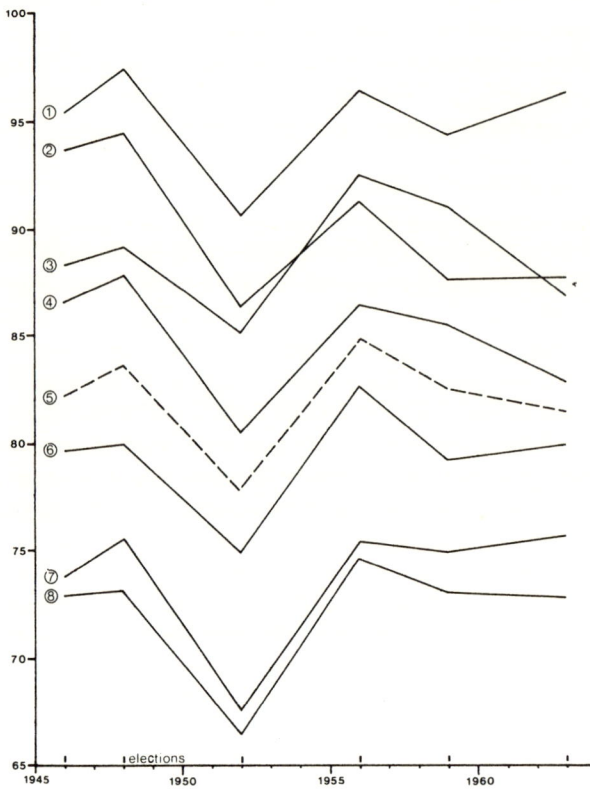

FIGURE 3.1. Percentage of Catholics Voting KVP by Context
Source: Houska and Leiden Ecological data sets. For details see Appendix 2.

KEY:
1. Catholics in non-urban municipal districts in the north (area above the Rhine) which are at least 60 per cent Catholic (non-urban = population less than 30,000).
2. Catholics in non-urban districts in homogeneous Catholic south (area below the Rhine encompassing provinces of North Brabant, Limburg, and part of Gelderland).
3. Catholics in all non-urban districts in the north.
4. All Catholics in the south.
5. Catholic population as a whole.
6. All Catholics in the north.
7. Catholics in urban districts in the south (urban = population more than 30,000).
8. Catholics in urban districts in the north.

points between Catholics residing in northern, urban areas and those in northern, non-urban areas where Catholics were in a majority (category 1 versus category 8). Factors such as urbanization and lack of Catholic concentration tended to hinder the efforts of the church in insulating and mobilizing Catholics.

The data shown in figure 3.1 reveal further aspects of the role played by the church in Catholic political life. After taking no active part in the election of 1946, the bishops intervened directly just before election day in 1948 by asking Catholics to support the KVP; the outcome was an increase in support for the party. In the 1952 election the bishops did not intervene and the dissident KNP under the leadership of Welter competed with the KVP for Catholic votes; the result was a drop of more than five percentage points in support for the KVP. In 1954 the bishops issued their *Mandement* urging Catholics to maintain social and political unity. This resulted in increased organizational activity by the KVP and in the return of the KNP to the KVP. Support for the KVP in the 1956 election reached its highest level, higher even than that attained by the prewar RKSP.

Finally, in spite of significant differences between the various categories as shown in figure 3.1, the support for the KVP in all categories was very high by cross-national criteria. Even the support given by Dutch Catholics residing in northern urban centres was substantially higher than the overall support given by Catholics to Catholic parties in other nations. One of the more important conclusions from these data is that the Catholic subculture was remarkably successful in maintaining political cohesion among Catholics in all sectors of Dutch society.

4. Summary

The dominant theme that comes through in this retrospect of Dutch Catholic politics is the overwhelming importance of the church in determining all aspects of Catholic political life. It was the ecclesiastical hierarchy which was responsible for keeping the Catholic party intact and holding defections and splinter parties to a minimum. It was the hierarchy in combination with a willing and able clergy which ensured that Catholics voted *en masse* for the Catholic party. During the interwar period the church was directly involved in mobilizing the Catholic vote for the Catholic party. Messages from the hierarchy were read by priests from the pulpit at election time. The clergy actively worked to deliver the vote, conducting special classes, for instance, on how to fill out the ballot. After the war the church was less directly involved in mobilizing the vote. Nevertheless it actively encouraged the preservation of unity, and the expectation that parishioners should and would vote KVP.

In the postwar period the Catholic party was still highly dependent upon the church in spite of its intention to turn itself into a programmatic party. Yet because the church was responsible for maintaining the political cohesion of Catholics, the Catholic party was able to be extremely flexible in carrying out functions such as interest group representation and regional representation. Since the party's role was not to proselytize it needed only to act defensively when issues involving the Catholic subculture such as broadcasting and education came into the political arena. Furthermore, the party was sufficiently competitive, catering to the needs of both working-class and non-working-class Catholics. Contextual factors such as urbanization and concentration of Catholics had an effect in varying the vote among Catholics. This was attributable to the way the social control of the church was affected by these variables, social control being more difficult in heavily urbanized regions of the Netherlands. At the same time the overall vote remained extremely high.

By the early 1960s the KVP was complacent. After the difficulties in reconstructing the party in the early postwar period and the problem of the KNP in the early 1950s, things were going smoothly. In the 1963 election the KVP obtained 31.9 per cent of the total popular vote, its best-ever result. One prominent KVP politician described the pleasant celebration which was held in the city of Den Bosch just after this election. It followed a four-year period in which the KVP prime minister De Quay had presided over a very successful government. Everyone at this gathering was blissfully unaware of what lay in store for them in the next few years (Interview 16).

The following chapters will examine the changes that occurred in the 1960s, and show how changes within the church resulted in a significant redrawing of the boundaries of the Catholic subculture, how voters responded to these changes, and how the KVP sought to rescue itself from a deteriorating position.

Chapter 4 **The Theological Revolt and Changes in the Catholic Community**

Without the authority of the church the Catholic party would not have enjoyed such a high level of support among Catholics in the Netherlands. And without the intervention of the church the Catholic party itself would have been rent asunder. The emphasis on unity among Catholics in both social and political life was maintained largely at the behest of the ecclesiastical hierarchy who could rely on a willing and able clergy to help foster appropriate expectations and, if necessary, apply the necessary sanctions.

Yet in the 1960s a number of remarkable changes occurred in Dutch Catholicism, changes initiated by the church itself. Catholics were given much greater individual responsibility in deciding what was appropriate or inappropriate behaviour, making it much more a matter of individual conscience. Catholics were asked by the church for advice in revising the liturgy and the catechism. In many places they were asked to aid in running the affairs of the parish. In 1965 the sanctions contained in the *Mandement* of 1954 were publicly repealed. And in 1967, just before the national election, one of the bishops announced on television that in his opinion it was no longer necessary to vote for the Catholic party in order to be a good Catholic.[1]

What was the nature and scope of the change in the Dutch Catholic Church? What caused this reorientation on the part of the church hierarchy and clergy? What were the consequences for subcultural cohesion?

1. Changes Within the Church

Theological Changes. The papal encyclical of 1891, *Rerum Novarum*, and its attempts to meet the challenges of industrialization, had a profound influence on many clergy and lay Catholics. The impetus for designing and implementing solutions to deal with social problems came from these people rather than the hierarchy. In 1900 a number of reform-minded priests and lay Catholics formed the Klarenbeekse Club, to discuss ideas concerning social reform.[2] In the interwar period, however, the work of progressive Catholics was largely overshadowed by the triumphalism of the "Rich Roman Life." Yet in spite of this, progressive-minded priests and laity continued with their work. In addition, in reaction to the cultural spirit of the "Rich Roman Life," a group of young Catholic writers appeared who were highly critical of many aspects of Dutch Catholicism. This rather amorphous group formed what has been referred to as an undercurrent in Dutch Catholic life which, though having no immediate impact in changing Catholic public opinion, nevertheless had long-term consequences.

This undercurrent persisted in the postwar period. In 1947 a group of priests, mainly because of their experiences during the war, wanted a changed church which would relax its attitude on matters such as family planning and political affairs.[3] In 1954, however, in an effort to ensure the political unity of Catholics the bishops invoked the spectre of severe church sanctions with the *Mandement*. This action stifled what few creative tendencies did exist in institutions such as the Catholic party (KVP). Instead of a general change within the Catholic subculture towards openness the opposite occurred.

Yet within the church itself, in spite of the 1954 *Mandement*, or quite possibly because of it, the undercurrent flourished, particularly in many of the seminaries and the new theological faculty at the Catholic University in Nijmegen. A Catholic priest, currently a dean and formerly a teacher at a seminary, noted: "When the *Mandement* came out in 1954 I was furious. I strongly disagreed with it and said as much to my students" (Interview 36).

In a number of Catholic publications, aimed mainly at intellectuals, such as *De Bazuin* and *Te Elfder Ure*, people who were critical of the conservative theology of the Dutch church aired their views.[4] A magazine for Catholic servicemen, *G-3*, also acted as a forum for those critical of the tenor of Dutch Catholicism. The critics generally were unhappy with what they saw as a dangerous physicalism or literalism and worked actively in their research and teaching to reinterpret many of the doctrines and symbols of the church. In 1957 Edward Schillebeeckx, a well-known reform-minded Catholic theologian from Belgium, arrived at the Catholic University in Nijmegen to take up a post in the theological faculty. Along with Dutch theologians such as Piet Schoonenberg, he played an important role in revising Catholic doctrine.[5] Evidence of their work and thinking can be seen in the contributions of the Dutch bishops to the Second Vatican Council.

These reform-minded theologians emphasized more worldly concerns in contradistinction to the supernatural. They were unhappy with the pre-Vatican II formulae of transubstantiation, the immaculate conception, and papal infallibility, and reinterpreted these doctrines as being symbols rather than concepts to be taken literally. In other words, they sought to demythologize the church. Prerogatives which the church held to be exclusively its own, were watered down. For example, the body of Christ came to be seen as "subsisting in" rather than identical with their own church. "The classical marks of the true Church—unity, holiness, Catholicity and apostolic faithfulness—were seen more as eschatological expectations and challenges than arrogant presumptions of faith."[6]

The debate on possible revisions concerning Catholic theology occurred at an elite level and was in the main restricted to Catholic theologians and intellectuals and published mostly in scholastic journals. Very little of this filtered down to the mass public. The Netherlands, of course, was not unique in having a prolific group of progressive theologians. Both France and Germany had like people with outstanding reputations; they also had journals like *De Bazuin* which involved lower clergy and lay elites in redefining church doctrine. The "new theology" of French thinkers like Congar and Lubac is often said to have become the theology of Vatican II.[7]

The Role of the Bishops. The major difference between the Dutch church and the church elsewhere did not lie so much in currents in theological thinking as in the role that the church hierarchy took upon itself. According to John Coleman, the behaviour of the Dutch bishops was unique in that they decided to deal with the pressures for change in an open and conciliatory manner, thereby commanding broad support from clergy and laity.[8]

In 1958, only four years after the *Mandement*, the bishops instituted a commission to look into problems of preaching and the catechesis, which were seen as the weakest points within the church.[9] This commission lasted from 1958 to 1965. Although only an advisory body, it had broad terms of reference. In one of its earlier reports it suggested that clergy should concentrate their efforts in a more pastoral and religious direction, while laity should become less dependent upon the support of spiritual advisers in the realm of socio-economic life. It offered a redefinition of tolerance which no longer implied that persons outside the church were by definition evil. Rather it argued that tolerance should mean acceptance of a person because of the unassailable worth of any human being, regardless of religious persuasion. This redefinition was significant in that it indicated a decline in the ultramontane sentiments evident in the *Mandement* of 1954.

In 1965, when the work of the commission was concluded, the bishops, acting on the advice of the commission, publicly rescinded all the negative sanctions applied to Catholic membership in so-called socialist organizations as outlined in the *Mandement* of 1954. Although it was this statement which most clearly indicated the changed position of the church with regard to its role in society, indications that changes were in the offing had already been manifested publicly. Thus in their Lenten message in the spring of 1959 the bishops stated: "While the hierarchy claims the teaching role in the Church and determines what belongs to the treasury of the faith, the hierarchy only teaches what is already to be found living within the community of the faithful."[10] The nuances of this carefully worded statement may not have been evident to ordinary Catholics. Nevertheless, argues Coleman, the message contained within it the "seeds of a view of authority involving a dialogue between shepherd and flock."[11]

In their Christmas letter of 1960 the bishops asked for lay suggestions on both liturgical renewal and revision in the catechism. A new organization, the Advanced Institute for Catechetics in Nijmegen, was commissioned to write a new catechism "which would speak to the faith of modern man."[12] Many of the initiatives of the bishops were taken in anticipation of the Second Vatican Council called by Pope John XXIII in 1959 and to be convened in 1962. Through Dutch theologians both in the Netherlands and in Rome the Dutch bishops were kept informed of the preparations that were being made for the council.

The most important contributions of the bishops were to popularize the reforms implemented throughout the decade of the 1960s and to give them practical effect. In 1960 a new bishop, Wilhelmus Bekkers, was appointed to head the diocese of Den Bosch, one of the three southern dioceses. Although previously quite conservative, upon his installation he announced that the church had found itself in a changed milieu and called for a new openness. He proceeded to introduce a number of experiments within his diocese, such as setting up a lay advisory board in each parish and entrusting the finances of the diocese and parishes to competent groups of laymen. This was in keeping with his deliberate aim to downgrade the status of the priest: "The priest of the future must remain an ordinary human being . . . a fellow man of the faith within the community of the faithful."[13]

When Vatican II began Bekkers instituted discussion groups of lay Catholics and clergy within his diocese to debate the various issues as they arose in the council.[14] Probably the most active of the Dutch bishops in Vatican II, he used the mechanism of the discussion group to keep in touch with the opinions of both ordinary lay Catholics and the lower clergy. He was also very close to theologians, in particular to Schillebeeckx. Neither a deep thinker nor an outstanding theologian, he had the great gift of being able to synthesize complex ideas, demands, and opinions, popularize them, and implement them. In 1964 he did away *de facto* with the confessional, which had become an odious practice in his view, and introduced the use of the para-sacramental confession.[15]

The other bishops watched with interest the experiments in the diocese of Den Bosch and soon adopted the new practices. The collective confession, for example, spread to virtually all parishes in the Netherlands shortly after it was introduced in the diocese of Den Bosch. By 1971 nearly 60 per cent of Dutch parishes had instituted a lay parish council and half of the parishes had their own liturgical commission.[16]

The other bishops also spoke out in favour of changes although they did not have the same flair as Bekkers. Mgr. de Vet of the southern diocese of Breda and Mgr. van Dodewaart of the diocese of Haarlem both considered themselves to be supporters of Bekkers. Ironically, the bishops themselves, including Bekkers, did not really see themselves as innovators. Rather they called themselves "bridge-builders," managers and conciliators of the conflict between conservative and progressive Catholics which occurred in a period of change.

His self-image notwithstanding, Bekkers was an innovator *par excellence*. His influence was restricted neither to the diocese of Den Bosch nor to Catholics. Through the medium of television, he had a direct link with most Dutch citizens. For some time before his death in 1966 he was a well-known figure through frequent appearances on a popular Saturday evening television program. He held regular fireside chats discussing the theological changes of Vatican II and the implication of these changes for Catholics, always discussing them with considerable latitude in interpretation. On 21 March 1963 he told his audience that the biological aspects of marriage were of concern only to couples themselves; they were of no concern to the church.[17] This statement was probably the most far-reaching that any member of an ecclesiastical hierarchy had ever made on the topic of birth control.

The changes popularized by Bekkers and others were important in two respects: they permitted the liberation of Catholics both spiritually and physically, especially in regard to birth control; they helped break down the boundaries between the Catholic bloc and other socio-religious groups in Dutch society. In 1965 Bekkers began friendly discussions with the Dutch Society for Sexual Reform, an organization advocating family planning which had been referred to pejoratively by Catholics as the Neo-Malthusian society. As recently as 1958 Bekkers himself had condemned it in no uncertain terms.[18] In 1966 a Catholic priest, Father Nico van Hees, actually became the editor of the official magazine of the society; previously he had been appointed editor of the major socialist daily newspaper *Het Vrije Volk*, which up to 1965 had been officially banned by the church under the prohibitions of the *Mandement* of 1954.[19]

Many of the major changes in Dutch Catholicism occurred in the first half of the 1960s. Yet they ended neither with Vatican II (1965) nor with the death of Bekkers (1966). In the latter year the bishops announced plans for a nation-wide Pastoral Council in order to decide how best to implement Pope John's call for *aggiornamento* (renewal of the church). The proposed council was to involve not only clergy, theologians, and lay Catholics but also Jews, Protestants, and non-believers. A series of post boxes was set up across the country to enable Catholics to make submissions to the council, and an extra effort was made to obtain submissions from those baptized as Catholics but who had ceased to regard themselves as such.[20] The council itself consisted largely of democratically selected delegates from the different dioceses as well as from the different Catholic socio-economic organizations. The bishops themselves reserved the right to appoint a certain number of delegates, but they exercised this right in the spirit of bridge-building by appointing members of conservative groups to ensure that the latter would not be left out or overwhelmed by the progressives. Lay Catholics were in the majority on the council of ninety-five. There was also a central commission of eleven members, again representing a cross-section of the Catholic subculture, presided over by Cardinal Alfrink. Finally there was a college of experts, 135 people from all walks of life who could give advice on various matters as they arose. Non-Catholics could deliberate in the proceedings but they had no voting rights. The Pastoral Council lasted from 1966 to 1969.[21]

Although several questions such as the celibacy rule were left unresolved by the council, some of the concrete changes subsequently undertaken by the church stemmed directly from council deliberations.[22] The seminary system of education for priests was abolished in 1967 and the hundred-odd seminaries were replaced by five theological schools, for the most part connected with universities. The principle of collegiality was introduced at the level of the parish, deanery, and diocese. The placement and transference procedure for parish priests was changed. Prior to 1969 priests could be moved at only a few days' notice regardless of the feelings of either priest or parishioners. The new system required all vacancies to be advertised. Candidates for positions had to apply on their own initiative and be interviewed by a lay committee from the parish. Priests were no longer required to wear clerical garb. Changes were introduced in interfaith marriages, divorce, and remarriage. Fasting rules were discarded.

Pressures within Clerical Ranks. Compared to the church elsewhere the ecclesiastical hierarchy in the Netherlands clearly took the initiative in introducing changes and allowed extraordinary latitude in the interpretation of the implications of Vatican II. To what extent were the Dutch bishops responding to pressures from rank-and-file priests? To what extent was there resistance among the clergy to the new changes?

According to Thurlings, in former times the Dutch priest *in foro externo*, that is, "in the open," had to hold firmly to the official teachings of the church. *In foro interno*, "in private," which usually meant the confessional, the priest could let himself be governed by his concerns for the well-being and happiness of the individual person.[23] Thus a Catholic who violated one of the teachings of the church could be forgiven within the sanctity of the confessional. This distinction, however, tended to encourage hypocrisy. Violations on a large scale would make a mockery of the official teachings of the church. In the postwar period the gap between the actual behaviour of Catholics and the teachings of the church widened. The Dutch clergy, who tended to be more literal in their interpretation of church edicts than clergy elsewhere, were unhappy about this. Furthermore, the distinction *in foro externo/in foro interno* did not really hold since many parishioners did not take the confessional seriously. As noted in chapter 2, it was usually treated as a ritual and served to increase the unhappiness of clergy who were concerned that in their pastoral work the teachings of the church could not be made to fit changed conditions.

In 1947 a group of Dutch priests had urged the bishops to soften their stand on issues like birth control. These appeals, however, were unavailing. The bishops, under the leadership of Cardinal de Jong, insisted on a strong, hierarchically structured church, and an obedient following insulated from the rest of Dutch society. Clerics continued to follow the directives of the church. There were, however, a number of indirect signs which, with hindsight, can be seen as indicators of major problems to come. The Dutch church had always had one of the best, if not the best, rates of recruitment to the priesthood in the

Roman Catholic church, and it had depended upon the large number of clergy available to help maintain the cohesiveness of the Catholic bloc. However, in the postwar period the recruitment rate had begun to drop. In the period 1943–47 the number of Catholic men admitted to the priesthood per 100,000 of the Catholic population was 160. In 1958–62 it was only 100 per 100,000.[24] Although the number of seminary students had increased, a KASKI memorandum of 1952 estimated that the proportion of students who successfully completed their studies and entered the priesthood had dropped by 40 to 50 per cent compared with the prewar completion rate.[25]

This decline may have entered the calculations of the bishops in the late 1950s when they first began tentatively to prepare for changes. What had the greatest impact upon them, however, was the departure of priests already ordained. A number of priests were showing their displeasure with the restrictions placed upon them, especially the celibacy rule, by voting with their feet. What confounded the situation further was that some departing priests voiced their complaints in public or announced that they were giving up their calling in order to get married.[26] In an interesting variation on the "exit-voice" theme some priests married and then refused to leave their posts; in certain cases priests involved in controversies of this sort had the support of their parishioners. The total number who left the priesthood between 1960 and 1965 (approximately thirty a year) was relatively low, though considerably higher than in the previous twenty-five years.[27] But the publicity these departures attracted was considerable.

There were other forms of protest. In 1962 Father Jan van Kilsdonk, moderator of the student parish at the University of Amsterdam, denounced the Roman Curia, claiming that its authoritarian and reactionary attitude was alienating large numbers of Catholics from the church.[28] Incidents such as this one forced the bishops either to condemn the participants out of hand or to meet the demands in some way. Their response in this and other cases was sympathetic. In the Van Kilsdonk incident the authorities in Rome reacted by demanding his removal from his post. The local bishop, Mgr. van Dodewaard, consulted with the Holy Office, which later issued a statement that it was leaving all disciplinary action to the Dutch church authorities. The bishop then informed the public that Van Kilsdonk was being left in his post of moderator.[29] In a parish in the diocese of Den Bosch the parish priest and one of his assistants decided to leave the priesthood in order to get married. Mgr. Bekkers himself took the pulpit in the parish to announce the event and to plead for special understanding from the parishioners.[30]

The incident with the widest ramifications was one involving a major Catholic news weekly called *De Linie* (The Line), until the early 1960s a Jesuit publication. The Jesuits responsible were publishing articles which were increasingly flamboyant as well as critical of the church in general and the Roman Curia in particular. In 1962 the magazine changed its name to *De Nieuwe Linie* (The New Line) and opened its board of directors to laymen. The director-general of the Jesuits in Rome ordered the three Jesuits involved to withdraw from the magazine. When they refused and left the order, Mgr. Bekkers stepped in and offered them positions as regular priests in the diocese of Den Bosch.[31] The Dutch church province was going to considerable lengths in risking an open schism with Rome in order to deal with the protests and demands of clergy within the Netherlands.

Clerics pushing for change, the so-called undercurrent, did not really have an organizational structure as such. They can best be described as groups of like-minded priests (and lay Catholics) centred around publications such as *Te Elfder Ure* or on the staff of the theological faculty at the Catholic University at Nijmegen. The seminaries had so many progressive clerics, particularly in the diocese of Haarlem, that they came to be regarded as being totally dominated by the progressive spirit. By the early 1960s the term "undercurrent" ceased to be meaningful since it had in fact become if not the dominant stream then at least the most visible.

In 1968 a number of priests in the diocese of Haarlem started an organization called *Septuagint* which took an uncompromising left-wing position. Its goals were a change in the celibacy rules and a completely democratized church having no institutional format whatsoever. Around the same time a group of conservative priests based in the southern diocese of Roermond (located in the southern part of the province of Limburg) started a group called Catholic Life which stressed unity of the church, faith, and obedience to Rome. *Septuagint* formally ceased to exist in 1973 after changing its name and transforming itself from a militant action group into a service-oriented "communication centre" for progressive clerical-lay groups at the parish level throughout the Netherlands. The Catholic Life group, although conservative, nevertheless accepted both the authority of the bishops and an element of democratization. It faded from existence in the mid-1970s.[32] Neither organization had a very large membership and more importantly neither group came into being until the late 1960s, well after many of the changes in theology and church organization had occurred.

The bishops were not the subjects of a well-organized attack by a specific group or movement within the church. The forces that the bishops were responding to were much more diffuse. How representative of the feeling among priests generally were the opinions of the more vocal progressives? To what extent had the Dutch priesthood changed with regard to attitudes on church doctrine and the carrying out of pastoral functions? Partial answers can be found in a 1968 survey of Dutch priests mainly on the question of celibacy.[33] It was in the form of a questionnaire mailed out to virtually all Dutch priests residing in the Netherlands. The response rate was over 85 per cent making for a sample of 7,381. The question on the celibacy rule permitted a variety of responses such as "abolishment of the celibacy rule with certain restrictions" or "maintenance of the rule but no opinion as to restrictions." Although some of the response categories were ambiguous certain results were clear: only 10 per cent of the sample were in favour of maintaining the celibacy rule for all priests. Forty-six per cent were definitely in favour of lifting the rule for at least "certain categories of priests."[34] In the same survey priests were asked their opinion of the 1968 Papal Encyclical *Humanae Vitae* which reaffirmed the papal prohibition against any and all forms of birth control. Forty-five per cent of the respondents disagreed with the encyclical while 35 per cent had no clear opinion.[35] The notion that 90 per cent of the responding priests would not be opposed to changes in the celibacy rule and that only 20 per cent would be in favour of the Pope's stand on birth control would have been unthinkable in the 1950s.

As shown in table 4.1, the younger priests were most likely to have liberal attitudes on the celibacy question. Older priests were more likely to favour ambiguous categories such as "no clear opinion." The authors of the report interpreted this to mean that while older priests may not have favoured changing their own celibate status they were quite willing to tolerate other priests doing so.[36] The push for reform was more likely to come from the younger generation of priests while at the same time older generations were receptive, or at least not unalterably opposed, to change. This is reflected in their reactions to the reforms as they were introduced. Most clerics welcomed the changes. They sensed that over the years their parishioners had changed. "The people were unhappy; we were unhappy. . . . Fewer people come to mass nowadays, that is for certain. But now people who attend mass come because they really want to come" (Interview 12). The secularization of the mass and the new catechism introduced in 1966 gained universal acceptance. One priest, aged eighty-two, still considered himself a staunch supporter of a hierarchical church and believed that faith was something that could be adequately safeguarded only by the

TABLE 4.1
Position on Celibacy by Age Cohort

	66+	61–65	56–60	51–55	46–50	41–45	36–40	31–35	<30	Total
Maintain celibacy	31%	21%	13%	10%	7%	6%	2%	2%	—	10%
No clear choice or willing to accept partial lifting of celibacy rule	64	70	72	69	62	59	53	50	41%	60
Lift celibacy rule	5	9	15	21	31	35	45	48	59	30
Total:	100%	100%	100%	100%	100%	100%	100%	100%	100%	100%
N:	(859)	(598)	(767)	(992)	(898)	(924)	(891)	(756)	(681)	(7366)

Source: Instituut voor Toegepaste Sociologie (ITS), *Ambtscelibaat in een veranderende Kerk*.

priests. Nevertheless he felt that through the new catechism and the use of the vernacular the church spoke much more directly to the people (Interview 17).

The introduction of collegiality at various levels of the church often meant a change in the personal lives of priests. Previously priests in different parishes had very little contact with one another. Instructions were received by mail and through occasional visits by the dean or an official from the diocese. Upon the introduction of collegiality most deaneries began having meetings of all priests in the deanery, some of them on a monthly basis. By providing opportunities for mutual support these meetings stood in contrast to the isolation and independence of earlier times.

Many of the changes that occurred in the church did not happen by fiat from the bishops. Particularly in the early stages there was a general sense that the rules had been relaxed, that a great many things were now permissible. "Take the structure of the mass, for example. Before everything had to be extremely precise. Then, I remember, in the early 1960s one would start changing certain aspects of the mass, leaving things out, experimenting a little. I am not quite sure why; there were no directives to that effect. One just felt somewhat more free to do these sorts of things" (Interview 18).

For priests the changes were not an unmixed blessing. They were the ones responsible for the difficult task of implementing the idea of parish councils with lay participation. Many priests discovered that it was very difficult to obtain a suitable level of participation or to find lay representatives who did in fact represent larger interests within the parish. Alternatively the pastor may have been faced with feuding lay factions, those in favour of changing the church and those who wished to preserve its traditional format. In such cases the pastor had to play the role of conciliator or bridge-builder to ensure that neither side felt aggrieved or left out. This role was in many ways much more demanding and time-consuming than the previous traditional role. The new sense of liberation had its drawbacks. Although preferring the new openness to the old closed, hierarchical system many priests nevertheless wished for more direction from the bishops. Some felt, too, that perhaps the changes had come too quickly. One priest noted: "The time of the Pastoral Council (1966–70) was particularly bad, what with the conflict with Rome and so on. There was a lot of confusion among people, myself included. Many had the feeling of being left behind" (Interview 19).

Yet there was no question among the clergy of ever turning the clock back. A highly conservative group of lay Catholics known as

Changes in the Catholic Community | 109

TABLE 4.2
Clerical Defection and Recruitment 1955–1975

Year	Entering the Priesthood	Leaving the Priesthood
1955	345	Not available
1960	318	30
1965	237	45
1966	227	74
1967	193	155
1968	143	155
1969	110	244
1970	48	243
1971	42	217
1975	32	94

Source: J. Thurlings, *De wankele zuil*, pp. 166–67; KASKI, *Vijf jaar kerkontwikkeling in Nederland*, p. 45.

Confrontatie (Confrontation), who wanted to do precisely that, had great difficulty in finding sympathetic priests to accompany them on their retreats.[37] A small number of clergy who were highly disturbed by the changes moved to West Germany where they were accepted by some of the more conservatively oriented German bishops.

It would be misleading to say that the bishops allowed changes to take place because of overwhelming pressure from rank-and-file clergy. The bishops probably saw a somewhat different situation, one in which there had been a drastic drop in the amount of clerical manpower available and a virtual certainty that this would drop even further in the future. The Catholic population had risen from 3.7 million in 1947 to 5.2 million in 1971.[38] The number of priests had declined so that by 1971 the ratio of Catholics to priests in the Netherlands had risen by about 50 per cent.[39] As can be seen in table 4.2 the defection rate rose dramatically in the 1960s and the recruitment rate dropped. Whereas in 1955, 345 priests entered the priesthood, only forty-two did so in 1971.

Not only were their numbers growing fewer, particularly in proportion to the rest of the Catholic population, but the age-structure had become skewed. The mean age-level of priests in 1971 was in the mid-fifties rather than the low forties of a decade earlier. This meant a large age discrepancy between priests and their parishioners, one which would continue to grow. Even if the bishops had wanted to

TABLE 4.3
Mass Attendance by Age

	Age Cohorts				
	60+	44–59	31–43	21–30	Total
Percentage who always attend mass	60.2%	57.7%	45.7%	38.6%	49.3%
N =	(59)	(113)	(85)	(73)	(330)
Total sample = 669					

Source: Dutch Election Study, 1970.

maintain a rigorous, traditional posture on the part of the church it would have been extremely difficult given the lack of adequate manpower.

2. Changes in the Clientele

Was the reorientation of the church merely a means of keeping up with changes occurring among Catholics generally in the Netherlands? Or alternatively to what extent did the church stimulate, initiate, or mould changes among Catholics?

The Dutch Catholic population in the late 1960s was definitely different from that of the early postwar period. For one thing it was generally better educated. In 1947 only 14 per cent of all Dutch secondary school students were Catholic. In 1971 35 per cent of secondary students were Catholic although the Catholic proportion of the school age population had risen only slightly.[40] The clergy sensed that people were becoming increasingly unhappy with required practices like compulsory attendance at mass and, of course, the church's stand on birth control. They noticed a drop in church attendance, particularly among the young.[41] As can be seen in table 4.3, there was a distinct generational difference in attendance at mass.

Increasing affluence had altered recreational practices. Figure 4.1 shows the rise in prosperity in the Netherlands which had begun in the late 1950s and accelerated rapidly throughout the 1960s. The advent of television allowed people to stay at home and at the same time be exposed to wider influences. In 1956 there were only 99,000 television sets. This number grew to 1,040,000 in 1960 and 2,113,000 in 1965. By 1974 there were 3,086,000 registered television sets in the Netherlands.[42]

With the rise in affluence and the number of television sets there was

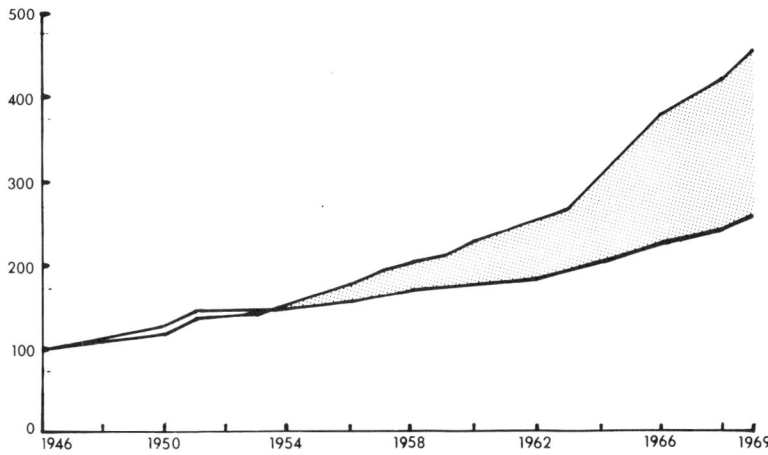

The upper line indicates the rise in the wage index (1946 = 100), the lower line that in the price index.

FIGURE 4.1. Dutch Wages and Prices, 1946–1969
Source: J. de Vries, "Spiral and Miracle: The Dutch Economy since 1920," *Delta* 13, no. 3 (Autumn 1970): 28.

a concomitant decline in attendance at sporting events and cinemas. Car ownership rose dramatically as well. In 1955 there were only twenty-five passenger vehicles per 1,000 inhabitants; in 1974 the number was 254.[43] By the early 1960s Catholics were better educated, more affluent, less dependent upon the church for spiritual and practical help, and more dependent upon their recently acquired consumer goods. One priest noted difficulty in making visits to the homes of parishioners: "If there is a soccer game on television you know for sure that you will not be welcome" (Interview 22).[44]

The occupational structure of the Netherlands changed as well. In 1947 19 per cent of the labour force was employed in agriculture; in 1960 only 11 per cent.[45] Much of the Netherlands' recent prosperity has been based on continuous industrialization throughout the postwar period, particularly in the southern provinces. Thus the labour force in the province of North Brabant grew by 25 per cent in a relatively short period (1953–60).[46] The new housing that resulted from the massive population increase in the same period was largely confined to non-urban areas, leading to the suburbanization of large amounts of rural land. Thus in the western provinces, where the major cities of Amsterdam and Rotterdam are located, the population in the agricultural areas grew by 22.9 per cent between 1951 and 1963, while the major cities in this area grew by only 13 per cent.[47] The development of large apartment block complexes helped lead to the attenuation of the relationship between the priest and his parishioners in urban areas. Pastors residing in these areas noted that it was now impossible to visit parishioners on a regular basis. They lacked the manpower and cited the large turnover rate among apartment dwellers.

Yet in spite of these developments there were no massive dislocations of the sort that occurred when the Netherlands first began industrializing, no large-scale flow of Catholic migrants to western cities like Amsterdam and Rotterdam. A detailed study has been done of both inter- and intraprovincial migration since the turn of the century. During the 1920s the migration index (measuring both types of migration) was around 120, reaching a high of 130 in 1930.[48] In the depression period the figure dropped to around 100. During the 1950s and early Sixties it stood at around 80, but in 1964 it began to rise again, reaching 100 in 1969. Virtually all of this increase was due to intraprovincial mobility, while interprovincial mobility remained constant at 80. The authors of the report attribute most of the increase since 1964 to the movement of people to the suburbs, increasing affluence making it possible for many of them to purchase their own homes.[49] At the same time an improved transportation system and access to the automobile made it possible for people to commute to work. This differed from the interwar period when a Catholic in the province of North Brabant who wished to work in the harbour in Rotterdam had to move himself and his family to that city.

Thus one cannot attribute the process of deconfessionalization in the 1960s to the occurrence of massive social dislocation. When geographical mobility on a large scale occurred, mainly between 1890 and 1930, the church managed to maintain its hold over most of its flock. When mobility did begin to rise in 1964 the bishops had already taken several important steps in reorienting the church. The rise in consumerism as well as in the general level of education was important in helping to attenuate the relationship between the parish priest and his parishioners. This manifested itself in a decline in church attendance and visits to the confessional. Yet there was no organized movement of revolt. Lay Catholics who were critical of the church and many of the institutions of the Catholic subculture were critics of long standing. Among them were members of the PVDA Catholic faction, intellectuals, and people who wrote for and read journals like *De Bazuin* and *Te Elfder Ure*.

In the 1960s a number of groups organized by lay Catholics did come into being. The more militant ones, however, tended to be conservative. The above-mentioned group calling itself *Confrontatie* was formed by two lay Catholics in 1964. Estimates of its membership have varied between 900 and 10,000. Its supporters tended to be older and middle-class, residing in the southeast. In publications and speeches its members attacked the bishops and institutions like the KRO and the KVP and made frequent references to the prewar church in the era of the "Rich Roman Life." When the new Catechism was announced in 1966 *Confrontatie* circulated a petition destined for the pope claiming that 80 per cent of the Catechism was false.[50] The very name of the group, however, is indicative of its character and the way it related to the rest of Catholic society. It appealed to only a very small minority and felt the need to use shock tactics in order to get its point across.

In 1968 a lay Catholic, who was formerly a promoter of devotions to visions of the Blessed Virgin, founded an organization called the Saint Michäel Legion which was even more reactionary than *Confrontatie* and disavowed any connection with it. It regularly attacked the ecclesiastical hierarchy in a virulent fashion and tried, though not successfully, to set up its own broadcasting organization and political party.[51]

A lay group calling itself Action Group World Church, moderately left-wing but without any clear profile, came into being in 1969.[52] Its *raison d'être* was opposition to the demands and tactics of *Septuagint*. It failed to become a focus for promoting change and faded from view in 1971. In 1972 an organization named Action Group Open Church was founded by prominent lay Catholics and clerics largely in response to the papal nomination of an extremely conservative candidate, Johan Gijsen, as the new bishop of Roermond.[53] Its general aim was to promote democratization within the church, but its specific aim was to provide support for the Dutch bishops in what the group saw as a battle between the church in Rome and the Dutch church concerning the Gijsen appointment. The latter purpose is indicative of the relationship between the hierarchy and most Catholics in the Netherlands. Although the actions of the bishops during the 1960s were disapproved of by a number of traditional older Catholics, on the whole the bishops enjoyed wide acceptance. A public opinion poll in 1969 indicated that 88 per cent of Dutch Catholics had "strong confidence in the leadership of the bishops."[54] When asked what they thought of their local parish priest 73 per cent of the same sample indicated that they were either satisfied or highly satisfied. Exactly the same percentage said they were satisfied with the changes in the liturgy. Interestingly, a fairly high proportion of the sample, 41 per cent, considered themselves to be "conservative Catholic," while 54 per cent saw themselves as "progressive Catholics."[55]

One of the greatest changes introduced by the Dutch church was the new set of guidelines on birth control which essentially stated that the church was no longer interested in interfering in "the biological aspects of marriage." To what extent did this *de facto* withdrawal of the objection to birth control coincide with the wishes of Catholics? The data in table 4.4 on attitudes towards birth control in 1965 and 1968 show that only a small minority held that birth control of any sort was objectionable. Moreover, between those two years the minority objecting to birth control dropped from 10 to 3 per cent, while the figure for those having no objection rose from 46 to 58 per cent. More and more Catholics were adopting more liberal attitudes on birth control.

In 1968, following the Papal Encyclical *Humanae Vitae* which condemned all forms of contraception except the rhythm method, a further survey showed that 81 per cent of Dutch Catholics disagreed with the statement, "the Pope has brought great joy to Catholics with this encyclical." Seventy-two per cent of the sample agreed that "the Pope has set the clock back several years." Eighty-nine per cent were of the opinion that birth control methods other than the rhythm method should be permitted. Of those who actually did use a method other

TABLE 4.4
Attitudes of Dutch Catholics towards Birth Control, 1965 and 1968

	1965	1968
Opposed to contraception under any circumstance	10%	3%
Permissible under certain circumstances	38	37
No objection whatsoever	46	58
No opinion	6	2
Total:	100%	100%

Source: Attwood Statistics, cited in Thurlings, *De wankele zuil*, p. 160.

than the rhythm method such as the pill (61 per cent), 93 per cent said that the encyclical would have no effect on changing their behaviour.[56] Dutch Catholics clearly preferred the leadership of their bishops to that of the pope.

The concerns of many Catholics were ordinary ones and usually not related to questions of high theology, as the content of the letters posted in the boxes instituted by the Dutch Pastoral Council indicated. The most serious problems for individuals were caused by remarriage after divorce; other letters came from groups in villages wanting another parish priest. The change in discipline caused by the dropping away of many compulsory rituals was a psychological relief for most Catholics. One of the more popular figures in the 1960s was a cabaret artist by the name of Fons Jansen. His special theme was the pre-Vatican II Catholic church and he kept Catholic audiences laughing with his routines on Roman Catholic moral teachings.[57]

Although the changes were generally welcomed, the lack of constant guidelines and the falling away of many traditions left many people with the feeling of being lost. This was particularly true of older persons, who tended to remember with a certain fondness the cultural trappings of a bygone era, pushing the harsher aspects of that era into the background. One parish priest noted that he occasionally acceded to the demands of older women for prayer sessions for the Virgin Mary (Interview 8).

In the pre-Vatican II church an ordinary Catholic who more or less lived by the rules of the church received in return a certain comfort and a high degree of predictability in his life. In several ways the new church with its emphasis on personal responsibility was much more demanding since it required active participation on the part of lay

Catholics. A number of pastors reported difficulties in maintaining a sufficiently high level of enthusiasm among parishioners to keep committees and parish councils operating.

The main form of participation in religious life was still the mass. However, if mass attendance is an indication of how much of their time and energy Catholics are willing to devote to their religious life then the prognosis is not good. Mass attendance in the Netherlands has shown a constant decline as documented by KASKI statistics (see table 4.5). Attendance in 1974 was similar to that of Catholics in West Germany and Belgium in the same year although in those countries it had previously been much lower than in the Netherlands. By 1979, however, the rate in the Netherlands was considerably below that of both West Germany and Belgium.[58]

Mass attendance has remained relatively high only in the rural areas where older Catholic traditions still persist (56.4 per cent in rural areas in contrast to 18.3 per cent in major cities in 1974).[59] These traditions persist in the more rural, isolated areas not so much because of the demands of the church as because of the wishes of the local population. A parish priest in a largely Catholic village in the northeast told of considerable difficulty in changing old practices. When he arrived in the parish in 1971, incense and Latin were still being used in the mass. It took some time for him to phase out these practices and introduce parishioners to some of the changes brought about by Vatican II (Interview 12). Such traditional parishes, however, are rather few in number since most Catholics were introduced to the changes well before that time.

Even more dramatic than the decline in mass attendance has been the decrease in the number of people who regard themselves as Catholic. In the census of 1971 40.4 per cent of Dutch citizens said they were Catholic.[60] In surveys done in 1977 and 1979, however, only between 31 and 33.9 per cent of the respondents still considered themselves as Catholic.[61] The 1981 census will confirm or disconfirm the accuracy of these estimates. If they are true the Dutch church will have suffered its greatest decline in numbers since the seventeenth century. This does not bode well for the future of the Dutch church and it is quite possible that by the year 2000 Catholics will constitute less than 20 per cent of the population in the Netherlands.

During the 1960s and 1970s ordinary Catholics accepted and felt liberated by many of the post-Vatican II changes but they probably experienced a degree of alienation as well. Thurlings sees this alienation as resulting in part from conflicts within the Catholic subculture between groups like *Confrontatie* and *Septuagint*, between the Dutch

Changes in the Catholic Community | 117

TABLE 4.5
Mass Attendance by Year, 1966–1979

	Year and Month							
	Jan. 1966	Jan. 1968	Oct. 1970	Jan. 1972	Jan. 1974	Jan. 1976	Jan. 1978	Oct. 1979
Percentage of Catholics attending mass	64.4%	58.4%	47.2%	41.1%	35.1%	31.1%	27.8%	26.1%

Source: KASKI, "De ontwikkeling van het misbezoekcijfer, 1966–1979," Memorandum No. 213 (1980), p. 7.
Note: Data based on counts taken in 1,608 of the 1,810 parishes in the Netherlands. Counts represent average of counts taken on two separate weekends in month indicated.

church and Rome, and, more recently, among the bishops themselves. The new conservative bishop of the diocese of Roermond, Johan Gijsen, has in the last few years openly attacked the other bishops and engaged in bitter feuds with even moderate clerics in his own diocese. The call for greater orthodoxy in the Netherlands by Pope John Paul II is unlikely to help matters. As Thurlings noted in 1971: "The conservatives are now obliged to advocate the maintenance of the strict norms and in so doing give the impression that they are in favour of a rigorism that was unknown in the traditional Catholic Church. And though the progressives reject many burdensome traditional norms, they demand at the same time a personal commitment that the rank and file is incapable of producing."[62]

3. Mobilization

The decline in attendance at mass during the 1960s and early 1970s must be seen largely as a result of the abolition of social control by the church and the substitution of an individualized form of authority as the rationale for participating in religious activities. The church took the initiative in instituting these changes. Yet the rapidity with which they were accepted and the impact they had requires further explanation. One can say there was a ready market for many of these changes, especially for those concerning birth control. However, the attitudes of Catholics were also in part shaped by the church and the impact of the changes was magnified because of the mobilization resources that were available. The very institutions which, in the previous era, helped insulate Catholics from the rest of Dutch society during the

1960s helped expose Catholics to outside influences generally and the influences of a new church in particular.

The Catholic Broadcasting Organization (KRO) did not become committed to the new theology in the way that certain periodicals did. It did, however, provide detailed coverage of both the changes and the events that accompanied them. Mgr. Bekkers used the medium of television in an extremely effective way. His message, couched in the terminology of love and understanding and containing concrete guidance, was beamed into millions of homes. From 1962 to 1965 the proceedings of the Vatican Council received intensive coverage. A fulltime studio with staff was located in Rome on a permanent basis during that period. No television network in other countries provided a similar service to viewers. The Dutch Pastoral Council (1966–70) also received considerable attention, and many of the letters to the council were read and discussed on the air by the KRO.[63] The Dutch Catholic daily and weekly press also provided extensive coverage of matters related to change. Since virtually every Catholic home received at least one Catholic daily, there was very little chance that anyone would be unaware that something new was afoot in the church. Catholics would have found it difficult to insulate themselves from events by switching to the media of the other blocs since they also provided extensive coverage of both Vatican II and related events in the Catholic subculture.

Many of the problems discussed such as the celibacy question were of a topical nature and provided considerable publicity value. A priest's housekeeper wrote in the official weekly of the diocese of Breda that the question of celibacy was at best an academic one because most priests were not fit to marry anyway. "They do not even notice that somebody looks after them, let alone that it is a woman who does it all."[64] This unleashed a storm of protest from the clergy, many of whom were convinced that they would make excellent husbands. This incident was greatly amplified in the press and provided cartoonists with ample material for several weeks as priests went to great lengths in pressing their case.

The highly centralized structure of the Dutch church and the longstanding tradition of collegial decision-making among the bishops themselves helped to ensure that changes spread quickly to all parts of the Dutch church province. Many of the changes in the 1960s involved the lifting of sanctions and a degree of democratization. Yet there was still a large element of control from above with regard to the behaviour of clergy. While in the previous era the object was to ensure that the priest did not deviate from church doctrine and ritual, in the

Changes in the Catholic Community | 119

1970s there was pressure on many priests to ensure that they did in fact implement or try to implement the changes accepted by the bishops and the Dutch Pastoral Council. Today the pressure may no longer be as direct and may also involve peer group pressure from fellow-priests. Nevertheless, there is a perception among some of the clergy that they would be "rapped across the knuckles" (Interview 8) if, for example, they tried to prevent lay participation in parish affairs.

Thus many of the very structures that were critical in maintaining the unity of the Catholic subculture up to the early and mid-1960s were used in the period of change to make Catholics aware of their altered status vis-à-vis the church.

Continuity with the Past. The implication so far has been that the Dutch hierarchy deliberately broke with the past to set the church on a new course. The Dutch church, which was formerly seen by Rome as among the most loyal of all the ecclesiastical provinces, has since the early 1960s been seen as one of the most rebellious. In Ireland the bishops announced in 1965 that people need have no fear of what was discussed at Vatican II, since the orientation of the Irish church would remain largely unchanged.[65] In West Germany also, the bishops remained conservative. Although the secularization of the liturgy was accepted by most of the world church, most of its bishops still held to the principles of hierarchy. The question remains why the Dutch bishops took the course they did.

In the Netherlands during the early 1960s it was obvious that Catholics were drifting away from the church, that the teachings of the church were becoming less and less relevant. The bishops faced more direct pressure than before from clergy and theologians. But this still does not explain the course they took. This period was marked by generational change among members of the hierarchy; by 1962 Cardinal Alfrink was the only member who had been involved in the 1954 decision concerning the *Mandement*. Yet prior to their appointment the new members of the ecclesiastical hierarchy were for the most part considered to be quite conservative. For example, Bekkers, the television bishop, was considered very traditional up to 1958. Most members of the hierarchy changed their views quite late in their careers.

The evidence suggests that the behaviour of the bishops in their policy of church renewal was consistent with many of the cultural traditions of Dutch Catholicism. This can best be illustrated by putting forward a number of the alternative courses of action that were open to the bishops at the crucial threshold in the late 1950s and early 1960s. First, they could have maintained the posture of the church as outlined in the *Mandement* of 1954. Sanctions might have been applied against those who transgressed the rules. Those Catholics who did not wish to follow the wishes of the church could, as Professor Romme noted in the 1950s, have left the church. The second option would have been to have held to orthodox doctrine, at least officially, but in practice to have been lenient in the application of sanctions, to have turned a blind eye to many of the transgressions. This would have involved bending the rules rather than breaking them.

If the bishops had taken the first option, large numbers of Catholics would have left the church and a schism would have been a very real possibility. The Dutch church would have been left with an aging clergy rapidly diminishing in size. The clientele would have become increasingly restricted to the older age groups, and younger generations would basically have been lost to the church.

In 1954 Alfrink had strong misgivings about the *Mandement*[66] and these were confirmed by the reactions that the document evoked. It is highly likely, therefore, that Alfrink as well as the newer bishops were aware of the practical consequences of a firm position. Those consequences would have been difficult to reconcile with traditions emphasizing the unitary nature of Dutch Catholicism. The faith which had been carefully nurtured over the centuries by previous generations of bishops and clergy would have been snuffed out in a large proportion of the Catholic population.

To have taken the second course, leniency in enforcing official doctrine, would have been even more inconsistent with Dutch Catholic cultural traditions. As noted in chapter 2 Dutch Catholics have always been known for their literalism in applying rules and edicts, a tendency often associated with Calvinistic and Jansenist influences. As Thurlings has argued, to a Dutchman rules exist either to be followed or to be broken. Rules are never bent.[67] In the case of the Dutch church an alternative to breaking the rules was to revise them. The initiatives taken by the bishops have had a distinct affinity with the past. Their concept of bridge-building, that is, maintaining links with all elements within the Catholic subculture, can be seen as a modern version of the tradition of maintaining unity among Catholics. The democratization of the church generally and the demythologizing of the clergy in particular is not inconsistent with Calvinist and Jansenist tendencies that have always been present in Dutch Catholicism. The much greater stress on personal responsibility, personal commitment, and lay participation also falls into this category.

The various objectives of the Catholic subculture had long been met. Catholic institutions were safe. In terms of educational achievement Catholics were nearly equal to the rest of the population. Institutional emancipation which was particularly important during the interwar period gave way to a more personal sort of emancipation whereby Catholics were expected to achieve their aims as individuals in the wider society rather than as part of a collectivity. This development was akin to the sort of emancipation a number of liberal Catholic intellectuals had in mind during the first half of the nineteenth century. The events of the 1960s can also be seen as a reversion to an earlier type of isolation. The Catholic progressive movement had a curiously apolitical cast. Many argued that the church should retreat to a safer position, that it was harmful for it to venture into the realm of political controversy. This was not unlike the policy advocated before World War I. Then it was argued that direct interference by the church in politics would only evoke negative reactions from non-Catholics in the Netherlands.[68]

At Vatican II the Dutch bishops were probably the most active members of the council in the attempt to redefine church doctrine, to make that doctrine more relevant and applicable to modern conditions. Rather than bending rules, or attempting to apply rules no longer relevant to changed conditions, or breaking them and thus risking their relationship with Rome, the Dutch bishops chose deliberate action to remedy a difficult situation, much as they had at a time of massive social dislocation during industrialization and again when National Socialism posed a threat.

4. Socio-Economic Organizations and Deconfessionalization

How did the winds of change that blew through the Catholic church and the Catholic community affect Catholic socio-economic life? The Catholic hierarchy, it has been noted, had reoriented its attitude towards the sanctions applied in the past to ensure that only Catholic organizations were patronized by church members. There was also a definite psychological change among Catholics. Many no longer felt compelled to attend mass on a regular basis or to embark upon the formation of large families.

In assessing the effect of these changes on various socio-economic organizations it is useful to look at the membership figures for the major radio and television broadcasting organizations (table 4.6). The KRO declined in membership but not severely. The socialist VARA also underwent a decline and the libertarian VPRO declined the most sharply. Since the basic threshold for broadcasting organizations in order to obtain "A" status is 400,000 paid members the KRO is in no danger of disappearing.[69]

The figures for trade union membership reveal a similar pattern (see

TABLE 4.6
Broadcasting Organizational Membership by Year

Year	KRO (Catholic)	NCRV (Protestant)	VARA (Socialist)	VPRO (Libertarian Protestant)	AVRO (Liberal)	TROS (Neutral)
1939	160,791	126,000	108,571	—	196,699	—
1947	84,566	101,072	101,146	46,000	86,394	—
1960	604,243	435,945	533,678	214,875	405,994	—
1965	566,713	465,448	484,713	160,000	385,172	—
1970	545,262	476,000	485,652	139,215	835,000	250,000*
1976	556,000	502,000	495,000	146,000	825,000	682,000

Source: Thurlings, *De wankele zuil*, p. 139; *Omroep ABC*, p. 110; Thurlings, "Pluralism and Assimilation in the Netherlands," *International Journal of Comparative Sociology* 20, no. 1–2 (March–June 1979): 94.
*as of 1971.

TABLE 4.7
Trade Union Membership by Year

	1947	1950	1955	1960	1965	1970	1973
NVV (Neutral)	300,300	381,600	463,100	486,000	526,400	562,500	656,600
NKV (Catholic)	224,900	296,400	361,000	400,400	406,700	400,000	396,000
CNV (Protestant)	119,000	155,000	199,000	219,000	228,900	238,500	234,900

Source: Centraal Bureau voor Statistiek, *Statistiek van de vakbeweging*, 1973, p. 2.

table 4.7). In the period from 1947 to 1973 the Catholic Trade Union Federation (NKV) managed to expand its membership, thus keeping up with the growth of the industrial labour force, although its growth rate was not as high as that of the neutral NVV. Membership figures by themselves offer only slight evidence that the changes in Dutch Catholicism have had an impact on Catholic trade unions. There are a number of Catholic organizations whose rates of growth equalled or exceeded those of their neutral and Protestant counterparts. For example, the Catholic health care organization, the White-Yellow Cross, had a membership growth rate of 30 per cent in the period 1958–67. In the same period the neutral Green Cross had a growth rate of 25 per cent.[70]

The circulation of Catholic newspapers also grew in direct proportion to the Catholic population. In 1955 76 per cent of all Catholic households subscribed to a Catholic newspaper. In 1969 the figure was 75 per cent.[71] Van Kemenade noted in 1969 that virtually every Catholic child at the kindergarten and grade school levels attended a Catholic school. This figure of 100 per cent has remained constant over the last four decades. At the academic secondary school level the figure was estimated to be about 80 per cent in 1969, an increase from 60 per cent in 1947.[72] The Catholic Farmers' Association had a drop in membership from 76,181 in 1960 to 59,989 in 1976.[73] This drop, however, is consistent with the general drop in the percentage of workers employed in this sector.

The figures for some of the Catholic organizations and institutions mentioned above give some indication of their economic viability and chances for survival in the future. However, they say very little about the character of these organizations and the changes they underwent during the period of church renewal. Thurlings described those running many of the Catholic socio-economic organizations as loyal bureaucrats with little imagination.[74] Many of these bureaucrats were caught unawares by the change in Catholicism and as a result were unable to adapt themselves to changed conditions. However, their distribution varied from organization to organization. Furthermore, the amount of adaptation required of the organizations varied in accordance with the services offered, that is to say, their role in the social, cultural, and economic marketplace.

Some Catholic institutions took to heart the reforms of Vatican II and the Dutch Pastoral Council. One of the first institutions to embrace the spirit of ecumenicalism was the Catholic marriage bureau. In 1967 it joined with the humanist, Reformed, and Calvinist bureaus to form a single agency for the purpose of bringing potential marriage partners together.[75]

In the same year the White-Yellow Cross along with the other two cross organizations set up a Foundation for Cooperating Cross-Associations,[76] with the object of arranging that in areas where the existence of more than one such organization meant unnecessary duplication of facilities, they would merge or one or more of them would be disbanded. The slogan became "Cooperation wherever possible. Separation only when necessary."

A number of other organizations merged or federated, or attempted to do so, with their neutral or Protestant counterparts. These actual or attempted mergers were due not so much to the spirit of ecumenicalism as to economic pressures. The influence of deconfessionalization meant that members no longer felt morally obligated to support their Catholic organization, particularly when it seemed less relevant or efficient. With the withdrawal of church support such organizations were now subject to the forces of economic rationalization.

For example, the Catholic Retailers' Organization (KNOB) suffered a decline in membership during the 1960s. A number of member organizations such as the Catholic Plumbers' Association had already merged with their neutral and Protestant counterparts. When members balked at paying higher fees, the Catholic Retailers' Organization decided in 1971 to enter into a federation with the Protestant Retailers' Organization. Within a few months the executives of the two groups discovered that they could not get along with one another, and so the partners in the Christian Federation of Retailers' Associations decided to part company. The building which they had newly acquired was divided into two and Catholics and Protestants reverted to their original organizational formats. The financial pressures on the Catholic organization did not subside, however. Economic rationalization and the decline in small retailers continued to diminish the number of potential members. In 1976 the Catholic Retailers' Organization and the Royal Retailers' Organization (the neutral organization) agreed upon a formula for a merger which came into effect in 1977.[77]

The Catholic Employers' Federation faced similar economic pressures. During World War II a number of mergers had taken place among the larger industrial organizations at the behest of the German occupiers. After the war many of these mergers remained in force although when the separate employers' federations reappeared the interconfessional organizations would often join two or perhaps all three of them. In the 1960s many of these organizations began dropping one or both of their confessional memberships. And, as in the case of many small businessmen's organizations, the larger bodies which had not already done so also began to federate or merge. In 1970 the Dutch

Christian Employers' Federation (NCW) came into being, a result of the merging of the Catholic and Protestant employers' federations.[78]

Currently a number of the sixty-two organizations affiliated with the NCW are also members of the neutral federation. This dual membership is maintained partly out of loyalty to the confessional federation but also because of the somewhat different services the two federations offer. In fact, the clientele of the NCW is different in character. The neutral federation counts large multinational firms like Shell and Unilever among its members, whereas the NCW still caters to small and medium-sized firms and claims to help protect their interests against those of the multinationals. Thus, aside from its confessional character, it also has a definite economic function to perform which helps to explain its viability. Until the creation of the unified Christian Democratic Appeal (CDA) in 1980, the NCW was the only example of a successful merger between major Protestant and Catholic organizations.

In the trade union sector matters took a different course, demonstrating pressures towards deconfessionalization but also the difficulties involved in achieving a merger or federation between quite similar bodies. In the postwar period the three trade union federations had developed a very close working relationship and by 1967 they had come out with a common program. There was, however, a divergence in views on the form and intensity of future cooperation. Van Eiberger, leader of the Protestant Trade Union Federation (CNV), called for closer cooperation in terms of the existing structures, while Mertens, leader of the Catholic Trade Union Federation (NKV), indicated that his organization favoured a federation of the three bodies. Only Kloos, leader of the neutral Trade Union Federation (NVV), urged that a complete merger take place.[79]

Within the NKV there was a distinct difference between the leadership and the rank-and-file on the merger question. A survey of members of all three federations, commissioned by the NVV in 1968, indicated that among rank-and-file members 70 per cent of NVV members, 61 per cent of NKV members, and 56 per cent of CNV members favoured the idea of a merger.[80] Another survey done by the NKV among its own members showed that 66 per cent of the rank-and-file wanted a merger.[81] The NKV leadership, however, persisted in pursuing the federation rather than fusion plan and starting in 1968 commissioned a series of committees to look into the question of the NKV, its Catholic identity, and the meaning of deconfessionalization. They concluded that the organization did indeed have a separate identity which was worth preserving though they admitted to not knowing precisely what it was.[82] Preying heavily upon the minds of the leaders were the problems associated with the merger of a smaller organization (NKV) with a larger one (NVV). They may well have wondered about the influence they were likely to have in the new scheme of things. Conflicts also occurred between individual Catholic and NVV trade unions. Thus in 1971–72 there was a rather prolonged one between the leaders of the industrial unions of the NKV and NVV concerning a proposed collective agreement in the metal industry.[83]

The NKV leadership also faced pressure from certain member unions not to proceed with merger plans. The Catholic Policemen's Union and the Catholic Civil Service Union threatened to leave the NKV if it continued its courtship of the NVV, and they did in fact leave in 1975 when federation appeared inevitable. At the same time the NKV was faced with other adverse developments, including a decline in the porcelain and textile sectors where much of its strength lay. Thus while the membership of the NVV was still growing in the 1970s, NKV membership was stagnant (see table 4.5). The NKV was bypassed when new sectors in the Dutch labour force became unionized, as in the case of the full unionization of school teachers in the early 1970s. The result was that Catholic teachers became affiliated with the NVV but not the NKV.

The NKV leadership was in a dilemma. The majority of rank-and-file members were in favour of a merger with the two other trade union centrals. A significant minority, however, did not want it. At the same time NKV leaders were concerned about their own futures in the event of union with the NVV, and were hesitant about going ahead with a merger which did not include the CNV. It was clear that the CNV was cool towards the idea of a federation let alone a merger. A NKV-NVV merger would leave it isolated and serve to split the Dutch labour movement rather than enhance cooperation.

In the fall of 1970 the NKV officially proposed a federation of the three trade union centrals. The negotiations that followed were long and protracted and were not helped by conflicts between individual NKV and NVV unions. By 1974 the CNV made it clear that it was no longer interested even in a federation.[84] In the fall of 1975 an agreement was finally reached between the NVV and NKV to form a federation based on equal partnership.[85] The path to this successful union was a difficult one and illustrative of the myriad of conflicting interests involved in such a procedure. In spite of virtually identical interests, structures, programs, and services, and a membership whose majority favoured a merger, sufficient incentives still existed for NKV leaders to maintain a separate organization. In spite of deconfessionalization they managed to preserve their influence as well as to hold on to their clientele.

Changes in the Catholic Community | 127

The leaders of the Catholic Farmers' Association (KNBTB) never had any doubt about their position on mergers.[86] Even though the number of agricultural workers was declining, the membership could be relied upon to continue supporting the organization. Since most members were from the rural areas where Catholics tend to be more traditional, it would have been very difficult to sell the idea of dropping the title "Catholic" to the members even if the leadership had wished to. A spiritual adviser to one of the regional organizations felt that many Catholic farmers were unhappy and considered themselves to have been bypassed by the changes in Dutch Catholicism (Interview 7).

The areas where deconfessionalization made the least impact in terms of diminishing support or altering organizational structures were broadcasting, the press, and education. During the late 1950s and early 1960s the KRO came under criticism from radical periodicals like *De Nieuwe Linie*. It had always been one of the crown jewels of the Roman Catholic edifice and for the most part it faithfully catered to the wishes of both the church and the Catholic population. In the postwar period the KRO distanced itself from some of the excesses of the Dutch church by minimizing, for example, discussion on the air of the 1954 *Mandement*. By 1960 it had phased out all programs which basically provided free air time for the KVP. During the 1960s it never took a distinctive progressive or conservative stance on issues, but remained relatively neutral and broadened its coverage of events as they unfolded. The more progressive elements were given ample air time to discuss their views. Bishop Bekkers's monthly appearances on the Saturday evening *Brandpunt* program have already been noted.

Among its employees and executives the need for maintaining the KRO as a separate organization was never questioned. "There were some discussions within the organization about taking on a sharper profile. But they never got very far. I'll tell you frankly that a major reason was one of employment" (Interview 3). A sharper profile would have meant fewer paid subscribers resulting in smaller subsidies from the government and therefore a cut in staff. Given the system of broadcasting in the Netherlands no incentive exists to merge with other broadcasting organizations if one's own subscription figures are reasonably healthy. The minimum number of paid-up members required for maintaining "A" status was (and still is) 400,000 and the KRO is still well above that figure.

Catholic newspapers have fared reasonably well although deconfessionalization has led to a de-emphasizing of their Catholic identity. The Catholic daily national newspaper stopped calling itself the "Catholic" *Volkskrant* and became known simply as *De Volkskrant*. The major single characteristic which still indicates the Catholic origins of *De Volkskrant* are the names of priests, brothers, and nuns that tend to predominate among the death notices. It portrays itself as a secular nonconfessional newspaper and as a result has gained many non-Catholic readers.[87]

Catholic journalism has had a long and honourable tradition. The Catholic newspaper *De Tijd*, for example, played an important role in starting the emancipation movement in the first half of the nineteenth century. The sociologist G. Marsman claims that the healthy position of certain Catholic newspapers has been largely due to the improvement in quality when the protection of the church dropped away.[88] Of the quality daily press *De Volkskrant* was one of the few papers that survived intact the financial difficulties which afflicted all newspapers during the 1960s. In contrast the socialist national daily newspaper *Het Vrije Volk* underwent a severe decline in its circulation and its readership became centred only around Rotterdam. The two quality liberal newspapers, *De Nieuwe Rotterdamsche Courant* and *Het Algemeen Handelsblad* merged in 1971 in order to resolve their respective financial problems.

Aside from the church itself the Catholic educational system has always been considered the most precious of Catholic institutions. It was the issue of Catholic schools which acted as a catalyst for Catholic political organization. By assimilating children into the Catholic culture, the educational system functioned as the cornerstone of the Catholic pillar. And it is still the institution to which Catholics have the greatest attachment. In Van Kemenade's survey in 1967 of Catholic parents, school teachers, and school principals, the parents showed the strongest support for the Catholic school system: 57 per cent regarded the maintenance of the system as "necessary," while 30 per cent and 52 per cent of teachers and principals, respectively, were of this opinion.[89] Contrary to the case of Catholic trade unions, the clientele of the Catholic school system is more inclined to favour continuation of the institution than are those running it. Respondents were also asked about the necessity of other Catholic institutions. The Catholic press received the support of 42 per cent of the parents, but only 13 per cent of them thought that a separate Catholic sports organization was necessary.[90]

In spite of the more traditional conception of Catholic education on the part of the parents, the orientation of Catholic schools changed considerably during the 1960s. The Catholic school authorities adopted a new revised catechism even before the official revised one came out in 1966. Former priests and nuns were often hired by schools to teach the catechism and related subjects long before this practice became socially acceptable. Until the early 1970s there was still much stigma attached to those who left the priesthood and as a result had difficulty in finding employment related to their previous duties such as social work. The number of lay teachers increased. Many of the traditional hallmarks of Catholic education such as the retreat fell away. Some of the Catholic party politicians interviewed alleged that several teachers in the Catholic school system were propagandizing on behalf of left-wing parties such as the PPR or the PvdA. Thus the image of the stern schoolmaster helping the parish priest in inculcating orthodox Catholic values was certainly not applicable to the post-Vatican II school system. Nevertheless, the Catholic school system is the institution, other than the church itself, which is least likely to disappear.

Catholic institutions of higher learning are also not likely to disappear. Since 1965 they have been open to non-Catholics. At the Catholic University at Nijmegen there was considerable discussion about dropping the title "Catholic."[91] The bishops, however, indicated that they wished to see the title retained. The same was true of the Catholic Higher School of Economics at Tilburg. But although these institutions have been opened to non-Catholics, most of the students are still Catholic since both institutions are located in the south and tend to draw students from that area. The theological faculty at the Catholic University at Nijmegen played and continues to play a crucial role in changing the nature of Catholicism in the Netherlands. There was considerable turmoil at both Nijmegen and Tilburg in the early 1970s, but this related to conflicts between Marxists and non-Marxists and only to a lesser extent to the question of the Catholic identity of these institutions. It is highly unlikely that Catholic institutions of higher learning will cease to regard themselves as Catholic or to play a role in future developments concerning the church and Catholic life in the Netherlands.

The Search for Identity. Catholic socio-economic institutions in the period up to the 1960s remained viable because, in part, they catered to the social and economic needs of Catholics. Many organizations and institutions put a great deal of emphasis on providing a high level of service and accordingly employed large numbers of people. Leaders and employees had a direct incentive to ensure their organizations were viable in socio-economic terms. The title "Catholic" was used as an additional lever to ensure that most Catholics would patronize only their institutions but the meaning behind the title was often taken for granted. In the 1960s, however, many organizations were forced to question their Catholic identity. Some like the Catholic Farmers' Association could rely on traditional bases of support since many of their clientele still held to a traditional conception of Catholicism.[92] Many others, however, felt compelled to start examining what it meant to be a Catholic organization, either because of the spirit of church renewal and Vatican II or because they could no longer depend upon their Catholic identity to maintain a high level of support.

The attitude of the ecclesiastical hierarchy toward Catholic organizational life was highly ambiguous. Although the bishops removed the sanctions against patronizing non-Catholic organizations, they did not deliberately go about informing Catholics that they no longer needed to support Catholic organizations. The closest they came to doing so was in the case of the Catholic party. The bishops were well aware that the numerous organizations employed thousands of people. To have suggested, in the spirit of church renewal, that they were no longer necessary might have had an adverse effect on the market for the services they provided. Hence the Pastoral Council (1966–70) deliberately left off the agenda the question of the need for specifically Catholic socio-economic institutions.[93]

Several organizations, however, did remain uneasy, wondering what it meant to be a Catholic organization and how the new Catholic values were to be implemented and reflected in their work. In 1970 the bishops, specifically responding to requests from the confessional organizations, called into being a special commission entitled "Church and Everyday Life" to look at their problems. The commission, however, had a very difficult existence. An organizer described one of the meetings, at which virtually all Catholic organizations were represented, as a gigantic babylonian talk festival. "We had the complete works: the women's groups, the unions, the social welfare organizations . . . and they could just not understand one another" (Interview 41). After two years a report appeared which essentially concluded that it was no longer possible to have one vision of Catholic organizational life. The report satisfied no one. So a much smaller committee was set up by the bishops in late 1975 to continue grappling with the problem. Only the major organizations such as the NKV, KRO, and the Catholic Social Welfare Council were represented and representation was unofficial so as not to bind organizations to decisions made by the committee. By 1979 the committee had produced discussion papers on youth unemployment, homosexuality, and women and the church. However, major questions such as trade unions and their Catholic identity were left untouched. As of early 1981 the committee was continuing its deliberations.[94]

In spite of the efforts of these two bodies, organizations remained in a quandary. Before Vatican II the church provided the over-arching umbrella and the justification for the existence of Catholic socio-economic organizations. Many of their officers were psychologically uneasy about the disappearance of the umbrella; some spoke of an authority crisis or noted that they would like a more positive stand by the bishops. "We would prefer closer contacts with the bishops. We really feel that they have let the bonds become too loose" (Interview 41). For others, however, the concerns were more concrete. The Christian Employers' Organization (NCW) undoubtedly hoped that an affirmation of some sort of Catholic identity by all organizations would mean closer cooperation between themselves and Catholic trade unions.[95] But the work done by bodies like the Everyday Life Commission probably increased the problem of cooperation by bringing home to each organization that there was no one Catholic vision and that its own vision differed drastically from that of some of its fellow organizations.

As the authority of the church receded in socio-economic life the debate between organizations with conflicting socio-economic interests became more acrimonious. The Council of Discussion, the forum in which Catholic labour, employers, farmers, and retailers met to discuss their differences, fell into disuse. In earlier years it had at least served to establish a climate of mutual respect, and the willingness to meet was in turn based on the fact that all the participants were Catholic. However, after 1973 only two meetings were scheduled, one of which never took place (Interview 41).

5. Summary

An undercurrent of discontent on the part of Catholic intellectuals, theologians, and clerics within the Catholic subculture suddenly became highly prominent in the early 1960s. Members of this group were unhappy with the unusually strong emphasis by the church on unity and the use of negative sanctions to maintain this unity. The Dutch ecclesiastical hierarchy changed course in the early 1960s by legitimizing critical debate within the church, and the subculture generally, and by instituting major changes. The church became less hierarchical and more collegial. Sanctions were withdrawn and Catholics were given a large degree of personal responsibility in the scope and form of their participation in religious activities.

One result was the decision by many Catholics to devote much less time and energy to the spiritual aspect of their lives, a tendency reflected in the decline in mass attendance. The effect of this deconfessionalization on Catholic socio-economic organizations and institutions has been much less pronounced. Despite a sense of uneasiness among many executive officers most Catholic organizations remain viable and still tend to carry the label "Catholic." Some, in order to maintain their viability in the face of changing economic conditions, decided to federate or merge with their neutral or Protestant counterparts. They could no longer make appeals on the basis of their Catholic identity in order to maintain an adequate level of support. Such organizations usually had a particular and somewhat narrow base, for example, small businesses in the case of the Catholic Retailers' Organization.

Catholic institutions such as the educational system, health and welfare organizations, and the media, which served a much wider clientele, had much greater success in meeting changed conditions. One mass appeal Catholic organization, the Catholic People's Party (KVP), did not survive. The reasons why deconfessionalization and the changed orientation of the Catholic church had such an impact on its viability will be examined next.

Chapter 5   **The Catholic Party**

Decline and Fall, 1963-1980

In 1963 the Dutch Catholic party (KVP) received over 84 per cent of the Catholic vote. In 1967 its share dropped to 63 per cent and by 1972 it was down to 38 per cent. In 1976 the use of the party label for electioneering purposes ceased when the KVP federated with the two major Protestant parties to form the Christian Democratic Appeal (CDA). In 1980 the three parties completely merged. What accounted for the decline in KVP support, particularly in view of the relative stable support for Catholic institutions such as the educational system and the broadcasting organization (KRO)?[1]

The answers are to be found in the way the bishops deliberately altered their support for the KVP; in the way its leaders reacted to deconfessionalization; and in the manner in which deconfessionalization affected the political attitudes and behaviour of rank-and-file Catholics.

1. Organizational Decline

To have members elected to a legislature, a party must have a modicum of cohesion and organization. Moreover, it needs at least to go through the motions of running for office. As David Butler and Donald Stokes point out, the importance of electioneering must be seen in terms of what would happen if one or all parties did no campaigning at all before an election.[2] The KVP managed to remain largely intact until the mid-1960s. And although heavily dependent upon the authority of the church, Catholic party leaders did put a reasonable amount of energy into waging election campaigns. Considerable effort was also devoted to ensuring that slates of election candidates were representative of the major socio-economic groupings in the Dutch Catholic bloc. The situation was then altered by a series of events. In 1966 the KVP was responsible for the sudden collapse of a government, led by a KVP prime minister, which the party had been instrumental in forming. In 1967, 1971, and 1972 the party waged admittedly ineffective campaigns. In 1968 a number of prominent parliamentarians left the KVP to sit as a separate bloc in the Second Chamber and later formed their own party.

Commitment and Adaptation. Ironically, some of the factors which helped speed the process of disintegration of the KVP were also ones which had been important earlier in keeping the party together. In chapter 3 it was argued that one of the reasons for cohesion was the low degree of commitment to the party. Most individuals and factions saw the party in pragmatic terms. They were persuaded that a Catholic party was necessary to defend basic interests such as the Catholic school system but also realized that it was in fact a rather fragile coalition of disparate interests. No one tried to impose a particular Catholic or socio-economic ideology upon others, knowing they might well decide to leave the party.

Dutch Catholics have always been ambivalent about politics generally and the Catholic party in particular. Father Schaepman in the late nineteenth century did not wish to see a Catholic party but rather preferred a single Christian party encompassing both Catholics and Protestants. After lying dormant for many decades the idea of a Christian Democratic Union was reactivated not long after the 1963 election. A number of the leading intellectuals within the KVP were conscious of the developments taking place within the church, including the forthcoming revisions in the guidelines originally laid down in the *Mandement* of 1954. Hence they argued that the nature of the party's Catholic identity should be reexamined in view of Vatican II and changes in Dutch Catholicism.

As a result, in 1964 the KVP instituted a committee to look into the question of "Foundation and Character of the KVP." Two years later its report concluded that for the foreseeable future the Catholic character of the KVP should be maintained.[3] At the same time the report noted the existence of a close working relationship with the two other Christian parties and it did not rule out a possible union of the three major confessional parties at some indeterminate date in the future. Since the KVP was the largest party in the Second Chamber and had done quite well in the 1963 election, there was no logical reason for its leaders to start actively pursuing a merger with other parties. Nevertheless, the fact that the topic was broached does indicate that the KVP was not a highly valued institution. This is further evidenced by the debate which broke loose within the party upon submission of the report. Some members of the parliamentary party argued against the long-term conclusions of the report and urged that the KVP turn itself into a secular party. Others, including most of the executive, spoke in favour of a Christian Democratic party. Only a very small minority favoured maintaining the KVP as a distinctively Catholic party in the long run.

I. Lipschits has identified five separate factions or "streams" within the KVP in the mid-1960s, all of which came into full bloom after the report was tabled:[4] the pro-KVP faction, smallest in size; the Democratic Centre faction which wanted secularization of the party; the KVP-Radicals faction, left-wing Christians who wanted close cooperation with the PvdA; the "Brabant" faction, a group pressing the interests of the Brabant region and favouring ties with the PvdA; and finally the pro-Christian Democratic faction.[5] The acid test for these groups came in 1967. The election results gave party leaders a concrete indication that the KVP could no longer count on the nearly unanimous support of Dutch Catholics. Two days after the election the chairman of the "Foundation and Character" committee, who was also chairman of the KVP, visited the leaders of the ARP and the CHU to urge them to enter into discussions concerning a merger of the three confessional parties. On the basis of this initiative an interparty committee comprised of six members from each party proceeded to look into the question of a merger.[6]

By 1968, however, the KVP radicals had become increasingly disenchanted with the course of events within the party. They realized that any coalition resulting from the merger discussions would probably be right of centre. Unsuccessful in transforming the KVP into a radical Christian party, some of them left the KVP to sit as a separate bloc which was named the Party of Political Radicals (PPR). It included a number of prominent Catholics such as the chairman of the KRO and a former director of the KVP research bureau.

The drop in support suffered by the KVP in the 1967 election was substantial by Dutch standards. Although it still had 63 percent of the Catholic vote and remained the largest party in the Second Chamber, the possibility of rebuilding the party and regaining or stabilizing the vote was never seen as a serious option.[7] Their unwillingness to try to retrieve the situation was in part a function of the low degree of commitment most KVP leaders had towards the party.

Not only was there a lack of willingness but also a lack of understanding of the situation which might have enabled the leadership to undertake some kind of rescue operation. Many were unable to adapt.

An air of fatalism was coupled with a high degree of incomprehension. Most KVP leaders attributed the party's losses to the deconfessionalization of the electorate and, to a lesser extent, to the collapse of the government in 1966. However, some were perplexed about the causes of deconfessionalization and about its implications. The chairman of a major Catholic socio-economic organization, a long-time member of the Second Chamber and later of the First Chamber, found the changes which had occurred in his hometown in the south inexplicable. "In the last ten years things have changed completely. Before, the parish church was always filled with people at Sunday mass. Now whenever I go back the church is virtually empty. . . . I just don't know what has happened" (Interview 24). For some it was almost as if their world had been turned upside down. As a result they depicted the changes in the darkest possible way. One former member of the KVP executive steering committee stated: "Don't talk to me about changes in the Catholic pillar. It hasn't changed; it has simply disintegrated. As far as I am concerned it no longer exists. Do I make myself clear?" (Interview 40).

The incomprehension of many KVP politicians was due in part to the structure of the Catholic subculture. As it developed and became increasingly differentiated, contact between the different sectors became less frequent. The KVP had essentially been by-passed by the changes in Dutch Catholicism. As Van den Berg and Molleman point out, most of its officials were far too busy with the operation of the party apparatus as well as the affairs of whatever socio-economic organizations they represented.[8] While they were experts in their particular policy area and internal party politics, they always left theological affairs to the church.

An indication of this division of labour was the party's connection with the Dutch Pastoral Council of 1966 to 1970 in which the changes of Vatican II and their implementation were discussed. Only a few figures from the KVP were actively involved in the council, namely Dr. Marga Klompé and Professor Piet Steenkamp.[9] Klompé, then minister for Culture and Recreation (1967–71), had considerable influence within the council, but within the KVP she was unsuccessful in trying to induce the party to discard its confessional image. Most KVP leaders were too preoccupied with politics to become involved with theological questions, or alternatively they took a rather cynical view of the goings on at the Pastoral Council. An important member of the executive of a *kieskring* in the south noted that the council was mainly for those who had been "complainers" of long standing or "overly sensitive intellectuals" (Interview 6). For him, therefore, it was of little relevance. The Pastoral Council was definitely marked by an apolitical character and reflected a basic characteristic of the church renewal movement which was to have profound consequences, namely the withdrawal of church authority from the realm of politics.

The Rise of Intraparty Conflict. Ever since the period of internal tension in the early 1950s, resulting from the appearance of the Catholic National Party (KNP) organized by Welter and the conflict between left and right-wing factions, conditions within the party had been relatively quiescent. A member of the KVP caucus from 1954 to 1965 described it as a "very happy club" (Interview 4). By 1966 the situation had changed. Soon after the publication of the "Foundation and Character" report in 1966 the five different streams emerged. The debate on whether or not the title Catholic should be retained was actually of minimal importance, most of the controversy revolving around socio-economic issues. Major changes in the nature of the KVP were bound to occur and the factions had definite and differing interests in the various alternatives. The KVP radicals, the Brabant group, and to a lesser extent the Democratic Centre faction, favoured a more progressive course, which in concrete terms meant closer cooperation with the PVDA rather than the Liberals. The Christian Democratic faction, encompassing a plurality if not a majority of the party's parliamentary caucus, tended to be more conservative.

These divisions were exacerbated by a number of events. In 1965 a coalition government which included the KVP and the Liberals but not the PVDA collapsed over the broadcasting issue. A Liberal cabinet member was seen as having brought about its fall by trying to push through a policy which would have done away with the pillarized structure of broadcasting.[10] A new government was formed with the KVP and the PVDA as the major partners. Although the KVP parliamentary leader, Norbert Schmelzer, was apprehensive about this coalition, he saw no alternative and consented to its formation.[11] In the fall of 1966, however, the PVDA-KVP government, under the leadership of the KVP prime minister J. M. L. Th. Cals, suddenly collapsed. The cause was withdrawal of support by the KVP parliamentary party led by Schmelzer during a vote on one of the spending estimates, an event which became known as the "Night of Schmelzer."[12]

Those within the KVP supporting the Cals government were furious and the chairman of the Catholic Trade Union Federation (NKV) made it known that he was extremely unhappy. In the election of 1967 the KVP had great difficulty in finding candidates from Catholic labour. These events helped set the stage for the departure of a number of the KVP radicals in 1968. The absence of real attachment to the KVP made it easier for individuals to leave when the opportunity presented itself. Beyond this, additional factors enhanced the possibility of conflict and decreased the chances for its containment. The style of leadership and the unwritten rules governing conflict had changed.

Traditionally the Catholic party would not deliver to cabinet unusually powerful figures. However, Cals, prime minister of the ill-fated government of 1965-66, was a strong-willed political leader who was determined to lead his colleagues in a distinctively left-wing direction.[13] He was quite different from previous Catholic party prime ministers who tended to be conciliatory, affable men capable of holding a diverse cabinet together and at the same time not alienating bases of support within the Second Chamber. The elevation of Cals broke a tradition which had long been important in maintaining harmony within the Catholic party.

A further change occurred in the style of leadership. As noted, the Catholic party had always had a strong parliamentary leader. Nolens and Romme, for example, would, at crucial points in caucus debate, assert their authority and resolve contentious issues in short order. When Romme retired in 1961 there was no logical successor capable of his kind of leadership. Yet even if there had been such a candidate it is doubtful whether he would have been acceptable to the KVP caucus. The choice of Norbert Schmelzer in 1964 was probably indicative of the marked change of climate.[14] Schmelzer's style was friendly, flexible, and democratic. He did not assert himself publicly, but attempted to maintain order within the caucus by using his charm on individual members. He was an expert in behind-the-scenes management and in finding a middle ground between conflicting interests.[15]

When it came to important socio-economic issues, however, Schmelzer was not prepared to compromise. Historically the Catholic party had always tried to avoid taking responsibility for specific political actions. In 1966 the so-called "Night of Schmelzer" broke that tradition. Never before had the Catholic party been seen to be responsible for the collapse of a government under the leadership of one of their own party members. A close supporter of Schmelzer during this period noted that the party knew Schmelzer's move would be an unpopular one. Yet it was prepared to pay the cost, namely the tarnishing of the reputation of the KVP, of bringing down what was generally conceded to be a reasonably good government. Members of the KVP caucus representing the interests of employers, small businessmen, and farmers were highly perturbed by the scale of deficit financing proposed by the cabinet. "Politically we had to pay the price but we knew that in economic terms we were correct. We could not let the Cals cabinet continue on the course it was on" (Interview 27).

Decline and Fall of the Catholic Party | 139

During the 1960s the deferential relationship between the party in the regions and the central party executive began to change. The Brabant group is a good example of this. It included members of both the KVP parliamentary party and the executives of *kieskring* organizations in Brabant and Limburg, and represented the distinct regional interests of the south.[16] Regional interests, as opposed to class interests, had never before been so clearly articulated. The mines in Limburg had been shut down in 1965 and government policies designed to retrain workers and to attract and develop new industries in the area were regarded as ineffective.[17] The Cals cabinet had developed a detailed policy for economic redevelopment. However, the government which took office after the "Night of Schmelzer" decided to devote less in the way of resources to this scheme and watered down several of the promises contained in the original plan.[18] A member of the Brabant group said the "Night of Schmelzer" indicated to him that the KVP had become much too conservative. He argued that their concern with balancing the budget and minimizing expenditures was a typical example of the traditional Catholic inferiority complex. "They were afraid of tackling the problems of the south for fear of appearing openly to be favouring Catholics" (Interview 6).

Factions within the KVP were much more concerned with policy and with aggressively pushing their particular interests than party members had been in earlier times. In doing so they appeared to have little concern for the party itself. Ironically these developments can be seen in part as the fruition of the emancipation process. The dropping away of feelings of caution, isolation, and inferiority permitted many within the KVP to pursue their own interests.

During the election campaign in 1967 a haphazard unity was maintained, although the NKV refused to endorse the KVP and a number of KVP candidates stated publicly that they disagreed with the views of many of their colleagues, particularly those of Schmelzer, the party leader.[19] Nevertheless, there were no defections before 1967. The KVP was still the largest party and each faction thought it could employ sufficient leverage to swing the party behind its particular orientation. They may have been aware that the political, social, and cultural climate in the Netherlands had changed but were uncertain of its possible consequences and were probably only dimly aware of the way in which changes in the nature of Dutch Catholicism were affecting their own behaviour.

The reality of these changes became apparent following the election of 1967. Those favouring a merger with the other confessional parties immediately initiated negotiations with the ARP and the CHU. The KVP radicals, in order not to be left behind, contacted a number of like-minded "Christian Radicals" in the ARP and the CHU, and formed an interparty "Christian-Radical Steering Committee."[20] Members of the Brabant group, some of whom were also members of the KVP radicals group, loosely affiliated themselves with the latter. The KVP Youth movement, though not supporting the radicals directly, criticized the party executive for making unkind remarks about them.[21] The various groups all spoke in favour of political renewal but it was quite clear that for some (the KVP radicals and the Brabant group) renewal implied close cooperation with the PVDA and possibly with the Democrats '66, whereas for others, mainly the party executive, this was not the case.

In November 1967 the leader of the KVP radicals declared that if the executive did not speak out in favour of a radical, progressive party, the radical wing would have to find a home elsewhere.[22] In December, at a meeting of the party council, a series of resolutions was passed which satisfied most factions at least temporarily. However, in January 1968 the radical group nominated P. Bogaers, their spokesman, for the position of deputy vice-chairman of the party. When the executive declared this to be unacceptable, the radicals considered its action to be against the spirit of the resolutions passed by the party in December. In February some of them decided to leave the party and in April they founded the Party of Political Radicals (PPR).[23]

Political Cohesion and the Church. In the past, when a fracturing of the Catholic party seemed imminent, or had in fact occurred, cohesion was maintained by pointing to the views of the bishops on the need for Catholics to maintain their unity in the political sphere. In the 1960s this was no longer possible. The slogan "maintain our sacred unity" would have sounded strangely old-fashioned and inconsistent given the calls for a renewal of the party system and in the context of Vatican II and the Pastoral Council. Furthermore, virtually the entire party was committed to doing away with its specifically Catholic character. In 1961 the bishops refused to name a replacement for Father Stokman who was retiring from the Second Chamber;[24] in 1965 they officially withdrew the provisions of the 1954 *Mandement*. The KVP leaders, even if so inclined, could no longer point to the wishes of the bishops as a basis for maintaining political unity.

No alternative rationale existed for maintaining the unity of the party other than a purely pragmatic one. Because the KVP radicals emphasized that they were Christian radicals, it was difficult to accuse them of being unchristian. They had impressive academic credentials, were loyal Catholics, and had a well-articulated Christian vision of life and politics. After the departure of part of the KVP radical group

Schmelzer noted that the split had been unavoidable and resigned himself to a permanent separation.[25]

The Catholic party had always been the forum in which the major socio-economic interests in the Catholic bloc could interact and attempt to resolve their differences. After 1967 this was no longer the case. There was never an open break between the KVP and the NKV but relations became distinctly cooler as time went on. The NKV was just beginning to move in the direction of a merger or federation with the socialist NVV, which had strong links with the PVDA. The KVP on the other hand was aiming for a merger with the ARP and CHU, parties usually seen as being slightly right of centre. From 1967 on the PVDA managed to attract candidates for its electoral lists from NKV-affiliated unions,[26] while the KVP had increasing difficulty in finding representatives from the NKV. By 1976 communication between Catholic labour and the KVP had become extremely poor. A KVP member of the Second Chamber, a former member of the executive of the NKV, complained of the changed climate in which it was no longer possible to talk rationally with many of the NKV leaders (Interview 32). In the same year the official magazine of the Catholic Transport Workers' Union published a photograph of this KVP member with the single word "traitor" as a caption.

In 1973, after ten months of unusually protracted negotiations for the formation of a government, the KVP agreed to a coalition which included the PVDA. This upset a number of interests in the KVP, in particular the Catholic Retailers' Organization. An officer of the organization claimed that there was considerable pressure from member associations to drop all ties with the KVP (Interview 24). The middle ground which the Catholic party had successfully occupied for so many years had shrunk considerably. Being Catholic was no longer a sufficient motivating force for different interests to arrive at a compromise solution. "Before when we came to a difficult problem we said, 'well, we have to find some kind of solution because after all we are all Catholic'. Now this doesn't operate anymore" (Interview 5).

Mobilization of the Vote. The fatalistic attitude of the KVP was amply reflected in the way it conducted election campaigns. In 1967 the party produced a program which differed little from those used in previous elections. Its preamble emphasized that the KVP favoured "safeguarding marriage and the family."[27] The party's candidates openly disagreed or contradicted one another. "I could pretty well say what I wanted about the 'Night of Schmelzer'. No one reprimanded me. They [the party] were probably glad to have me since I was from the labour movement" (Interview 5).

In 1963 the KVP still depended heavily on volunteer labour to decorate neighbourhoods with placards and deliver pamphlets. By 1967 the party began to place more emphasis on the media, focusing in particular on television. However, campaign organizers found it difficult to package the KVP as a marketable product. One organizer noted: "Our people [candidates] didn't come across very well. We had very little experience with television. . . . We had meetings with public relations types to help think up slogans but it was very difficult. Compromise is not an easy thing to sell. It is much easier to develop liberal or socialist slogans like 'promote free enterprise' or 'abolish private property'. . . . We were way behind, especially in comparison with flashy new parties like the Democrats '66" (Interview 28).

After 1967, rather than rebuilding the party, the KVP leadership spent most of its time and energy trying to promote a merger between the three confessional parties. Most were fully expecting the merger to be completed before the next election, but this did not occur.[28] At election time in February 1971 there was still no Christian Democratic union. The party did manage to find a relatively young and attractive candidate to head the election list, Gerhard Veringa, who was untainted by the events surrounding the "Night of Schmelzer." At the same time he had had political experience as a major portfolio-holder in the 1967–71 cabinet. Campaign organizers touted him as the Dutch version of John F. Kennedy.[29] However, KVP fortunes declined even further in the 1971 election, providing an additional shock for the party. "No one thought that deconfessionalization would go this far" (Interview 5). Furthermore, Veringa became seriously ill shortly after the election and had to resign. In the election of 1972, little more than a year later, there was still no Christian Democratic union and the party was ill prepared, not having selected its list leader until shortly before the election. Its support sagged even further to only 38 per cent of the Catholic vote.

The efforts of the KVP to conduct election campaigns were further hampered by the lack of funds. One of the more important sources had been membership fees. However, membership had dropped from 430,000 members in 1955 to 73,204 in 1972[30] and the days of membership drives and bicycle rallies were in the past. Furthermore, the Catholic Retailers' Organization, which had long been active in soliciting funds from its members, reported that the task was becoming increasingly difficult in the early 1970s.[31] One KVP official noted that in 1963 the party had one million guilders available ($380,000). In 1972 he estimated that the party needed four million guilders to run a proper election campaign but had only two million (Interview 34).

Enthusiasm among KVP officials and workers at the local level diminished. Fewer people came to party meetings. Party headquarters began to take a more important role in making up the election lists, in part to have the central control necessary to run a national campaign focusing on the media. Furthermore, after 1967 the central executive, realizing that fewer seats could be regarded as safe, assigned a smaller number of these to the regionally oriented candidates. This upset local organizers in provinces like Limburg.[32] Much less in the way of financial assistance was made available to the *kieskring* organizations. "Before we had considerably more money. We could rent sky-writing planes, loudspeakers, and so on. Now we're lucky if we have enough for a few leaflets" (Interview 29).

Particularly in the south, where unemployment was running higher than the national average because of the mines closure in 1965, party workers and even some *kieskring* chairmen were less than enthusiastic.[33] Only in the more remote rural areas such as those in the east did party organization remain intact and in a relatively healthy state. Although party headquarters in The Hague stated in 1976 that the KVP was no longer selling memberships, since the formation of the CDA was imminent (Interview 2), the chairman of the local KVP organization in a village in the eastern Netherlands was still conscientiously selling memberships in that year (Interview 34). However, even in this village matters had changed. Since 1970 attendance at party meetings had declined considerably, and it was becoming increasingly difficult to sell memberships. "People will tell me that they'll vote for the party but buying a membership? No, they won't do that anymore" (Interview 34). In the mid-1950s virtually every family in the village had been a paid-up member of the KVP.

The party newspaper *De Opmars*, which at one point appeared biweekly, was appearing only on a bi-monthly basis by 1965. In that year the title, *De Opmars* (The Upward March), which had been used since 1934, was changed to simply *De KVP*. A shift had already occurred in terms of content. From 1961 onwards there had been no mention of the notion of Catholic unity or of the importance of the KVP in safeguarding Catholic interests. Articles concerning the minority status of Catholics in the Netherlands or depicting the PvdA in highly uncomplimentary terms no longer appeared. *De KVP* was still very much aimed at a Catholic audience, however, as evidenced by the numerous advertisements for Catholic missionary work, Catholic book clubs, and Catholic periodicals. Moreover, Father Stokman still managed to contribute the occasional article.

In March 1968 *De KVP* ceased publication. It was revived in 1971

144 | Catholic Power in the Netherlands

when it became once more propagandistic in tone. This time, however, it was propaganda not for the KVP but for that elusive goal: the formation of a Christian Democratic party. The title was changed again in 1972 from *De KVP* to *Politiek Nieuws* (Political News). Henceforth virtually the entire content of the paper was devoted to one theme: the necessity for a Christian Democratic party. Contributors discussed the role that members of the KVP would play in the new party; the successful development of CDA lists in a number of municipalities for town councils was highlighted. By 1976 *Politiek Nieuws* was carrying thick black, almost desperate headlines stating "The CDA must come: there is no alternative."[34] Such desperation may have been the result of public opinion polls, one of which indicated in 1974 that the KVP would receive only 10 per cent of the popular vote if an election were to be held.[35]

The NKV had distanced itself from the KVP before the election in 1967 but NKV leaders made no effort to persuade Catholic trade unionists to vote for a different party. Before 1960 the KRO had provided free air time for the KVP to the exclusion of other parties. After this date they took a much more neutral stance. Catholic party officials complained that whereas the KRO had largely disassociated itself from the party, the socialist broadcasting organization (VARA) was still very much oriented towards propagandizing for the PvdA.

The only organization which remained loyal to the KVP until the end was the Catholic Farmers' Association, which continued to advise its members to support the party. In its monthly publication the chairman of the association, who was also a member of the First Chamber for the KVP, would discuss political affairs and urge Catholic farmers to vote KVP, a practice which continued right up to the provincial elections of 1974.

The Public Withdrawal of Church Authority. The church had been distancing itself from the KVP since the late 1950s and the KVP for its part placed much less reliance on its links with the church. Fewer articles in *De Opmars* pointed out the relationship between Catholicism and the Catholic party in the Netherlands. And fewer items played on the emotions of Catholics concerning their place in Dutch society. Yet advertisements and notices in *De Opmars* indicated that the KVP was still closely linked to Catholicism and the Catholic subculture.

The repeal of the 1954 *Mandement* in 1965 did not come as a sudden blow since the bishops had given prior indications of this action. Given Vatican II and the changes in the Dutch church it was only to be expected. Furthermore, the repeal concerned all organizational life in the Netherlands and was not specifically directed against the KVP. The

Catholic party did become highly defensive, however, when members of the PvdA in the Second Chamber made a point of noting that Catholics could now vote or join the PvdA without fear of contravening the wishes of the bishops. Indeed, it accused the PvdA of taking unfair advantage of the situation.[36] More significant for the KVP was Mgr. Bluyssens's statement, in a television broadcast shortly before the 1967 election, that it was perfectly acceptable for a Catholic to vote for a party other than the KVP. Naturally the leadership of the KVP considered it extremely ill-timed.[37] The statement confirmed in the minds of many Catholics that the church had indeed disassociated itself from the KVP. Other actions indicated publicly that the clergy were no longer willing to support the KVP. Some clerics in embracing the tenets of the New Theology also embraced those of left-wing parties like the small Pacifist Socialist Party.[38] The number of clerics involved was relatively small but their actions were often calculated to yield maximum publicity.

In distancing itself from many aspects of Catholic organizational life, the church was most explicit in disavowing its connection with the KVP. Why was the KVP treated differently from organizations such as the KRO? Among clerical and lay Catholics who had been critical of church orthodoxy in the past, the expectation of support for the Catholic party was seen as one of the more odious aspects of that orthodoxy. It infringed upon notions of basic democratic rights. For many Catholics, particularly educated ones, voting for the Catholic party was put on the same plane as the church's expectations concerning birth control, the confession, and compulsory attendance at mass; all of them were aspects of religious orthodoxy that many people wished to see abolished.

In the early 1960s, as we have seen, the church changed the rules on birth control and attendance at mass and *de facto* did away with the confessional. A number of clerics and Catholic intellectuals lobbied at that time for an explicit statement on the relationship between Catholicism and politics.[39] What was wanted, however, was not a realignment of the church with a different political party but a more definite separation of the political world from the sphere of religion. The reorientation of the church can be seen as a response to these pressures.

The withdrawal from political affairs marked not an entirely new phase in the history of the church but rather a return to a centuries-old tradition. In the period up to World War I the Catholic church had always remained outside of politics. In the 1920s both church leaders and certain lay Catholics were highly ambivalent about the formation of a Catholic political party. Those in favour of church renewal in the

1960s were primarily apolitical in a manner not unlike many of their brethren in the eighteenth and nineteenth centuries.[40] This is reflected in the attitudes of ordinary parish priests towards involvement in politics. Of the fifteen priests interviewed in 1976 none expressed a preference for either the PPR or the PSP. One reported voting for the PVDA and had recently become a member of that party. Nevertheless, he made no effort to press his political beliefs on parishioners or even on colleagues. "It is my own private affair" (Interview 36). Two other priests said that if asked they would indicate their own political choice. In the past they had both supported the KVP but by 1976 they had had enough of the party and wished to see the new CDA become a reality. Only one priest, aged eighty-two and retired, expressed a wish for the continuation of the KVP as a separate political organization. For the most part priests indicated an unwillingness to become involved in the political affairs of their parishioners. On the rare occasions when the question did arise, they would refuse to give instructions and would point out that voting was a matter of personal choice.

As the church withdrew its support the KVP made no effort to develop a rationale for the maintenance of a separate Catholic party. From the beginning of the postwar period the KVP had tried to develop itself as a "programmatic" party. The overwhelming presence of the church had stifled those efforts and had ensured that the KVP would never be perceived as a policy-oriented party by the majority of Catholics. Interestingly, even in the period following Vatican II the KVP would still make occasional use of religious issues in order to help improve its chances at election time. Thus in 1970 Schmelzer, the party leader, explicitly made use of the abortion issue during the provincial elections of that year. By his own admission, he did this in a highly calculated fashion: "I knew the vote would decline because of deconfessionalization. If I hadn't used the abortion issue the vote would have gone down even further."[41]

Thus even in its dying phase the KVP was unable to disassociate itself from the church. "The irony of the Catholic party has always been its inability to develop a stance independent from that of the church. But the church in turn found it easy to untie itself from the party when it felt the time had come to do so" (Interview 43).

2. The Vote, 1963–1972

In Chapter 3 it was noted that for the most part Dutch Catholics did not see voting for the Catholic party as a form of behaviour distinct from other forms of behaviour such as subscribing to Catholic news-

Decline and Fall of the Catholic Party | 147

papers and attending mass. Voting for the Catholic party and religious loyalty were virtually indistinguishable. This behaviour in turn tended to be dependent upon social control by the church which was more effective in non-urban areas and in areas where Catholics were in a majority. How did the reorientation on the part of the church affect this relationship? Did the vote decline because large numbers of Catholics ceased to be actively loyal to the church (as indicated by regular mass attendance) or did the relationship itself change so that even those regularly attending mass stopped voting KVP? What role did factors such as class, the urban-rural cleavage, and gender play in the process of change? What was the importance of political issues involving the KVP, such as the "Night of Schmelzer," in changing the vote? *Confessional Attachment and Voting.* In the 1960s the church divested itself of virtually all its links with the KVP. Catholics were told it was no longer necessary to vote for the party. In addition the church deliberately removed the strictures on social and religious behaviour. Catholics were left to decide for themselves what the appropriate forms of behaviour should be. Many decided to attend mass no longer on a regular basis, and in doing so may have distanced themselves simultaneously from the church and the KVP.

Thus in the decline of the KVP vote two processes may have been at work. Catholics who were still loyal to the church as demonstrated by regular mass attendance may nevertheless have chosen to support a new political party because they had begun to differentiate increasingly between forms of behaviour, perceiving politics as an area quite distinct from religion. Secondly, Catholics may still have lumped the KVP and the church together and abandoned them both when they became less strongly attached to the church. The situation was not necessarily such that only one process operated to the exclusion of the other. They could well have been operating simultaneously among either individuals or groups.[42]

Table 5.1 shows the relationship between mass attendance and voting KVP in four different election years. The percentages in parentheses indicate the proportion of the sample who attended mass regularly and those who did not. The data show that the drop in support for the KVP was due not only to a decline in the proportion of those regularly attending mass but also to a weakening of the link between mass attendance and voting KVP. In 1956 90 per cent of those attending mass on a regular basis voted for the Catholic party. By 1972 only 53 per cent of those in this category did so. Irregular mass attenders in the post-Vatican II period have also been less inclined to vote KVP compared to those in 1956. Interestingly, the decline among irregular attenders

148 | Catholic Power in the Netherlands

TABLE 5.1
Vote by Deconfessionalization by Year

	1956	1967	1971	1972
Regular mass attenders voting KVP (% of sample)	90% (89%)	77% (75%)	70% (58%)	53% (46%)
Irregular mass attenders voting KVP (% of sample)	45% (11%)	37% (25%)	25% (42%)	25% (54%)
All Catholics voting KVP (% of sample)	85% (100%)	67% (100%)	51% (100%)	38% (100%)
N =	Not available	(1122)	(544)	(602)

Source: S. Wolinetz, "Party Re-Alignment in the Netherlands," pp. 90, 166; Werkgroep Nationaal Verkiezingsonderzoek 1972, *De Nederlandse kiezer '72*, p. 32.

reached its lowest point in 1971 and remained constant at 25 per cent in 1972. It was among the regular attenders that the sharpest drop occurred (17 per cent from 1971 to 1972).

The Effect of Context. What variables account for this simultaneous deconfessionalization and rejection of the KVP? In chapter 3 it was argued that certain conditions had helped to make social control by the church more effective with beneficial effects for the KVP. In smaller communities the parish priest was likely to know his parishioners better and have more contact with them. Moreover, in those areas where there was a high concentration of Catholics the close proximity of fellow-worshippers had provided an additional means of social control. In the 1960s most priests ceased making regular calls on parishioners unless they were ill or specifically requested a visit. The mass was secularized, the liturgy and the catechism were altered, and the confessional was done away with. Lay parish councils were introduced in most parishes. The abolition of a number of restrictions was widely publicized in the popular press and on television.

Figures 5.1 to 5.4 depict the level of KVP support among registered Catholic voters residing in the different contexts for the period 1946–72. The graphs are a continuation of the graphs presented in chapter 3 ·for the period 1946–63 (see Appendix 2 for details on the data). The differences prevailing between these groups before 1967 continued to prevail up to 1972, though to a lesser degree. As can be seen, there has been a distinct tendency towards convergence among these Catholic

Decline and Fall of the Catholic Party | 149

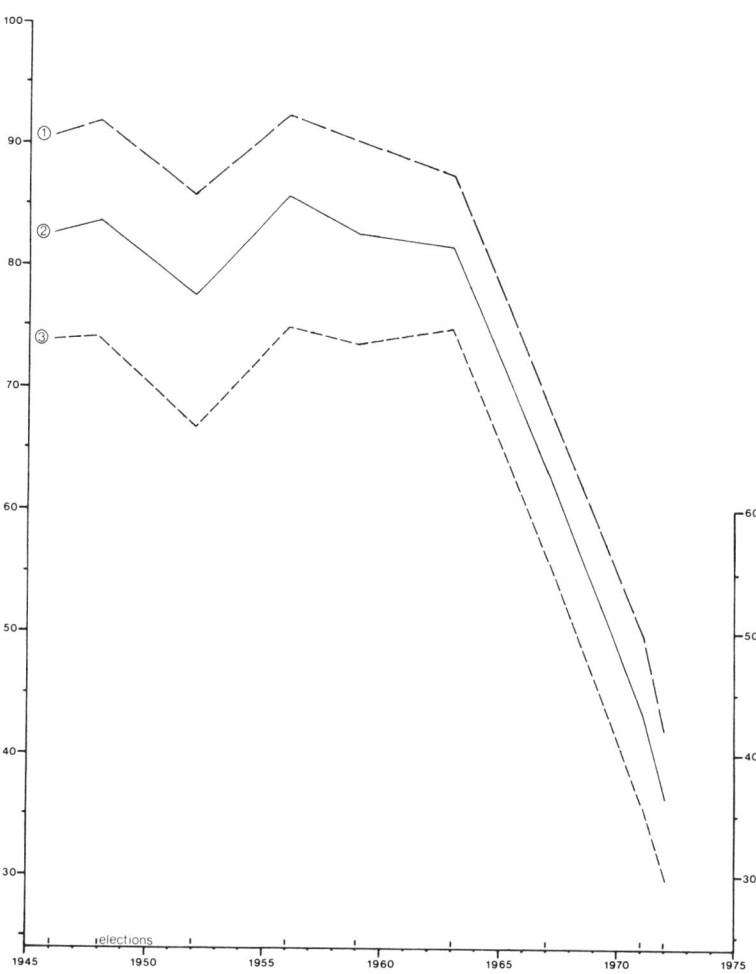

FIGURE 5.1. Percentage of Catholics Voting KVP by Urbanization
Source: Houska and Leiden data sets. See Appendix 2 for details.

KEY:
1. All Catholics residing in non-urban areas (non-urban = municipal districts with population of less than 30,000).
2. Catholic population as a whole.
3. All Catholics residing in urban areas (urban = municipal districts with population of more than 30,000).

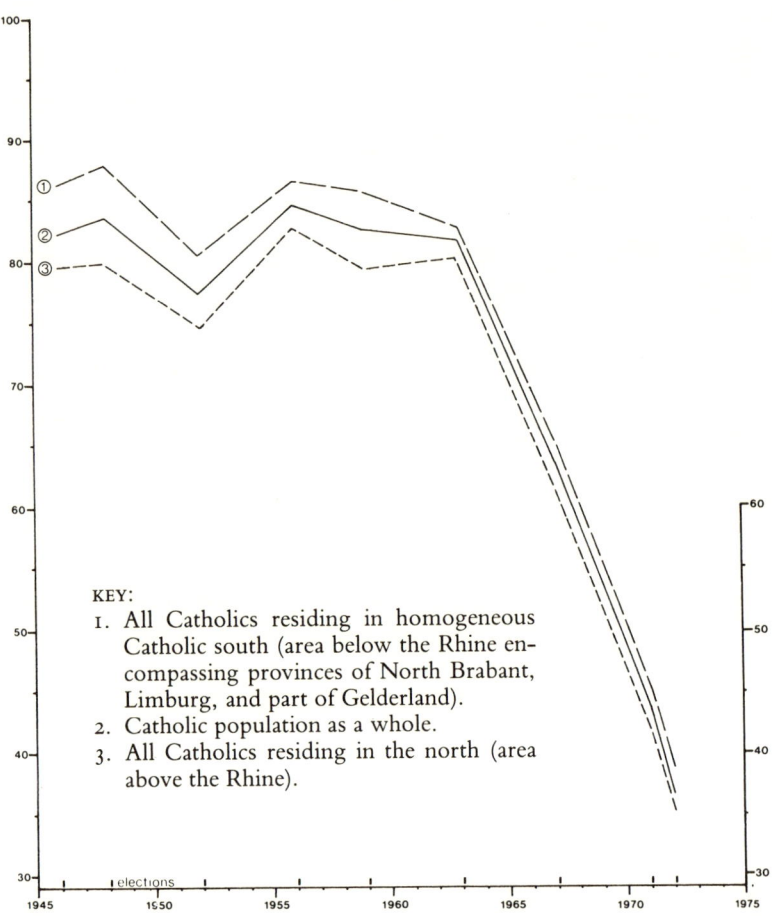

FIGURE 5.2. Percentage of Catholics Voting KVP by Region
Source: Houska and Leiden data sets.

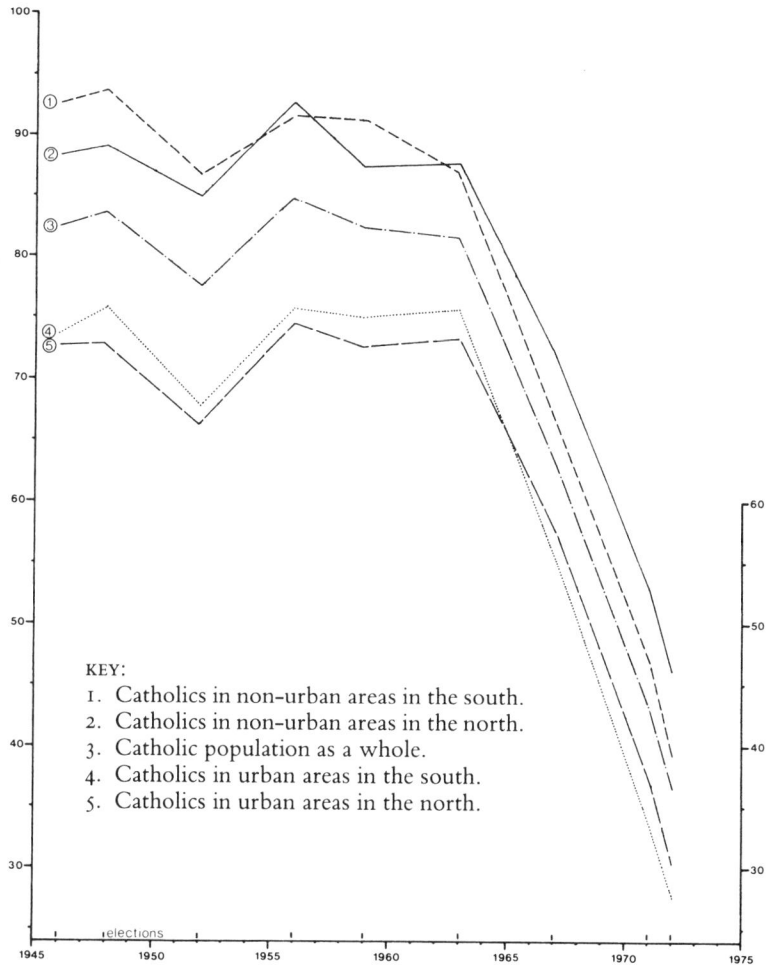

FIGURE 5.3. Percentage of Catholics Voting KVP by Urbanization and Region
Source: Houska and Leiden data sets.

152 | Catholic Power in the Netherlands

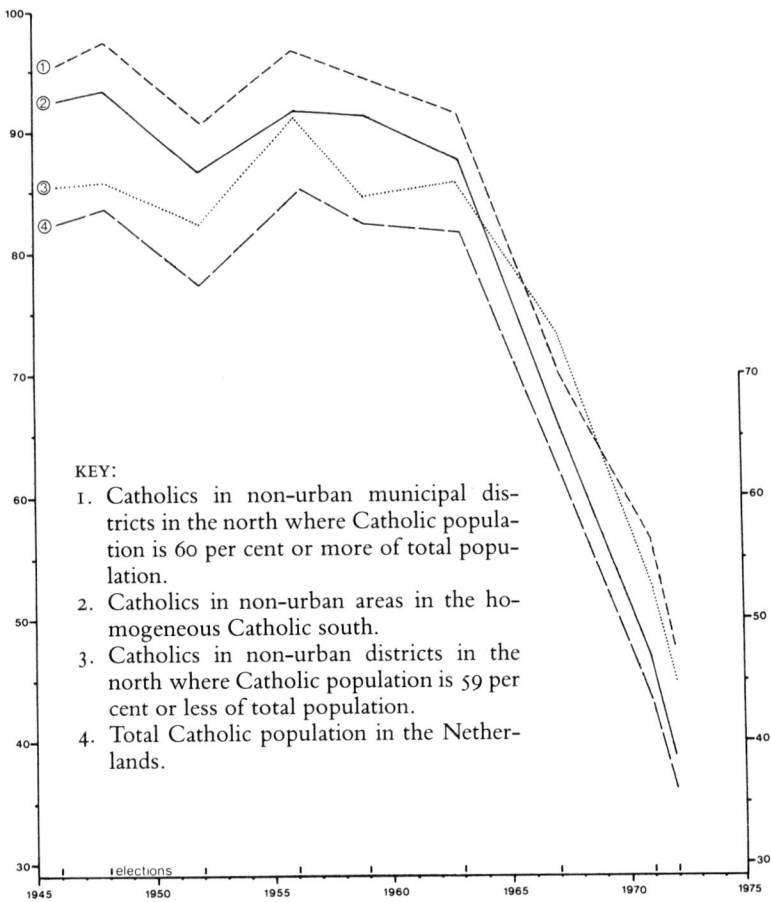

FIGURE 5.4. Percentage of Catholics Voting for KVP by Catholic Concentration, Urbanization, and Region
Source: Houska and Leiden data sets.

subpopulations. The most important finding is that the KVP vote declined no matter what the context. There is virtually no group which was immune from the changes which occurred in the latter half of the 1960s and in the 1970s. Support for the KVP among Catholics living in urban areas decreased from a high of 74.9 per cent in 1954 to 29.8 per cent in 1972 (see figure 5.1). Among those Catholics residing in homogeneous Catholic areas outside the solidly Catholic south, support for the party dropped from a high of 97.2 per cent in 1948 to 48.0 per cent in 1972 (see figure 5.4).

Context did have some effect on the magnitude of the change as may be seen by comparing the voting behaviour of residents of rural areas in the south with that of rural residents elsewhere (fig. 5.3). In 1948 the former gave 93.7 per cent of their vote to the KVP compared with 89.0 per cent for the latter group. By 1972, however, only 39.1 per cent in the south voted for the KVP compared with 46.0 per cent elsewhere. Since the south is virtually homogeneously Catholic changes were probably communicated more quickly. In the past the continual pressure from one's neighbours provided an additional means of social control. When attitudes changed, however, the presence of a high concentration of Catholics would have helped to accelerate change. It was also in the south that mass attendance rates dropped somewhat more quickly than in other regions.[43]

The vote of those living in rural areas outside the Catholic south, but where Catholics nevertheless form a majority (over 60 per cent), has not dropped in quite the same fashion as that of rural Catholics in the south (see fig. 5.4). Homogeneous Catholic villages and towns outside the south are essentially islands in a non-Catholic sea. Changes would more likely have been introduced via the media or visitors. The ripple effect, by which changes introduced in one parish spread to contiguous parishes, would be less likely to have occurred outside the south.[44]

Class, Organizational Membership, and Gender. It is possible that other variables were associated with the change in the Catholic vote for the KVP. The fall of the Cals cabinet in 1966 as a result of withdrawal of support by the KVP caused considerable ill will among Catholic trade union leaders. One might expect, therefore, that working-class Catholics, particularly those belonging to trade unions, would be less inclined to vote KVP in the post-1966 period than would middle-class Catholics, particularly the self-employed middle class. In other countries with Catholic or Christian Democratic parties the middle class is much more prone to support such parties than is the working class.[45] One might also posit that women would be less likely to withdraw

TABLE 5.2
Voting Choice by Self-Assigned Social Class, 1970

	Social Class			
	Working Class	Middle Class	Upper Middle Class	Total Sample
KVP	57.5%	58.3%	57.7%	57.8%
Other parties	32.1	35.6	32.7	33.7
Do not intend to vote	10.4	6.1	9.6	8.5
Total %:	100.0	100.0	100.0	100.0
N:	(268)	(247)	(52)	(567)

Source: 1970 Dutch Election Survey (provincial elections). Respondents were asked how they would vote if a national election were held. Designation Catholic is based on assignment by respondents themselves.

their support from the KVP. In countries such as West Germany, France, and Italy women are much more likely to vote for Christian Democratic parties than are men. Men, it is argued, are exposed to left-wing or secular influences at the work-place whereas women are more often religiously inclined.[46]

There is no survey evidence available for analysis from the period prior to 1963. However, Arend Lijphart, in *The Politics of Accommodation*, has analysed data from a survey carried out in 1964. He reports that the class composition of the KVP electorate was virtually a mirror image of the class composition of Dutch society as a whole. Middle-class Catholics were just as likely to vote KVP as were lower-class Catholics.[47] Thus if the interpretation concerning working-class alienation from the KVP in the late 1960s has any validity, one would expect a significant difference between middle-class and working-class Catholics in terms of their support for the party.

The data do not support this interpretation. Table 5.2 is a cross-tabulation for party choice and social class among Dutch Catholics in the year 1970.[48] Social class is defined according to the respondent's own definition of his or her class. There is clearly no difference between those who call themselves either working, middle or upper-middle class. A certain amount of variation becomes evident if we distinguish between those earning wages and those involved in agriculture (see table 5.3). Only Catholics working in agriculture are much more likely to support the KVP than is the rest of the Catholic population. The

Decline and Fall of the Catholic Party | 155

more wealthy Catholics earning salaries are somewhat less likely to vote KVP compared with other occupational groupings.

Table 5.4 cross-tabulates organizational membership with party choice. Rather than abandoning the KVP, it appears that Catholic trade union members were somewhat more likely to vote for the party than was the Catholic population as a whole. Given the disenchantment of the NKV as expressed by the leadership, one would have expected Catholic trade unionists in the year 1970 to have supported the KVP at a rate less than that of the total Catholic population. Particularly striking is the contrast between Catholic trade unionists and those belonging to the Catholic Retailers' Organization. Representatives of that organization in the KVP played an important role in the collapse of the Cals cabinet. Nevertheless, they were less likely to vote KVP than were Catholic trade unionists (55.6 per cent versus 64.1 per cent). On the other hand those belonging to the Catholic Farmers' Association were most likely to vote KVP. The evidence in relation to gender is also inconclusive: 55.2 per cent of male Catholics support the KVP compared with 59.2 per cent of female Catholics.

As noted, long-term time series analysis is not possible. However, using the 1967 and 1970 surveys one can discover whether relationships between KVP voting and variables like class and gender changed between those years. In 1967, in the case of middle-class and working-class Catholics, the rates of support were 75.1 and 73.6 per cent respectively (58.3 versus 57.5 per cent in 1970 as per table 5.2). Thus differences which existed in 1967 and 1970 were virtually of the same magnitude. The drop in KVP support occurred in both categories. In the case of gender, in 1967 72.0 per cent of male Catholics voted KVP compared with 74.3 per cent of female Catholics (55.2 versus 59.2 per cent in 1970). Female Catholics were somewhat more likely to support the KVP in 1970. However, apart from this minor difference it cannot be said that Catholic men were more susceptible to change than Catholic women.

Thus on the basis of the available evidence one cannot accept the argument that in their voting behaviour Catholics in the Netherlands became more like Catholics in countries such as Germany and Italy. In the Netherlands in 1970 Catholic workers were just as likely to vote KVP, even more so if they belonged to a Catholic trade union, as members of the Catholic middle class. And there was no disproportionate tendency among Catholic women, compared to Catholic men, to vote KVP. It appears that relationships between KVP voting, class, and other variables, which prevailed in the early 1960s, continued unaltered throughout the period of the decline in Catholic party support.

TABLE 5.3
Voting Choice by Occupational Level, 1970

	Self-Employed	Upper Middle-Class Wage Earner	Middle-Class Wage Earner	Lower-Class Wage Earner	Agriculture	Total
KVP	51.4%	40.0%	50.0%	52.2%	83.6%	54.6%
Other parties	35.7	50.0	43.6	36.8	10.9	35.6
Do not intend to vote	12.9	10.0	6.4	11.0	5.5	9.8
Total %:	100.0	100.0	100.0	100.0	100.0	100.0
N:	(70)	(20)	(94)	(272)	(55)	(511)

Source: 1970 Dutch Election Survey.

TABLE 5.4
Voting Choice by Organizational Membership, 1970

			Organization			
	None	NVV	NKV	Catholic Retailers' Organization	Catholic Farmers' Association	Total
KVP	55.6%	34.1%	64.1%	55.6%	90.0%	57.5%
Other parties	34.1	59.1	29.7	27.8	6.7	33.3
No vote	10.3	6.8	6.3	16.7	3.3	9.1
Total %:	100.0	100.0	100.0	100.0	100.0	100.0
N:	(349)	(46)	(128)	(20)	(30)	(573)

Source: 1970 Dutch Election Survey.

Decline and Fall of the Catholic Party | 157

Mobility. As people become geographically mobile or shift from one occupational level to another, they are prone to break with past traditions and familial bonds, and become receptive to new influences.[49] Combined with the dropping away of church influence, both geographical and occupational mobility may have given Dutch Catholics an opportunity to develop new socio-economic ties and a different political orientation. There was no significant increase in geographic mobility in the postwar compared with the prewar era. In fact, as noted in chapter 4, there was a decrease. Nevertheless, a large proportion of the population did change its locale. Furthermore, given the expansion in industrial capacity after the war and the higher level of education attained by Catholics, one might expect a greater rate of intergenerational mobility.

Table 5.5 indicates that geographically mobile Catholics, those moving from one environment where they were resident between the ages of ten and sixteen to another environment, do differ somewhat from those continuously resident in one locale. Yet the rate of KVP support among those geographically mobile cannot be taken as evidence that moving to a new environment leads to a loss of attachment to traditional forms of behaviour such as voting KVP. Those moving from a rural or semi-urban to an urban environment are slightly more likely to vote KVP than those continuously resident in an urban environment. As shown in table 5.5, people moving from a rural to a semi-urban environment or vice versa tend to have a rate of KVP support falling between the rate in the case of the non-mobile residents of rural areas and that of the non-mobile in semi-urban areas. In no category of those geographically mobile does the rate of KVP support deviate drastically from the national mean, nor does any category of geographically mobile Catholics fall below the rate of KVP support of those continuously resident in urban environments. Overall there is virtually no difference between those who are mobile and the non-mobile.[50]

A significant proportion of the Catholic population is intergenerationally mobile, although much of this mobility is in a downward direction (see table 5.6). Class is defined in objective terms (i.e., by the interviewer as opposed to self-placement by the respondent). The low to high and high to low categories have been eliminated from the table since they contained too few cases. Of those who are mobile, the low to middle-class and the upper middle to middle-class deviate most from the overall mean. What is unusual about the data, however, is the degree to which they reveal considerable variation within the standard occupational categories. Thus the KVP vote in the upper middle, middle, and lower classes is 40.7, 60.4, and 55.1 per cent respectively (not

TABLE 5.5
Voting Choice by Geographical Mobility, 1970

	Non-Mobile			Mobile			Total Non-Mobile	Total Mobile	Total Sample
	Rural*	Semi-Rural	Urban	Rural to Semi-Rural and Vice Versa	Rural and Semi-Rural to Urban	Urban to Semi-Rural and Rural			
KVP	76.5%	55.9%	41.6%	68.1%	44.2%	50.8%	57.0%	56.8%	57.0%
Other	12.2	37.8	49.6	24.5	44.2	40.0	34.5	34.3	34.2
No vote	11.2	6.3	8.8	7.4	7.4	9.2	8.5	8.9	8.7
Total %:	100.0	100.0	100.0	100.0	100.0	100.0	100.0	100.0	100.0
N:	(98)	(127)	(113)	(94)	(52)	(65)	(338)	(211)	(549)

Source: 1970 Dutch Election Study.
*Rural includes all those residing in rural areas with at least 20 per cent of the economically active male population in agriculture; Semi-Rural includes all those residing in urbanized rural municipalities with over 50 per cent of the economically active male population in manufacturing, industry, and small and medium-sized towns of up to 50,000 inhabitants; Urban includes all those residing in cities of more than 50,000.

Decline and Fall of the Catholic Party | 159

shown in table 5.6). In the upper middle category it is apparent that the figure of 40.7 per cent conceals the fact that whereas the non-mobile upper middle class support the KVP at a rate of only 18.2 per cent, those moving into that class from the middle class support the party at a rate of 56.3 per cent. It should be noted that the non-mobile middle-class category contains most of those who are in agriculture (N = 51) and who tend to be overwhelmingly KVP (88.9 per cent). This also tends to obscure the fact that the non-agricultural middle class votes KVP at a much lower rate (55.8 per cent). A considerable proportion of those in the middle to lower-class category (N = 24) are Catholics with agricultural backgrounds moving to non-agricultural occupations. Again there is very little difference between the non-mobile and the mobile.[51]

Generational Change. To what extent is the decline in the KVP vote related to age? David Butler and Donald Stokes argue that when political realignment occurs it usually involves younger voters, who are the most susceptible to changed conditions since the political allegiances they inherit from their parents are still rather fragile.[52] Older age cohorts have loyalties which are firmer and therefore more resistant to change. Large-scale change, according to Butler and Stokes, is mainly a function of generational discontinuity and the inevitable replacement of older by younger voters.

Ronald Inglehart, in a variation of the age cohort theme, has argued that younger generations in Western Europe, brought up under conditions of relative affluence, have developed political values and allegiances markedly different from those of their parents.[53] Younger voters who have developed so-called "post-bourgeois" values in reaction to the materialistic values of their elders, are much more likely to support political parties and movements emphasizing change and progress. Inglehart claims that this generational difference is quite pronounced in the Netherlands.[54] In addition to the changes he refers to, there are those specifically related to the Dutch Catholic population. Many Catholics came of voting age during the era of Bishop Bekkers and Vatican II and as a result they have felt much less bound to older Catholic traditions. Furthermore, younger Catholics are much better educated than previous generations and perhaps for this reason are more critical of traditional beliefs and practices. One would expect, therefore, that younger Catholics in the Netherlands would be much less likely to vote KVP than older Catholics.

Table 5.7 does indeed show clear, although not extreme, differences between age and KVP support. The rate for the youngest age cohort is approximately 16 per cent below the overall mean while the rate for the oldest age cohort is roughly the same amount above the mean.

TABLE 5.6
Voting Choice by Intergenerational Mobility, 1970

	Non-Mobile			Mobile				Total Non-Mobile	Total Mobile	Total Sample
	Upper Middle	Middle	Low	Middle to Upper Middle	Upper Middle to Middle	Low to Middle	Middle to Low			
KVP	18.2%	68.0%	50.8%	56.3%	30.0%	44.0%	62.1%	57.2%	55.2%	56.5
Other	45.5	26.0	38.3	43.8	50.0	44.0	28.4	33.3	34.8	33.8
No vote	36.4	6.0	10.9	0.0	20.0	12.0	9.5	9.5	10.0	9.7
Total %:	100.0	100.0	100.0	100.0	100.0	100.0	100.0	100.0	100.0	100.0
N:	(11)	(150)	(183)	(16)	(10)	(50)	(116)	(344)	(192)	(536)

Source: 1970 Dutch Election Survey.

Decline and Fall of the Catholic Party | 161

TABLE 5.7
Vote by Age Cohort

	Age Cohort				Total
	60+	44-59	31-43	21-30	
KVP	73.0%	63.5%	56.3%	41.6%	57.2%
Other	22.5	30.9	34.8	42.2	33.7
No vote	4.5	5.6	8.9	16.2	9.2
Total %:	100.0	100.0	100.0	100.0	100.0
N:	(89)	(178)	(158)	(154)	(579)

Source: 1970 Dutch Election Survey.

Furthermore, the age cohort effect appears to differ depending upon the context. In table 5.8, where age is controlled for urbanization, one can see that in rural areas only the youngest age cohort is less likely to support the KVP. Table 5.9 divides the age cohorts into south and non-south groups. In the homogeneous Catholic south the difference between the different age cohorts is much smaller. A difference of only 20 per cent separates the youngest age cohort from the oldest age cohort compared with a separation of 42 per cent within the non-south group. The high concentration of Catholics in the south may have helped to diffuse change more uniformly.

How stable is the age relationship over time? Are older voters likely to remain loyal to the KVP or have they changed as well? On the whole, the older age cohorts appear to be more resistant to change although not immune to it. Table 5.10 documents levels of KVP support among the age cohorts at different stages during the 1960s and 1970s. The 1970 data set was used for 1967 and 1970. Respondents were

TABLE 5.8
% KVP Vote by Age Controlled for Urbanization

Urbanization	Age Cohort				Total
	60+	44-59	31-43	21-30	
Rural	85.7%	80.0%	76.6%	51.7%	73.7%
(N)	(21)	(40)	(47)	(29)	(137)
Semi-Rural	73.5%	62.2%	54.7%	46.6%	57.3%
(N)	(34)	(82)	(64)	(73)	(253)
Urban	64.7%	53.6%	38.3%	28.8%	45.0%
(N)	(34)	(56)	(47)	(52)	(189)

Source: 1970 Dutch Election Survey.

TABLE 5.9
% KVP Vote by Age Controlled for North-South

North-South	Age Cohort				Total
	60+	44-59	31-43	21-30	
Non-South	78.3%	66.7%	61.0%	36.6%	58.7%
(N)	(46)	(90)	(82)	(82)	(300)
South	67.4%	60.2%	51.3%	47.2%	55.6%
(N)	(43)	(88)	(76)	(72)	(279)

Source: 1970 Dutch Election Survey.

asked what party they voted for in 1967 and what party they would vote for in 1970 if an election were to be held. The 1971 survey asked people how they would vote in the forthcoming election of that year.[55] From 1967 to 1971 the data show a definite drop in KVP support in all age categories except the oldest. This change cannot be attributed to the movement of voters in and out of the electorate through the coming of age of young Catholics and the death of older ones. The same age cohorts are followed through from 1967 to 1971. Thus the oldest age cohort category containing those born in 1909 or earlier has the same cutting point (1909) for 1970 and 1971. Furthermore, the 1967 and 1970 data are from the same survey. On the right-hand side of the table is an additional column for the 1970 and 1971 categories for voters who were not yet old enough to vote in 1967. Thus generational change is important but decline in KVP support is not restricted to the younger age cohorts.

TABLE 5.10
% KVP by Age Cohort Controlling for Year

Year	Age (as in 1970)				New Voters (21-23)	Total
	60+	44-59	31-43	24-30		
1967	77.4%	77.0%	76.2%	58.0%	—	73.3%
(N)	(93)	(183)	(168)	(100)		(544)
1970	73.0%	63.5%	56.3%	47.9%	31.0%	57.2%
(N)	(89)	(178)	(158)	(96)	(58)	(579)
1971	77.4%	61.7%	48.9%	35.1%	26.1%	52.5%
(N)	(115)	(201)	(176)	(94)	(92)	(678)

Source: 1970 Dutch Election Survey; Dutch Parliamentary Election Study, 1971.

TABLE 5.11
Voting Choice by Attitudes on Social Welfare, 1970

	Strongly Agree	Agree	Disagree	Strongly Disagree	Don't Know	Total
A. "There should be more social reform."						
KVP	52.4%	55.6%	54.2%	46.7%	72.5%	57.1%
Other	37.9	35.7	41.7	40.0	15.4	33.7
No vote	9.7	8.7	4.2	13.3	12.1	9.2
Total %:	100.0	100.0	100.0	100.0	100.0	100.0
N:	(145)	(277)	(48)	(15)	(91)	(576)
B. "There should be a decrease in social benefits and subsidies."						
KVP	66.0%	58.5%	51.0%	53.5%	71.3%	57.0%
Other	23.4	35.8	39.9	35.4	20.0	34.0
No vote	10.6	5.7	9.1	11.0	8.8	9.0
Total %:	100.0	100.0	100.0	100.0	100.0	100.0
N:	(87)	(106)	(208)	(127)	(80)	(568)

Source: 1970 Election Survey.

Decline and the Lack of Variation. Prior to 1963 virtually the entire Catholic population voted for the Catholic party. According to the ecological data only, variables such as Catholic concentration and degree of urbanization accounted for only a limited amount of the variation in the Catholic vote. In statistical terms there was not much variance to be explained. The influence of the church and the Catholic subculture was such that other factors were given only a limited role to play.[56] Little evidence exists to indicate that variables such as class have become more important during the period of decline since 1963.[57] Only age and degree of urbanization have some predictive power as to which Catholics continued to vote KVP and which were less likely to vote for the party in the early 1970s. However, the explanatory power of these variables is limited. Up to the end of its life as a distinctively Catholic party the KVP still managed to draw support from a wide cross-section of Catholics albeit at a much lower rate. No single group, whether trade unionists or urban dwellers, was completely alienated from it.

The significance of the overall low explanatory power of the above variables must be seen in the way they highlight the role of the church. If these variables are involved in the decline of the KVP vote only in a limited way, what then is the explanation? In earlier times the church was the crucial force in impelling Catholics to vote for the Catholic party. In the 1960s the church withdrew from this role and,

TABLE 5.12
Voting Choice by Political Interest, 1970

	Level of Political Interest					
	High			Low	Don't Know	Total
KVP	50.0%	53.3%	57.1%	58.8%	73.3%	57.1%
Other	46.2	44.0	37.2	26.5	13.3	33.7
No vote	3.8	2.7	5.8	14.7	13.3	9.2
Total %:	100.0	100.0	100.0	100.0	100.0	100.0
N:	(52)	(75)	(191)	(245)	(15)	(578)

Source: 1970 Election Survey.

in effect, cast its adherents adrift. Catholics were asked to be personally responsible for a whole range of matters including political choice. Given the well-developed communications network of the Catholic pillar, most Catholics would have been aware of the changed orientation of the church.

Political Interest, Attitudes, and Change. Guidance from the church to the effect that it was no longer the duty of Catholics to vote KVP need not by itself have led to the decline in KVP support. If Catholic voters were reasonably satisfied with the performance of the party they might not have perceived a need to change their vote. However, from 1965 onwards the KVP was under considerable pressure concerning its performance. Catholics, within and outside the party, who favoured a close working relationship with the PVDA were extremely upset by the actions which led to the fall of the Cals cabinet in 1965, and as we have seen in 1968 a number of important figures in the progressive wing left to form a new party. The issues at stake mostly involved expenditures for social welfare programs and aid to the Third World. The progressives favoured increased expenditure and deficit financing. Those supporting the party leader Schmelzer tended to favour limiting expenditure and balancing the budget.

The 1970 survey contained a number of questions about the scope of government activities. Respondents were asked whether social welfare problems required more social reforms and whether equality of income distribution should be a goal. They could agree, disagree, or indicate that they did not know. As can be seen in table 5.11 those who strongly disagreed were somewhat less likely to vote KVP compared with those expressing mild disagreement or agreement of any kind. The largest difference, however, was between the "don't knows" and the rest of the sample. The former were much more likely to vote KVP.

Decline and Fall of the Catholic Party | 165

The major difference, then, was not really between those who agreed or disagreed but between those who had an opinion on issues and those who did not. This suggests that those who were generally uninterested in political affairs were more likely to see voting as a form of traditional behaviour requiring little personal motivation, and therefore were more likely to vote KVP.

This point can be examined further by looking at the relationship between level of interest in politics and support for the Catholic party. Table 5.12 shows a slight but nevertheless linear relationship between voting KVP and level of interest. Those less interested in politics were somewhat more likely to vote KVP. In addition, as level of interest went down an increase occurred among those who did not intend to vote. Thus if one puts the question in the form of "which Catholics are most likely to vote for a party other than the KVP?" the difference between the highly interested and the uninterested becomes 33 per cent.

Those having a higher level of interest, aside perhaps from being more self-motivated, were also more likely to be exposed to news of events in the Catholic subculture and politics, and would therefore be more aware of the changed orientation of the church. They might react unfavourably to the behaviour of KVP parliamentarians or stands taken by the party on particular issues. As the growing dissension within the KVP demonstrates, during the 1960s and 1970s it became increasingly difficult to achieve compromise solutions. A middle-of-the-road position was sure to offend people on both sides of the question. Table 5.11 illustrates that Catholic voters having negative or positive opinions were less likely to vote KVP than those having no opinion at all (questions A and B). Thus Catholics interested in politics may well have decided that an alternative party like the Liberals or the PvdA had an orientation which was more in keeping with their own views and may have changed their vote accordingly. This interpretation can be partially confirmed by comparing switchers (i.e., those who voted KVP in 1967 but supported another party in 1970) with constant KVP voters in level of political interest. Switchers were less likely to fall into the "low" interest category than constant KVP voters (30.2 per cent versus 45.2 per cent).[58]

There was little attachment to the Catholic party itself. In a survey inquiring into the role of religion in the Netherlands carried out in 1966, respondents were asked whether or not they favoured deconfessionalization of the political parties.[59] The results are given in table 5.13, in which Catholics are compared with other socio-religious groupings in the Netherlands. Slightly more than half of all Catholics

166 | Catholic Power in the Netherlands

TABLE 5.13
Depillarization by Religion

	Catholic	Dutch Reformed	Calvinist	No Religion	Total
"Politics and religion should be separated."					
Yes	52%	54%	14%	78%	58%
No	35	35	80	16	33
Depends	8	8	4	5	6
Don't know	5	3	2	1	3
Total %:	100	100	100	100	100
(N's not available)					

Source: G. Zeegers et al., *God in Nederland*, pp. 216–17; W. Goddijn et al., *Opnieuw: God in Nederland*, p. 216.

favoured the uncoupling of religion and politics, only marginally less than the proportion of the entire sample in favour of it, and considerably more than in the case of the Calvinists. It should be emphasized that the survey was carried out in the same year in which over 80 per cent of Catholics still supported the KVP in the provincial elections.[60] In the election for the Second Chamber in 1967, 63 per cent of all Catholics still supported the party. Evidently many Catholics who voted for the KVP in those two elections did not believe that a Catholic party was necessary.

A similar question was asked in the 1971 election survey. This time 83.8 per cent of all Catholics indicated they were in favour of either one general Christian party or a secular party independent of religion. Only 9.5 per cent of Catholic respondents wished to see the continuation of the KVP. In comparison, 20 per cent of Calvinists wished to see the continuation of their party. Of the Catholics who voted for the KVP only 9.6 per cent wished to see it continue as a separate party.

In 1967 the sociologist J. A. van Kemenade asked a sample of Catholic parents about the perceived necessity of a number of different Catholic institutions.[61] The survey indicated that the Catholic educational system ranked at the top with 57 per cent while the KVP was much lower with only 36 per cent. Only the Catholic trade union federation and Catholic sports organizations were perceived as being less necessary (34 per cent and 12 per cent respectively). Thus the low level of attachment to the KVP displayed by the leadership of the party was matched by that of the Catholic electorate. A political party, because of the nature of the services it provides, and because it is much more likely to attract attention, is more prone to have dissatisfied clients than other organizations. The KVP, unlike the KRO, could not attempt to maintain a neutral position. Although Catholics may not be strong-

Decline and Fall of the Catholic Party | 167

ly attached to Catholic sports organizations, they will continue to patronize them if the services rendered are of reasonable quality. Such organizations are unlikely to venture into controversial areas.
Where Did Catholics Go? By 1972 only 37 per cent of Catholic voters who voted KVP in 1967 were still voting for the party.[62] What happened to the remainder? This question is worth raising for two reasons: those who no longer voted for the KVP, as well as younger age cohorts who in earlier times would probably have voted for it, represent a substantial portion of the Dutch population. A development in which a bloc of voters constituting more than 20 per cent of the total electorate leaves one party and disperses to a number of other parties can have major consequences for a political system. Secondly, an examination of the patterns of dispersion of ex-KVP voters may well reveal something about the nature of the Catholic vote. In particular, it can indicate the ways in which Catholics detached themselves from the KVP.

Political scientists like V. O. Key in his study of American electoral behaviour have developed the notion of the "critical election."[63] In such an election a large number of voters leave one party for another, and new, previously uncommitted voters are mobilized so that a major realignment of the electorate takes place. A realignment usually involves major issues; Roosevelt's "New Deal," for example, is seen as the key issue in bringing about a realignment of the American electorate in the elections of 1932 and 1936. Can we talk of a critical election or a series of critical elections in the Dutch case? According to Steven Wolinetz, party alignments in the Netherlands became unfrozen in the 1960s and 1970s; nevertheless, he argues, it is meaningless to talk of realignment.[64] Most of the major parties lost support and none made major gains. The chief beneficiaries were the smaller parties but none of them managed to achieve any degree of stability over time.[65]

A number of major issues such as the collapse of the Cals cabinet in 1966 agitated the KVP in this period. In the preceding section it was noted that Catholics who had an opinion on issues were less likely to vote KVP. However, ex-KVP voters did not shift to another party *en masse*. Instead they dispersed to a variety of alternative parties, and subsequently were likely to be highly unstable in their electoral behaviour.

Tables 5.14 and 5.15 indicate the nature of the traffic between the KVP and other parties in successive elections. In 1967 the largest proportion of ex-KVP voters went to the Democrats '66 (D'66) (table 5.14). The support of ex-KVP voters contributed heavily to the success of this brand-new party. Much smaller proportions went to the PvdA and the VVD. In 1971 the PvdA received a much larger proportion of

TABLE 5.14
Where Did the Ex-KVP Vote Go?

	Vote in 1967								
	KVP	PvdA	VVD	ARP	BP	D'66	Don't Know/ No Vote	Total	
Those who voted KVP in 1966	85%	2%	2%	1%	1%	4%	5%	100% (N = 1122)	

	Vote in 1971								
	KVP	PvdA	VVD	ARP	BP	D'66	PPR	DS'70	No Vote	Total
Those who voted KVP in 1967	79%	3.8%	2%	0	.3%	2.1%	2.5%	2.3%	7.7%	100% (N not available)

	Vote in 1972								
	KVP	PvdA	VVD	ARP	BP	D'66	PPR	DS'70	RKNP	No Vote	Total
Those who voted KVP in 1971	66%	8%	7%	1%	1%	0	2%	1%	4%	8%	100% (N = 249)

	Vote in 1977								
	CDA	PvdA	VVD	ARP	BP	D'66	PPR	DS'70	RKNP	No Vote	Total
Those who voted KVP in 1972	80%	10%	3.5%	0	1%	2.5%	0	0	0	3.5	100% (N = 198)

TABLE 5.15
Where Did the KVP Vote Come From?

Vote in 1966

	KVP	PvdA	VVD	ARP	BP	D'66	New/No Vote	Total
All those who voted KVP in 1967	91%	1%	1%	0	2%	0	5%	100% (N = 1045)

Vote in 1967

	KVP	PvdA	VVD	ARP	BP	D'66	New Vote	No Vote	Total
All those who voted KVP in 1971	86.4%	2%	2%	.2%	.5%	1.6%	3.6%	3.6%	100% (N not available)

Vote in 1971

	KVP	PvdA	VVD	ARP	BP	D'66	DS'70	New Vote	No Vote	Total
All those who voted KVP in 1972	77%	2%	1%	0	0	1%	2%	8%	7%	100% (N = 213)

Source: Vrije Universiteit Amsterdam, *De Nederlandse kiezers in 1967*, p. 17; H. Daudt, "Constante kiezers, wisselaars en thuisblijvers," *Acta Politica* 7 (1972): 32; Werkgroep Nationaal Verkiezingsonderzoek 1972, *De Nederlandse kiezer '72*, pp. 19, 21. G. Irwin et al., *De Nederlandse kiezer '77*, pp. 140–41.

newly defecting Catholic KVP voters and a smaller proportion went to the D'66. However, 2.5 per cent of 1967 KVP voters did go to the newly formed Party of Political Radicals (PPR), the party containing a number of ex-KVP politicians, and 2.3 per cent went to Democratic Socialists '70 (DS'70), a conservative breakaway faction of the PvdA. Thus the plurality of the ex-KVP vote in 1971 went to the newer, smaller parties, D'66, PPR, and DS'70. The largest single bloc of ex-KVP voters, however, is to be found in the category of those who elected not to vote at all in 1971. The increase in this category can, in part, be attributed to the elimination of the compulsory voting law in 1970.[66] In 1972 the situation was quite different. The PvdA and the VVD combined received by far the largest share of the ex-KVP vote. The D'66 received virtually none and the PPR and DS'70 a significantly smaller share. The newest party to arrive on the political scene, the Roman Catholic Party of the Netherlands (RKPN), received 4 per cent of the vote of those who voted KVP in 1971. The no-vote category increased slightly to 8 per cent.

An examination of where KVP votes came from (table 5.15) shows that there was some traffic coming back from the other parties. Particularly in 1971, the KVP appears to have recovered a considerable proportion of those who left the party for the PvdA or VVD in 1967 or earlier. In 1972 the KVP also received the votes of many of those who voted DS'70 in 1971. In 1972, however, the two-way traffic between the KVP and the PvdA/VVD became heavily biased in favour of the latter parties, both proportionally and in absolute terms. The traffic between the KVP and the PPR was strictly one-way since the KVP received virtually no votes from 1971 PPR voters. On the other hand, although the KVP lost 8 per cent of its 1971 electorate to the no-vote category, it received 9 per cent of its vote from those who sat out the election in 1971.

What does this flow of voters indicate? For years Catholics had been told that both the PvdA (and before the war the SDAP) and the VVD stood for all the things Catholics were opposed to: secularization of schools, hospitals, and the broadcasting system. It is highly probable that Catholics had been imbued with what might be called negative party identification. Many Catholics felt free to leave the KVP but felt incapable of moving directly to one of the old-line parties. In 1967 it was probably easier for many Catholics to support a new non-aligned, untainted party like D'66 which had not been involved in the earlier controversies concerning the role of the church in society. The same was true in 1971. Although the flow to the PvdA increased somewhat, the PPR, which presented itself as a radical Christian party, became a refuge for many ex-KVP voters. Over 40 per cent of PPR voters in 1971 were ex-KVP voters.⁶⁷ Moreover, a substantial number of Catholic voters decided not to vote at all. In 1972 a number of the more conservative orthodox Catholics moved to the Roman Catholic Party of the Netherlands (RKPN). This party took a strong stand on the abortion issue and claimed that the KVP was no longer a true Catholic party. Catholic voters were thus deserting the KVP on all sides, the orthodox going to the RKPN, the more radical to the PPR.

In 1972 the PVDA and the VVD received a larger share of the ex-KVP vote than previously. However, taking into account the number of non-voters in 1972, these two parties received slightly less than half the total ex-KVP vote. The Catholic vote for the PVDA and the VVD is also unstable. Thus 26 per cent of all those who voted PVDA in 1971 but did not do so in 1972 were Catholic. Only 35 per cent of Catholics who voted PVDA in 1972 had done so in 1971. In contrast Dutch Reformed support for the PVDA was much more stable: of those who voted for the party in 1972 69 per cent had done so in 1971.⁶⁸

Nevertheless, the trend does appear to be that ex-KVP voters are moving towards the VVD and PVDA. Many Catholics who first voted for the smaller parties moved to the larger parties at a later date. For them the smaller parties acted as a way station. Karl Dittrich's examination of some panel data provides further evidence on this point. His findings are presented in table 5.16. The sixty-two voters in the table are Catholics who voted KVP in 1967 but left in 1970 at the time of the provincial election. The data show that the smaller parties were indeed a temporary way station for many Catholics. A general trend towards the PVDA and the VVD is also apparent. Thus, of the eleven Catholics who voted D'66 in 1970 we find that not a single one was still voting for that party in 1972 (not shown in the table). Six of the eleven went to the VVD and three to the PVDA.⁶⁹

The patterns of dispersal of Catholics who left the KVP offer an interesting commentary on the nature of political change in the Dutch Catholic community. It is consistent with the notion that the reorientation of the church left many Catholics without clear guidance in the realm of politics. The KVP itself was unhelpful because it was in an obvious state of decline. The much hoped-for formation of a Christian Democratic party did not appear imminent. Many Catholics, the remnants of the all too recent past imprinted upon their consciences, were confused about where their interests lay.

Many felt inclined to abandon the KVP but had no clear-cut alternatives. One newspaper commenting upon this phenomenon headlined an article, "The Catholics are jumping off the roof tops but there are no safety nets."⁷⁰ A trend can be discerned towards some form of realignment. The data for 1972 show Catholic voters gradually moving towards the PvdA and the VVD. In the 1977 national election, however, the presence of the long-awaited CDA, based upon the three major confessional parties, altered this trend in important ways. As shown in table 5.14, an even greater proportion of voters leaving the KVP moved directly to the PvdA (10 per cent versus 8 per cent in 1972). However, the movement of ex-KVP voters to the VVD has slowed considerably (3.5 per cent versus 7 per cent) and the new CDA has been relatively successful in retaining previous KVP supporters within the confessional camp. The CDA also succeeded in retrieving a considerable number of Catholic voters from both the PvdA and especially the VVD, as the KVP had not done in 1972.[71] Although the PvdA obtained the largest vote share in 1977, the CDA federation did succeed in arresting the decline of the previous decade in the total vote for the confessional parties (see table 1.1).[72] To talk of realignment having taken place, without examining a series of elections in which the CDA is a participant, would be premature.

3. Summary

In the 1960s the Dutch church changed its views considerably on what constituted an appropriate role for both the church and individual Catholics in modern society. It placed several areas outside its jurisdiction and one of these was the realm of politics. Catholics were left free to vote according to their conscience: no one party was favoured by the church. The Catholic party could no longer use the symbols of church authority in order to cajole the electorate into supporting it. Largely in response to these new circumstances many Catholics ceased supporting the KVP. The proportion of people voting KVP from 1967 onwards declined uniformly in virtually all sectors of the Catholic population. Occupation, gender, and organizational membership determined only in a minor way whether or not an individual would vote for the KVP. Those most likely to remain loyal were those employed in agriculture, people residing in rural areas, and older people. Individuals who had little or no interest in politics were also more likely to remain constant KVP voters.

The KVP leadership felt both unable and unwilling to attempt a rescue operation. Virtually the entire party was committed not to the survival but to the disappearance of the KVP as a Catholic party. A majority was in favour of a merger with the two old-line Protestant parties. After 1967 most of the KVP's efforts were directed towards this goal, which was finally reached in the fall of 1980. To be sure, the KVP was in an unusually difficult position compared with other Catholic

TABLE 5.16
Vote in 1970, 1971, and 1972 of Catholics Who Voted KVP in 1967

Vote	1970	1971	1972
KVP	—	3.2%	—
PvdA	8.1%	9.7	21.1%
VVD	3.2	4.8	22.7
D'66	17.7	9.7	4.8
PSP	1.6	1.6	3.2
PPR	8.1	8.1	16.1
BP	1.6	—	4.8
DS'70	—*	6.5	4.8
CPN	—	—	3.2
RKPN	—*	—	1.6
Did not vote	59.7	30.6	17.7
Don't know/Can't remember	—	25.8	—
Total %:	100.0	100.0	100.0
N:	(62)	(62)	(62)

Source: K. Dittrich, "De gevolgen van de veranderingen in partijvoorkeur van de Nederlandse kiezers sinds 1966 voor KVP en PvdA," M.A. thesis, Leiden University, 1975, p. 18.
*Party did not compete in election of that year

organizations which had a specific clientele with a limited number of interests, such as the Catholic Farmers' Association, or else a well-defined product or service which was essentially non-controversial, such as the White-Yellow Cross Association. Any actions undertaken by the KVP were bound to alienate substantial sectors within the Catholic population, and during the late 1960s very few of its stances could be justified in terms of advancing specifically Catholic interests.

The perceptions of KVP leaders as to the eventual fate of the party were coloured by their own predilections, fears, and interests. Nevertheless, their perceptions were probably accurate. The Catholic party throughout its history was dependent upon the church for its electoral support and internal cohesion. It was never able to develop a character or identity which was distinct from that of the church. Ironically, the church, when the time came, found it relatively easy to make itself independent of the KVP, leaving the latter to flounder. The Catholic party leaders saw no alternative ideology, technique, or program with which they could retain the loyalty of a highly diverse electorate. Before 1967 the fact that all the members of this diverse group were Catholic was sufficient to unite them behind one political party. Less than a decade later this was no longer the case.

Chapter 6   **Conclusion**

Political Change and the Future of Catholic Power

This study began by asking some questions about the unusual electoral behaviour of Catholics in the Netherlands. Why did 85 per cent or more of Dutch Catholics regularly vote for the Catholic party and why did this level of support suddenly start to decline in the 1960s and 1970s? It was noted that this pattern of electoral stability and electoral decline was unique in Western Europe. In seeking an explanation for such behaviour it was decided that the concept of party identification, which emphasizes individual attachments to political parties, would be unsuitable in the European context. Most of the literature on West European electoral behaviour suggests that social characteristics such as class and religion are the major determinants. Researchers such as Phillips Shively argue that in Western Europe individuals identify with subcultural blocs rather than parties, take their cues from such blocs, and see political parties in instrumental terms.[1]

Unfortunately those arguing for the importance of subcultures have little to say about how subcultural blocs actually animate electoral behaviour or how subcultures remain viable and intact over time. How important are organizations or institutions such as trade unions, social clubs, and newspapers? Do social, religious, or political leaders play an active role? What are the characteristics of their clienteles? Is the influence of subcultures direct or indirect? In the light of these questions, the initial task in this study was to delineate the manner in which the Dutch Catholic subculture was organized and to account for its unusual cohesiveness. A further task was to show that the vote for the Catholic party was, in fact, a consequence of subcultural cohesion and that the change in the vote in the 1960s was integrally related to changes in the Catholic subculture.

Conclusion | 175

Findings. Evidence was presented to the effect that the Roman Catholic church had a dominant role in ensuring the cohesiveness of the Catholic bloc. The Dutch church was strongly influenced by an isolationist mentality and a feeling that Catholics in the Netherlands were a suppressed minority. Only through isolation, it was felt, could the Roman Catholic faith be adequately safeguarded. The church was characterized by distinct Calvinist and Jansenist tendencies, in many ways inherent in Dutch culture, which emphasized the rigorous application of rules and sanctions, thereby enhancing the effectiveness of isolationist policies. During the later nineteenth and early twentieth centuries the church became instrumental in the development of a wide range of Catholic socio-economic institutions. These institutions helped to insulate Catholics from the rest of Dutch society during the age of industrialization and beyond.

At the head of the church stood a compact and cohesive group, the bishops, who operated on a collegial basis, usually speaking with a single voice to the entire Catholic population. This collegiality was particularly strong from 1910 onwards. It was the ecclesiastical hierarchy which was most affected by the isolationist mentality, and through hierarchical control was successful in imposing its wishes on the clergy and the Catholic population as a whole. A number of the lower clergy, though interested in preserving the spiritual well-being of all Catholics by means of institutional isolation, nevertheless also favoured the development of Catholic socio-economic institutions in order to ameliorate the harsh conditions under which many lower-class Catholics existed.

Catholics of all classes remained within the boundaries of the highly institutionalized subculture, as it was from 1910 onwards, in large part because of a highly effective system of social control operated by a willing and able clergy. Clerics, through direct personal contact, ensured that their parishioners were well aware of the church's expectations. Catholics were provided with social, economic, and, of course, spiritual support that made it unnecessary or at least unattractive for them to move outside the Catholic subculture in order to obtain what they needed or wanted. In many ways Catholics can be seen as clients who were reasonably satisfied with the services provided by Catholic institutions.

The church played a crucial role in the maintenance of political cohesion. Among its expectations concerning the behaviour of Catholics, such as regular attendance at mass, the bearing of many children, and the reading of Catholic newspapers only, was the expectation that Catholics should "remain one" politically. This expectation was voiced several times by the bishops themselves before World War II and on four separate occasions in the postwar period. For most ordinary people, voting for the Catholic party was part and parcel of being Catholic—like attending Sunday mass. The idea of not voting Catholic rarely occurred.

The authority and ethos of the church was used by the leadership of the Catholic party not only to ensure electoral support but also to prevent the fracturing of the party itself. Although the leaders spent much time developing programs and reconciling conflicting economic interests within the organization, it was the authority of the church which proved to be most effective in ensuring compliance. Dissidents were persuaded from leaving, or to return if they had left, by having the wishes of the bishops pointed out to them. Dissident groups which did leave to set up a separate Catholic party invariably did poorly at election time.

The potency of church influence was dramatically shown by the events of the 1960s when bishops and clergy altered their authoritarian stance. The church, facing pressures from clerics and Catholic intellectuals, embarked on a program of critical self-appraisal. Sanctions imposed in earlier times concerning inter-faith marriage, weekly attendance at mass, and related matters were lifted. Church doctrine was demythologized and a large element of democratization introduced. A considerable amount of authority devolved upon the individual Catholic. Catholics were told that they were capable of deciding for themselves what constituted good Christian behaviour. And specifically they were told that voting was a matter of personal conscience. The result was that many decided no longer to participate in the activities of the church or support the KVP. Even a proportion of those still remaining loyal to the church ceased to vote KVP. The party's Catholic vote dropped from 85 per cent of the total vote in 1963 to 38 per cent in 1972. A public opinion poll in 1974 indicated that only 25 per cent of Dutch Catholics would still vote KVP if an election were to be held. The drop was consistent in most sectors of the Dutch Catholic population. Only among older voters, those living in rural areas, and those in agricultural occupations, did the KVP vote remain relatively high.

Although a number of political issues arose in the 1960s which involved the Catholic party and which embittered relations among conflicting socio-economic interests within it, this did not lead any one class, the working class for example, to desert the KVP. It is notable, however, that in all classes it was the younger, better educated Catholics possessing an interest in political affairs who were more likely to leave.

Without the authority of the church as a prop upon which to lean, the KVP ceased to be a viable operation. Its leaders either defected to form new parties or attempted to negotiate a merger with the two major Protestant parties to produce a middle-of-the-road Christian Democratic party. Their effort to create the latter, the Christian Democratic Appeal (CDA), was successful in 1980.

Theoretical Implications. These findings have important implications for the literature on electoral behaviour; at a minimum they highlight the need to explore further the problem of social and political cohesion. Some writers treat subcultures as given entities or as unspecific forces which lurk in the background but which nevertheless animate political behaviour.[2] Others who have examined the workings of subcultures more closely emphasize the insulating role of subcultural institutions such as the media.[3] In the case of the Dutch Catholic subculture the religious cleavage was not some unspecific traditional force but was actively fostered by elites, in particular by the religious authorities, namely the bishops. Political elites too played an important role by judiciously taking a guarded middle-of-the-road stand on various issues so as not to offend differing interests within the Catholic bloc. They were active as well in promoting the idea that the Catholic party was the one and only party for which Catholics should vote.

Dutch Catholic institutions did indeed play an insulating role, but this was not their sole function. They should also be seen in market terms. Catholic institutions helped cement the loyalty of Catholics to the subculture by providing services which were competitive with those of the other blocs in Dutch society. Particularly in the area of trade unions and broadcasting Catholics were generally aware what alternatives were available. Catholic organizations made a considerable effort to ensure that their clientele had no cause for transferring their loyalty to non-Catholic institutions. At the turn of the century Catholic trade unions, for the most part led by priests, had much success in organizing workers, especially in the south and east. In the postwar period the services offered by the Catholic Trade Union Federation were virtually identical to those offered by the socialist and Protestant federations.

Furthermore, the boundaries separating the Catholic subculture from the rest of Dutch society were not impermeable. Catholics preferred reading non-Catholic novels. They would frequently listen to non-Catholic radio programs. In the world of work there was interaction between Catholics and non-Catholics at all levels of society. Thus I. Gadourek describes how in the village of Sassenheim members of Catholic, Protestant, and socialist trade unions at local factories would meet to discuss problems concerning working conditions. Their views and recommendations would be forwarded to union leaders who in turn forwarded them to trade union centrals.[4] In the social and religious spheres considerably less interaction occurred between the different blocs. Nevertheless the view that interaction and cooperation between blocs was totally lacking at the mass level is a false one. Catholic institutions could not maintain a grip over their clientele solely by attempting to insulate them from outside influences. Catholics remained loyal to these institutions because for the most part they provided an adequate level of necessary or desirable services. And in the mid-1960s when church sanctions were revoked many Catholics remained loyal to institutions such as the Catholic Broadcasting Organization (KRO).

Thus for the Dutch Catholic subculture to have survived intact over a considerable period of time required a judicious blend of authoritarian social control, sanctions and rewards for the individual, and socioeconomic institutions which were viable in market terms. Furthermore, the whole system required the active participation of leaders at both local and national levels, as witnessed by the number of instances in which the Dutch bishops intervened in the realm of politics.

The charge can be made that the case of the Dutch Catholic subculture is unusual and not relevant for the study of intra-bloc cohesion elsewhere. The high degree of social and political cohesion on the part of Dutch Catholics was certainly unmatched by any other subculture in Western Europe.[5] However, their case does serve a useful purpose in acting as a benchmark with which to compare other examples.

Other subcultures, both within and outside the Netherlands, may have different ideological bases and perhaps different organizational techniques. Nevertheless, in their broad outlines the structures of many of the religious and ideological blocs in Western Europe are surprisingly similar. All tend to have trade unions (and other class-based organizations if the bloc cuts across class lines), youth movements, and other service organizations.[6] Furthermore, the manner in which the institutions of different blocs operate is not markedly dissimilar to that of the Dutch Catholic bloc. For example, Roth's study of the Social Democrats in Imperial Germany indicates that there was a strong tendency on the part of Social Democratic institutions, such as libraries and social welfare organizations, to provide services related almost entirely to the material and recreational needs of German workers.[7] These institutions did very little in the way of attempting direct ideological indoctrination. In contrast to the Dutch Catholic bloc, however, the German SDP had fewer direct sanctions available, other than group pressure, to strengthen their hold over the German working class. This probably helps to explain the failure of the SDP to increase its support significantly both before 1914 and later during the Weimar period.[8]

Thus comparison of less cohesive blocs with the Dutch Catholic bloc may help to explain why the former are less cohesive. The fact that subcultures do vary in their cohesiveness is very important and frequently neglected. This point becomes particularly acute in explaining the conditions underlying political change. Phillips Shively, for example, argues that in Weimar Germany, where high levels of party identification were lacking, it was possible for alternative political parties to compete successfully for the interests of specific blocs, and thereby displace parties which had previously represented these interests.[9] In the Netherlands, however, political change among Dutch Catholics occurred when the central institutions of the bloc changed. This resulted in a loosening of the grip of the church over its clientele. No other political party could successfully claim to represent the specifically Catholic interests of the Dutch Catholic subculture. Rather, other interests began to predominate over previous Catholic ones and a large proportion of the Catholic vote dispersed to a number of parties. Previous attempts to "raid" the Catholic vote had been unsuccessful because the subculture was sufficiently well organized to be able to control the voting behaviour of its members.

These considerations suggest that the subcultural blocs in Weimar Germany referred to by Shively lacked cohesion, and that they were in fact blocs consisting of aggregates of individuals with similar characteristics rather than well-organized subcultures. One need only look at the Catholic vote for the Centre party, which was designated by the German ecclesiastical hierarchy as the approved Catholic party. No more than 40 per cent of Catholics in Weimar Germany voted for this party,[10] considerably less than the support given by Catholics to the Dutch Catholic party in the period prior to 1967. Shively's statement that the choice for a Catholic in Weimar Germany was quite clear[11] thus appears to have been true for only a minority of the German Catholic population. The majority of Catholic votes in Weimar Germany went to Marxist and non-Marxist parties. It is quite probable, therefore, that like party identification, subcultural cohesion was not an important factor in Weimar Germany. Few blocs were sufficiently well organized. The interests and social location of many Germans were unclear, a fact which probably explains the tenuous links they had with political parties. The National Socialists successfully competed for the support of such voters, offering very general solutions to the economic and social malaise afflicting Germany during that era.

The major implication of the Shively argument is that electoral stability based upon the identification of people with subcultures is potentially highly unstable. Voters may move in massive swings to new political parties or movements. The case of the Dutch Catholic bloc and the Dutch Catholic party, however, demonstrates that where subcultures are well organized and cohesive, electoral behaviour is both stable and reliable. Furthermore, this type of electoral stability is highly resistant to efforts by other parties, particularly extremist ones like the National Socialist, to dislodge substantial numbers of voters locked into such a subculture. When change does occur it is likely due to large-scale changes within the subculture itself.

What implication does this have for the concept of party identification as used by Angus Campbell and others?[12] In the case of Dutch Catholics it was shown that party identification was unnecessary in providing a stable base for the Catholic party. The vote was determined, one can almost say over-determined, by the influence of the Catholic subculture. Thus, contrary to what is claimed by Dennis and McCrone, one can have party system stability without having a sense of identification with the parties "widely rooted in mass public consciousness."[13] It is possible, however, that when the protective boundaries of the subculture are removed or altered, political change will be much more rapid.

The Future. The Dutch party system is currently in flux. Large numbers of voters are basically adrift. Nevertheless certain patterns are discernible. Among ex-KVP voters there is a gradual movement towards the two major non-religious parties, the Labour Party (PvdA) and the Liberals (VVD). This movement appears to be animated by socio-economic differences. If we look at non-KVP/CDA voters only, it can be seen that in 1970 those of lower-class standing preferred the PvdA while middle and upper middle-class voters were more likely to prefer the VVD (see table 6.1). This trend continued in the 1977 election except that the situation was even more polarized along class lines than in 1970, much to the benefit of the PvdA.

In 1977 both the PvdA and the VVD improved their share of the total vote. Support for the smaller parties, with one exception (D'66), declined. It appears that the CDA succeeded in stemming the tide, receiving slightly more than the KVP, ARP, and CHU combined in 1972 (see table 1.1). Close to 50 per cent of Catholics voted CDA which compares favourably with the 38 per cent who voted KVP in 1972. The CDA also attracted 42 per cent of young Catholic voters entering the electorate, which contrasts with the 23 per cent support rate of the next youngest cohort, those twenty-three to thirty years of age who had been eligible to vote in the previous election. However, in comparison

TABLE 6.1
Vote by Self-Assigned Social Class for Non-KVP/CDA Voting
Catholics, 1970 and 1977

Vote	Lower Class		Middle and Upper Middle Class		Total	
	1970	1977	1970	1977	1970	1977
PvdA	27.2%	56.8%	12.8%	29.1%	19.7%	42.8%
VVD	7.9	7.5	29.6	35.9	19.2	21.8
D'66	20.2	6.6	31.2	14.1	25.9	10.5
Other*	20.2	5.0	10.4	7.5	15.1	6.3
Will not/ did not vote	24.6	25.0	16.0	11.6	20.1	18.5
Total %	100.0	100.0	100.0	100.0	100.0	100.0
N =	(114)	(120)	(125)	(118)	(239)	(238)

Source: 1970 Dutch Election Survey (provincial) (respondents were asked how they would vote if a national election were to be held); 1977 National Election Survey (respondents were asked how they voted in the election). The designation Catholic is self-assigned for both years.
*Including the CP, BP, PPR, etc.

with the other parties, the support base of the CDA as a whole is much older.[14] Working- and middle-class Catholics gave 49.7 and 48.2 per cent respectively of their votes to the CDA, indicating that the party, like the old KVP, still draws support from all classes within the Catholic community. However, it should be kept in mind that the ratio of Catholics to non-Catholics has decreased in recent years, many Catholics having left the church.[15]

What implications do these patterns have for the future? The development of widespread party allegiances to the CDA, PvdA, or VVD is a possibility. Catholics no longer receive cues or instructions from an authoritarian church. The world may appear to them to be considerably more ambiguous than formerly. Catholics may want to develop partisan loyalties in order to provide themselves with an element of order and stability. But these loyalties would have to develop over a series of successive elections and that would require that at each election the parties be perceived as a stable part of the political landscape and be distinguishable from one another.[16] Furthermore, the chosen party would have to take stands on political controversies which consistently coincide with the inclination of the voter. This would help to attract voters initially and in time reaffirm party loyalty.

There is a likelihood, however, that these conditions will not be met. The three major parties may not be perceived as distinct alternatives with the CDA occupying the political centre. Catholic voters may find it easy to switch from the PvdA to the CDA and back again in successive elections and therefore not develop a commitment to one party. Issues above and beyond socio-economic ones could arise which impel Catholics to leave a party for which they voted in a previous election. The abortion question, for example, is still a live issue in the Netherlands. Both the PvdA and VVD are in favour of liberal legislation; the CDA is more conservative.[17]

There is also the question of whether the CDA will indeed remain a permanent part of the political landscape. Between 1976 and 1980 the party was only a federation in which the KVP, ARP, and CHU maintained separate organizations, memberships, newspapers, headquarters, and the like. Several times during this period ARP leaders expressed dissatisfaction with the federation and the plans for a merger, and some even urged withdrawal of the ARP from the CDA. As a result the date for the merger was postponed a number of times. Only after some of the more recalcitrant members resigned from both the ARP and the CDA did the merger become a reality.[18] The disintegration of the CDA federation loomed as a distinct possibility between 1976 and 1980, which probably did not help in the development of strong CDA loyalties among voters. And even now, the merger of 1980 notwithstanding, the possibility remains that the Calvinists in the CDA may rebel and revive the ARP.

As part of the merger, procedures were devised to ensure that representation on the election list, executive council, and other party organs of the new CDA would continue to be based on the relative strengths of the KVP, ARP, and CHU as they stood just prior to the merger.[19] These arrangements were fixed for a four-year period beginning in 1980. Thus if a former KVP member resigns from the executive he or she will be replaced by another former KVP member. However, no one is sure what the subsequent arrangements will be, and long before the present agreement expires there will be considerable debate and conflict over its replacement.

An alternative possibility for Catholic voters is the development of loyalties to a *tendance* as it is referred to in France: that is, commitment to a group of parties representing a restricted range of ideological space.[20] The party system would be continuously in flux with several parties waxing and waning in rapid succession as they compete for the support of particular *tendances*. Parties would not be able to depend on an over-arching authority to ensure a stable support base but rather would face a situation similar to that of parties in Weimar Germany and the Third and Fourth French Republics. This was basically the situation which prevailed among Catholic voters in the period from 1967 to 1977 and which may well prevail again in the future.

Further scenarios involving the Catholic vote might see the resurgence of subcultural influences.[21] Some analysts have argued that in recent years, among socialists, Catholics, and Protestants, there have been efforts at "repillarization," attempts to bring back at least some of the elements of the past. Within the Catholic community Cardinal Willebrands, who succeeded Cardinal Alfrink in 1976, has tried to follow a somewhat more conservative course while at the same time accepting the changes of the 1960s and the ethos of collegiality. In 1970 Adrien Simonis, a conservative, was appointed bishop of Rotterdam. But he too has adapted himself to the changes in the Dutch church and has cooperated with his fellow bishops. In contrast, Johannes Gijsen, bishop of Roermond since 1972, finds that the tenor of the Dutch church is still too progressive. As a result he has boycotted meetings of the bishops' conference and has attempted to block many of its initiatives; its decisions frequently do not carry his signature. In the late 1970s the ambivalent attitude of Cardinal Willebrands and the other bishops towards Gijsen, and the public feuds between Gijsen and his own clergy, resulted in a leadership vacuum.

Both before and during the changes of the 1960s the hallmark of the Catholic subculture was the strong direction given by the bishops and their unified approach to political, social, and theological problems. By the mid-1970s this was no longer the case. In the fall of 1979 Pope John Paul II called a special synod in Rome of the Dutch bishops to discuss the problems of discord and church orthodoxy. The synod, held in January 1980 and lasting three weeks, resulted in an agreement signed by the pope and all seven bishops in which they jointly affirmed their belief in the hierarchical nature of the church. The bishops agreed to present to Dutch Catholics the official teachings of the church as determined by the Roman authorities and to make decisions collectively. They also agreed that the liturgy be celebrated "according to the official texts"; that Dutch Catholics be required to attend mass at least once a week and on all church holidays; that the practice of personal confession be reinstituted; and that new texts be prepared for the Dutch catechism. In essence the special synod rejected virtually all the common practices of the Dutch church of the preceding fifteen years. It marked a return to the authoritarian church of old.[22]

Its effect, however, will not necessarily result in greater orthodoxy among Dutch Catholics. In fact, rather than setting the Dutch church on a conservative bearing, the synod has prevented it from taking any bearing whatsoever. By April 1980 most of the officials in the secretariat of the Dutch church province, including the secretary-general, had resigned.[23] By early 1981 no new guidelines had been issued. Even aside from the lack of an effective secretariat, the implementation of new conservative guidelines would be difficult given the decentralized nature of the church, the consequence of several years of democratization. The priests themselves would be highly resistant to the reassertion of strict guidelines since they were probably the group most appreciative of the changes stemming from Vatican II and the Pastoral Council; more than any other group of Catholics, they were unhappy with the rigid practices and restrictions of the church of old.

The conservative lay group, "Confrontation," hailed the results of the synod as a victory for Church orthodoxy.[24] However, the group itself, given the limited circulation of its newspaper and its small membership, is evidence that the new orthodoxy will not find a wide market in the Netherlands. Should serious attempts be made to enforce orthodoxy the result might be, at best, a church with far fewer adherents than at present, or, at worst, a split within the Dutch church as a result of which a large group of Catholics would no longer pay homage to Rome. Whatever the future actions of the bishops, it is unlikely that they will result in the resurgence of a large cohesive subculture, whose members can be mobilized behind a single political party.

Ironically the lack of unity and leadership within the Dutch church has probably benefited the CDA by allowing it independence and an opportunity to fill at least in part the leadership vacuum. The former chairman, Piet Steenkamp, was once regarded as a relatively unimportant figure within the KVP. However, he played an active role in the Pastoral Council, and since 1973, when he was charged with the responsibility of bringing the CDA to fruition, he has successfully exploited his participation in the church renewal movement and the spirit of ecumenicalism generally to win support for the CDA both within and outside the three confessional parties. At present many of the important office-holders in the CDA are Catholic, notably the prime minister, Andries van Agt, and the leader of the parliamentary party, Ruud Lubbers. As the authority of the church recedes, Catholic political leaders, more than ever before, are in a position to have a powerful influence on Dutch political life.

Whatever the course of events, they are likely to be shaped to a considerable extent by the actions of elites. In the past, leaders of the Catholic party, in conjunction with church authorities, successfully used the religious cleavage in the Netherlands to gain influence. The future configuration of Dutch politics as a whole, and more particularly the fate of the CDA, will depend in large measure on the entrepreneurship of Catholic leaders and their Protestant brethren in exploiting sources of political cleavage to their own advantage.

Appendix I

Interview Procedures

A major source of data for this study is interviews with fifty-one individuals closely connected with the Dutch Catholic subculture. The sample consisted of members of the Catholic party (KVP) executive and parliamentary caucus, members of certain other parties, priests, and executive officers of the main Catholic socio-economic organizations. The actual breakdown of the sample is as follows: fifteen were priests, two were journalists, and six were members of parties other than the KVP. The remainder were members of the KVP and/or Catholic socio-economic organizations. There was considerable overlap between membership in the KVP and in the organizations. Seventeen of the twenty-one people who were active in the party were at some point employed by or involved in the organizations. Connections with these organizations were for the most part actively maintained by KVP members while sitting in the Second Chamber, on the executive, or acting as party organizers. Five individuals occupying executive positions in Catholic socio-economic organizations had no formal connections with the KVP, but tended to have considerable contact with those actively involved in the party.

Of the six persons in the other parties, two were from the Labour party (PVDA), two from the Party of Political Radicals (PPR) and two from the Anti-Revolutionary Party (ARP). All but those from the ARP were Catholic. Three of the four people in the PVDA and the PPR had been active in the KVP prior to changing their party affiliation. Thus a total of twenty-five individuals in the sample were or had been actively involved in the affairs of the KVP during the postwar period.

Given the limited number of individuals interviewed it cannot be said that the sample is totally representative of the Catholic pillar as a whole. Nevertheless, an effort was made to ensure some sort of balanced distribution. The priests interviewed were resident in different parts of the country: in the rural east, in the south, and in the rural and urbanized areas of the west. In the case of each of the major Catholic socio-economic organizations or sectors, for example, the Catholic trade union federation (NKV), the broadcasting organization (KRO), the self-employed middle class (KNOB), the employers (NCW), and the farmers (KNBTV), a minimum of two individuals were interviewed and in most cases at least three or four.

The interviews had two main goals. The first was to find out what went on inside the Catholic subculture, to gain information about the structure and activities of organizations, about the role of the church, about specific events. The second was to inquire into the values and beliefs of individuals; for example, why priests believed in the importance of insulating Catholics from non-Catholics. The interviews themselves were semi-structured. Certain questions were asked of all individuals concerning the influence of the church, actual instances of church control or intervention, their reaction to events like the *Mandement* of 1954, and their reaction to the changes in Catholicism during the 1960s.

In addition, there were questions for particular groups and specific individuals. Priests were asked what means were used to control the behaviour of parishioners and in what ways the bishops exercised their authority. Catholic party leaders were asked how they mobilized the vote, what relations were like between the party and the socio-economic organizations, and about the impact of the decline in the KVP vote on the party during the 1960s.

The length of interviews varied from forty minutes to well over six hours. Eight of the sample were interviewed more than once and one individual four times. The interviews are identified by numbers in the text. The same number has been used when referring to subsequent interviews with the same individual. Notes were taken by hand during the interview. Immediately afterwards additional time was taken to record as many impressions and details of the interview as possible. If there were gaps or points which were ambiguous, the interviewee would often be asked for clarification later by telephone or in a subsequent interview. The use of a tape recorder was rejected because it was felt that it might make subjects more guarded in their responses or lead to outright refusal on the part of certain subjects. Some individuals specifically asked for anonymity and all were told their names would not appear in the study. All information was double-checked with other individuals and with published sources. Forty-six of the interviews were carried out during a nine-month period in 1976; five were interviewed again in the spring of 1980; five additional individuals were also interviewed during the latter period.

Appendix II

Aggregate Data and the Catholic Vote

In examining the stability and decline of the Catholic vote for the Catholic party (KVP) during the period 1946–72, I have depended mainly on aggregate data. The election data were originally collected by Joseph Houska of the University of California (Berkeley). The data consist of election returns aggregated to the municipal district level, covering all Dutch national elections from 1946 to 1972.[1] These data were combined with ecological data, again aggregated to the municipal district level. The ecological data were collected by researchers at the Department of Political Science, University of Leiden, under the supervision of H. Daalder and J. Verhoef. The ecological data, based on census data and data collected by municipal registry offices, concern variables such as degree of industrialization and urbanization, proportion of Catholics, birth rate, and so on. Data for these variables are available at different time points, for some variables as far back as 1889, enabling the researcher to take into account changes over time in the socio-economic structure of municipalities.

There are over 900 municipal districts (the actual number varies from year to year as new municipalities are created and others disappear or become amalgamated in larger units). This results in a reasonably large sample with a high degree of differentiation between units and relative homogeneity within units. In analysing the data the assumption was made that only Catholics vote for the KVP, an assumption borne out by survey data.[2] This helps considerably to minimize some of the problems usually associated with analysis of aggregate data.[3]

Figures 3.1, 5.1, 5.2, 5.3, and 5.4 are based on the total registered vote in each municipal district multiplied by the percentage of Catholics in the district. Registered voters rather than actual vote turnout was used since for some election years the latter was not available. Thus to ensure consistency the registered voters' variable was used for all election years. This has the effect of systematically underestimating the actual percentage of Catholics who voted KVP since not all registered voters turned up at the polling booth at election time (e.g., some non-voters were actually deceased but still on the registration list). According to W. J. Kusters, in 1959 85.9 per cent and in 1963 84.8 per cent of all Catholics voted KVP.[4] In my analysis the use of the registered voters' variable results in figures of 82.8 per cent and 81.6 per cent for 1959 and 1963 respectively, a difference of approximately 3 per cent compared with the figures computed by Kusters.

The registered Catholic vote figures used in this study were multiplied by a correction factor to take into account the difference in age structure between the Catholic population and the rest of the population. Fewer Catholics are of voting age compared with non-Catholics. For example, in 1947 Catholics constituted 38.5 per cent of the entire population but only 35.5 per cent of those of voting age. Thus for the elections of 1946, 1948, and 1952 a correction figure of .922 was used (based on the 1947 census). For the elections of 1956, 1959, and 1963 the factor used was .932 (1960 census) and for 1967, 1971, and 1972 the factor used was .982 (1971 census).

Notes

CHAPTER ONE
1. Jean Laponce notes: "The Catholics of the Netherlands merit some attention. They are unique, in the states of Western Europe, in having a party with a religious basis which attracts all the votes of the members of that religion. . . . Because the proportion of Catholics to the total population is 35 percent, the ratio of communal support is close to 90 percent. This indicates a political cohesion comparable to that of the more unified racial groups. No other Catholic party in Europe offers a similar example." Jean Laponce, *The Protection of Minorities*, p. 139.
2. Arend Lijphart, *The Politics of Accommodation: Pluralism and Democracy in the Netherlands*.
3. Before 1918 a different electoral system based on districts and run-off elections provided a different set of incentives for electoral mobilization. Thus in the north and west where Catholics were in a minority, Catholics threw their support first behind the Liberals and later the Anti-Revolutionaries (Calvinists). This still indicates a high degree of control on the part of the clergy and Catholic political organizations. See Hans Daalder, "The Netherlands: Opposition in a Segmented Society," in *Political Oppositions in Western Democracies*, ed. Robert A. Dahl, p. 204; Jan Verhoef, "Kiesstelsels en politieke samenwerking in Nederland, 1888–1917," *Acta Politica* 6, no. 3 (July 1971): 261–68.
4. Laponce, *Protection of Minorities*, p. 139.
5. In the case of Italy, Hazelrigg notes that less than half the population could be called either moderate or strict Catholic. Lawrence Hazelrigg, "Religious and Class Bases of Political Conflict in Italy," *American Journal of Sociology* 75, no. 4, pt. I (January 1970): 502.
6. Ibid.; Steven B. Wolinetz, "Party Re-alignment in the Netherlands" (Ph.D. diss., Yale University, 1973), p. 97. It is worth noting that 89 per cent of Dutch Catholics fell into the "regular mass attendance" category in 1956. In France in 1966 only 66 per cent of regularly practising French Catholics supported Catholic-oriented Centrist and Gaullist parties (20

per cent of the sample). See Guy Michelat and Michel Simon, "Religion, Class, and Politics," *Comparative Politics* 10, no. 1 (October 1977): 169.
7. *Annuaire Statique de la Suisse 1965*, p. 41.
8. Ibid.
9. R. Morsey, *Die Deutsche Zentrumspartei, 1917–1923*, pp. 11–25.
10. Tom Mackie and Richard Rose, *The International Almanac of Electoral History*, p. 157.
11. Laponce, *Protection of Minorities*, pp. 154–55.
12. Paul Lazarsfeld et al., *The People's Choice*.
13. Angus Campbell et al., *The American Voter*.
14. Jack Dennis and Donald J. McCrone, "Pre-Adult Development of Political Party Identification in Western Democracies," *Comparative Political Studies* 3, no. 2 (July 1970): p. 247; see also Philip Converse, "Of Time and Partisan Stability," *Comparative Political Studies* 2, no. 2 (July 1969): 141–42.
15. David Butler and Donald Stokes, *Political Change in Britain: Forces Shaping Electoral Choice*. For a critique of their approach, see Ivor Crewe, "Do Butler and Stokes Really Explain Political Change in Britain?" *European Journal of Political Research* 2, no. 1 (March 1974): 47–92.
16. Butler and Stokes, *Political Change in Britain*, p. 17.
17. Ibid., p. 18.
18. Ed van Thijn, "Kritische kanttekeningen bij een trek naar rechts," *Sociologische Gids* 10, no. 3 (1963): 239; Wolinetz, "Party Re-alignment," pp. 85, 111. Wolinetz states that both "party and subcultural identifications were strong factors in the Netherlands" (p. 111, n. 1). Wolinetz may be referring to different subpopulations, some having strong party identifications, others subcultural identifications. I would argue, however, that at the individual level it is not possible to have both. Furthermore, if party identification is seen as a function of subcultural identification then this would considerably reduce the status of the former as an independent variable. At best it can only be seen as an intervening variable. For further discussion of the problem, see David Robertson, "Surrogates for Party Identification in the Rational Choice Framework," in *Party Identification and Beyond*, ed. Ian Budge et al., pp. 365–82; K. MacCorquodale and P. Meehl, "On a Distinction between Hypothetical Constructs and Intervening Variables," *Psychological Review* 55, no. 1 (March 1948): 95–107.
19. The survey on which this table is based was carried out shortly before the provincial elections in the spring of 1970. A stratified random sample was used resulting in a final sample of 1,838 cases. Principal investigators were Ph. Stouthard, F. Heunks, W. Miller, and J. Rusk. The data set was made available through the Inter-university Consortium for Political Research (ICPR), Ann Arbor, Mich.
20. Wolinetz, "Party Re-alignment," p. 90.
21. A. Campbell and H. Valen, "Party Identification in Norway and the U.S.," *Public Opinion Quarterly* 25, no. 1 (March 1961): 57.
22. W. P. Shively, "Party Identification, Party Choice, and Voting Stability: The Weimar Case," *American Political Science Review* 66, no. 4 (December 1972): 1203–25.
23. Ibid., p. 1214.

Notes to pages 9-12 | 193

24. Ibid., p. 1222.
25. I am using the term pillar in the sense that Lijphart and Rogowski use it. According to Rogowski, "In any highly stratified society, a faction that contains members of every stratum in rough proportion to their respective fractions of the total population of the society will be called a pillar." Ronald Rogowski, *Rational Legitimacy: A Theory of Political Support*, p. 102; see also Lijphart, *The Politics of Accommodation*, pp. 16 ff.
26. A new party which appeared in 1972, called the "Roman Catholic Party of the Netherlands" (RKPN), received only .9 per cent of the total vote. Another new party, the "Party of Political Radicals" (PPR), contains a number of ex-KVP members as well as former members of the Anti-Revolutionary Party. It has attracted some of the Catholic vote but it has not done so on an explicitly religious basis.
27. For an overview of this theme concerning the Netherlands as well as other countries, see Val R. Lorwin, "Segmented Pluralism: Ideological Cleavages and Political Cohesion in the Smaller European Democracies," *Comparative Politics* 3, no. 2 (January 1971): 163 ff.

CHAPTER TWO

1. S. M. Lipset and Stein Rokkan, eds., *Party Systems and Voter Alignments: Cross-National Perspectives*; Val R. Lorwin, "Segmented Pluralism: Ideological Cleavages and Political Cohesion in the Smaller European Democracies," *Comparative Politics* 3, no. 2 (Jan. 1971): 153 ff.; Richard Rose and Derek Urwin, "Social Cohesion, Political Parties and Strains in Regimes," *Comparative Political Studies* 2, no. 1 (April 1969), pp. 7-67.
2. G. Dekker, *Het kerkelijk gemengde huwelijk in Nederland*, p. 99.
3. Centraal Bureau voor de Statistiek (CBS), *Vrije-tijdsbesteding in Nederland winter 1955/56*, Deel 9, pp. 19, 21; Katholiek Sociaal-Kerkelijk Instituut (KASKI), "De pastorale funktie van het katholiek verenigingsleven. Een godsdienst-sociologisch onderzoek in een middelgrote stad van N.O. Nederland," Report No. 227, 1959, p. 47.
4. Guenther Roth, *The Social Democrats in Imperial Germany: A Study in Working-Class Isolation and National Integration*.
5. J. S. Furnivall, *Netherlands India: A Study of Plural Economy*; M. G. Smith, *The Plural Society in the British West Indies*.
6. Lorwin, "Segmented Pluralism," p. 143.
7. Richard Hoggart, *The Uses of Literacy: Aspects of working-class life with special reference to publications and entertainments*; Richard F. Hamilton, *Affluence and the French Worker in the Fourth Republic*, pp. 3 ff. See also Frank Parkin, *Class Inequality and Political Order*, pp. 79-102; E. Popitz et al., *Das Gesellschaftsbild des Arbeiters*.
8. W. P. Shively, "Party Identification, Party Choice, and Voting Stability: The Weimar Case," *American Political Science Review* 66, no. 4 (December 1972): 1220-23.
9. Kenneth D. McRae has also taken this approach, although I think he errs in seeing linguistic and racial cleavages as being similar in nature to religious and ideological cleavages. See K. D. McRae, ed., *Consociational Democracy: Political Accommodation in Segmented Societies*, p. 26. My approach is what Przeworski and Teune would call a "Most Different Systems" design. Adam Przeworski and Henry Teune, *The Logic of Com-

parative Social Inquiry, pp. 34–39. For a discussion of the difference between religiously and racially based blocs, see Ronald Rogowski, *Rational Legitimacy: A Theory of Political Support*, esp. p. 100.
10. Alvin Rabushka and Kenneth A. Shepsle, *Politics in Plural Societies: A Theory of Democratic Instability*, pp. 12–21; J. S. Furnivall, passim; M. G. Smith, passim.
11. Netherlands Central Bureau of Statistics (CBS), *Historical Statistics of the Netherlands, 1899–1974*, p. 37.
12. CBS, *Statistiek zakboek 1974*, p. 57.
13. See, for example, Gordon Weil, *The Benelux Nations: The Politics of Small-Country Democracies*, p. 60. Unfortunately Weil does not cite the source of his information.
14. For a critique of the literature on race in the Netherlands, see J. P. Kruijt, *De onkerkelikheid in Nederland: Haar verbreiding en oorzaken; proeve ener sociografiese verklaring*, esp. pp. 311–23.
15. Johan Goudsblom, *Dutch Society*, p. 59.
16. Ibid., p. 60.
17. I. Schöffer, "De Nederlands confessionele partijen 1918–1939," in *De confessionelen*, ed. L. Scholten et al., pp. 53–54.
18. I. Gadourek, *A Dutch Community: Social and Cultural Structure and Process in a Bulb-growing Region in the Netherlands*.
19. Hoggart, *Uses of Literary*.
20. Michel van der Plas, *Uit het rijke Roomsche leven: Een documentaire over de jaren 1925–1935*.
21. Harry Scholten, *Aspecten van het tijdschrift De Gemeenschap*.
22. For example, many Catholic families subscribed to a magazine written in Italian, emanating from Rome. It is highly unlikely that the majority of Dutch Catholics were conversant with the Italian language in the interwar period. See Van der Plas, *Uit het rijke Roomsche leven*, p. 11.
23. Ibid., p. 20.
24. Gadourek, *A Dutch Community*, pp. 220–21.
25. CBS, *Vrije-tijdsbesteding in Nederland winter 1955–56*, p. 20.
26. Gadourek, *A Dutch Community*, p. 221.
27. R. A. Knox, *The Belief of Catholics*; N. van Doornik, *Het Katholiek geloof in hedendaagse gestalte*, p. 190.
28. M. Williams, *The Catholic Church in Action*, pp. 3, 59.
29. J. Poeisz, "God's People on the Way," in *Those Dutch Catholics*, ed. Michel van der Plas and Henk Suèr, p. 89.
30. Franz Schurmann, *Ideology and Organization in Communist China*, p. 18.
31. Ibid., pp. 23 ff.
32. J. Ellemers, "The Revolt of the Netherlands: The Part Played by Religion in the Process of Nation-Building," *Social Compass* 14, no. 2 (1967): 96.
33. Ibid., p. 99.
34. J. A. de Kok, *Nederland op de breuklijn Rome-Reformatie*, p. 69.
35. R. Fruin, "De wederopluiking van het Katholicisme in Noord-Nederland, omstreeks den aanvang der XVIIe Eeuw," cited in Ellemers, "The Revolt of the Netherlands," p. 103.
36. L. J. Rogier, *Geschiedenis van het Katholicisme in Noord-Nederland in 16^e en 17^e eeuw*, 4:749–66.

37. P. Geyl, "De Protestantisering van Noord-Nederland," in *Vaderlands verleden in veelhoud*, ed. G. Beekelaar, pp. 209–21.
38. J. M. G. Thurlings, *De wankele zuil: Nederlandse Katholieken tussen assimilatie en pluralisme*, p. 56.
39. Ibid., p. 64.
40. Ibid., p. 77.
41. Rogier, *Geschiedenis van het Katholicisme*, 4:703.
42. Ibid., pp. 733 ff.
43. H. Laan, *De Rooms-Katholieke kerkorganisatie in Nederland: Sociologisch structuur analyse van het bisschoppelijk bestuur*, p. 91. Currently this sect has only about 10,000 adherents.
44. Rogier, *Geschiedenis van het Katholicisme*, 4:747.
45. Thurlings, *De wankele zuil*, p. 64.
46. J. P. Gribling, *P. J. M. Aalberse, 1871–1948*, p. 96.
47. *De Katholiek in het openbare leven van deze tijd. Bisschoplijk mandement van 1954*.
48. Thurlings, *De wankele zuil*, p. 73.
49. Cited in ibid., p. 24.
50. Ibid., p. 25.
51. L. J. Rogier, *Het verschijnsel der culturele inertie bij de Nederlandse Katholieken*.
52. Thurlings, *De wankele zuil*, p. 27.
53. Ibid., p. 91.
54. It was actually only a limited form of responsible government. Full accountability of cabinet to parliament rather than to the monarch was not fully established until after a protracted struggle with the king in 1866–68. See P. J. Oud, *Honderd jaren: Een eeuw van staatkundige vormgeving in Nederland*, pp. 73–85.
55. L. J. Rogier and N. de Rooy, *In vrijheid herboren: Katholiek Nederland, 1853–1953*, pp. 34–73.
56. J. de Jong, *Politieke organisatie na 1800 in West Europa* (The Hague: Nijhoff, 1951), p. 331; Arend Lijphart, *The Politics of Accommodation: Pluralism and Democracy in the Netherlands*, pp. 111–12.
57. Rogier and De Rooy, *In vrijheid herboren*, p. 623.
58. C. Ruygers, "De Katholiek in de PvdA," *Socialism en Democratie* 11, no. 4 (1954): 427.
59. Rogier, *Geschiedenis van het Katholicisme in Noord-Nederland*, 4:703.
60. F. van Heek, *Het geboorte-niveau der Nederlandse Rooms-Katholieken*, p. 126.
61. Ibid., pp. 125–28.
62. Thurlings, "The Case of Dutch Catholicism," *Sociologica Neerlandica* 7, no. 1 (Spring 1971): 136. For a description of the generally Calvinistic character of the Dutch population as a whole in the sixteenth and seventeenth centuries, see Rogier, *Geschiedenis van het Katholicisme in Noord-Nederland*, 5:1072 ff; for a discussion of the Dutch national character and its relationship to Calvinism in the twentieth century, see A. Chorus, *De Nederlander innerlijk en uiterlijk: Een characteristiek*.
63. Cited in Van Heek, *Het geboorte-niveau*, p. 169.
64. Ibid., p. 131.
65. De Jong, *Politieke organisatie*, p. 320; Hans Daalder, "The Netherlands:

Opposition in a Segmented Society," in *Political Oppositions in Western Democracies*, ed. Robert A. Dahl, pp. 200–201.
66. Laan, *De Rooms-Katholieke kerkorganisatie in Nederland*, p. 31.
67. Ibid., p. 155.
68. John P. Windmuller, *Labor Relations in the Netherlands*, p. 36.
69. Ibid.
70. See, for example, *Statuten van de Katholiek radio omroep*, pp. 18–20.
71. Laan, *De Rooms-Katholieke kerkorganisatie in Nederland*, p. 188.
72. Van Heek, *Het geboorte-niveau*, p. 164.
73. W. Goddijn, *De beheerste kerk*, p. 102.
74. Daalder, "The Netherlands," p. 208, n. 43.
75. Windmuller, *Labor Relations in the Netherlands*, p. 23.
76. Rogier and De Rooy, *In vrijheid herboren*, p. 469.
77. Ibid.
78. Laan, *De Rooms-Katholieke kerkorganisatie in Nederland*, p. 190.
79. S. Stokman, *Het verzet van de Nederlandse bisschoppen tegen Nationaal-Socialisme*, p. 23.
80. S. Vellenga, *Katholiek Zuid-Limburg en het fascisme*, p. 41.
81. Ibid., p. 27.
82. A. F. Manning, "De Nederlandse Katholieken in de eerste jaren van de Duitse bezetting," *Jaarboek van het Katholiek Documentatie Centrum* 8 (1978): 108–9.
83. Stokman, *Het verzet van de Nederlandse bisschoppen*, p. 40.
84. A. F. Manning, "Geen doorbraak van de oude structuren," in *De confessionelen*, ed. Scholten, p. 72.
85. Jean Beaufays, *Les partis Catholiques en Belgique et aux Pays-Bas, 1918–1958*, p. 410.
86. Ibid.
87. KASKI, "Enige aspekten van de religieuze en sociale achtergrond van het mandement van de nederlandse bisschoppen betreffende de katholiek in het openbare leven van deze tijd," Memorandum No. 7, 1954. This document presented evidence on the under-representation of Catholics in higher strata with particular reference to the civil service.
88. D. de Lange, "Dutch Catholicism," *Delta* 9, no. 4 (Winter 1966): 22.
89. *Bisschoplijk mandement van 1954*, pp. 38–46.
90. A. F. Manning, "Uit de voorgeschiedenis van het mandement van 1954," *Jaarboek van het Katholiek Documentatie Centrum* 1 (1971): 140–42.
91. KASKI, Report No. 227, p. 47.
92. Thurlings, "The Case of Dutch Catholicism," p. 132.
93. Van Heek, *Het geboorte-niveau*, p. 167.
94. KASKI, "Het beeld van en de waardering voor het geestelijk beroep; probleem-stelling voor een sociologisch onderzoek naar het roepingenvraagstuk in Nederland," Memorandum No. 155, 1964, pp. 35–36.
95. Ibid., p. 37.
96. Van der Plas, *Uit het rijke Roomsche leven*, pp. 40–59.
97. Mancur Olson, *The Logic of Collective Action: Public Goods and the Theory of Groups*.
98. One pastor had a parishioner with a chip on his shoulder who supported the Catholic caucus in the PVDA and liked to argue with the pastor. This was an exceptional case. "If people really disagreed with the church they just left. You never heard from them again" (Interview 23).

99. The document, *Codex-Juris Canonici*, contains the official canon law of the church and was handed down by the Pope in 1918. In 1924 the Dutch church province revised all its statutes to ensure that all rules and regulations were consistent with the provisions of the *Codex* of 1918. Among other things the detailed *Codex* of 1924 spelled out the colour of shoes to be worn by priests and the type of bicycle to be used. Attendance at a play or film required the permission of the priest's bishop. This latter regulation was changed in 1949 but the document remained essentially the same until 1965. See Laan, *De Rooms-Katholieke kerkorganisatie in Nederland*, pp. 52–53, 174–81.
100. KASKI, "Rapport over de priesterroepingen van sekulieren en regulieren in Nederland," Report No. 72 (n.d.), p. 1.
101. W. Goddijn, *De beheerste kerk*, p. 102.
102. Ibid.
103. KASKI, "Memorandum betreffende de priesterroepingen uit de boerenstand in het gebied van de noordbrabantse christelijke boerenbond," Memorandum No. 67, 1958; J. Poeisz, "Determinants sociaux des inscriptions dans les seminaires et des ordinations de nouveaux prêtres aux Pays-Bas," *Social Compass* 10, no. 4 (1963): 508.
104. KASKI, Report No. 72, p. 8.
105. Rogier and De Rooy, *In vrijheid herboren*, p. 464.
106. A. Querido, *De wit-gele vlam: Gedenkboek ter gelegenheid van het 50-jarig bestaan van de Nationale Federatie het Wit-Gele Kruis 1923–1973*, p. 80.
107. Rogier and De Rooy, *In vrijheid herboren*, pp. 460–63.
108. J. P. Gribling, *P.J.M. Aalberse*, pp. 47, 85. It is difficult to classify ideologically these lay Catholics and clergy concerned with the "social question." Some, like Aalberse, were definitely in favour of insulating Catholics from the rest of Dutch society as well as helping them in a material sense and thus they can be said to have been under the influence of the isolationist ideology. Others, more concerned with social welfare than isolation, can be broadly defined as emancipationist in outlook as well as activated by an acute sense of social justice. All, however, took the provisions of *Rerum Novarum* extremely seriously and the literalness with which they interpreted these provisions can be said to be in part a function of the Dutch Calvinist spirit.
109. Ibid., p. 86.
110. Windmuller, *Labor Relations in the Netherlands*, pp. 28–29.
111. Van Heek, *Het geboorte-niveau*, p. 135. For a detailed description of the life and work of Father Poels, see J. P. Colsen, *Poels*.
112. R. Dieteren, *De migratie in de mijnstreek 1900–1935*, p. 34.
113. Ibid., p. 37.
114. Van Heek, *Het geboorte-niveau*, p. 135.
115. Dieteren, *De migratie in de mijnstreek*, p. 24.
116. Windmuller, *Labor Relations in the Netherlands*, p. 70; Rogier and De Rooy, *In vrijheid herboren*, p. 624.
117. Interview with an official of the Catholic Retailers' Organization (Interview 37).
118. William Petersen, "Fertility trends and population policy: Some comments on the Van Heek-Hofstee debate," *Sociologica Neerlandica* 3, no. 1 (1967): 2–16.
119. Catholic Action was first organized by Pope Pius XI in 1922 (Papal en-

cyclical *Urbi Arcano*) in order to give the laity some role in apostolic work as well as to alleviate the widespread problem of a shortage of priests. In the Netherlands there really was no shortage of priests. Furthermore, since the Dutch church was much stricter in its interpretation of the rules and regulations of the church it could see no clear role for Catholic Action. As a result this organization performed mainly technical tasks such as setting up chairs at church functions, etc. See Rogier and De Rooy, *In vrijheid herboren*, pp. 832–36.
120. Windmuller, *Labor Relations in the Netherlands*, pp. 135–38.
121. Ibid., p. 125.
122. In the village of Sassenheim, for example, Catholic and Protestant organizations kept strictly to their own kind in looking for clientele. Gadourek, *A Dutch Community*, pp. 195–214, 238–71.
123. Thurlings, "The case of Dutch Catholicism," p. 133.
124. Rogier and De Rooy, *In vrijheid herboren*, p. 624.
125. Windmuller, *Labor Relations in the Netherlands*, pp. 69–71; Michael P. Fogarty, *Christian Democracy in Western Europe*, pp. 59–63; Rogier and De Rooy, *In vrijheid herboren*, p. 627; J. Veraart, *Beginselen der publiekrechtelijke bedrijfsorganisatie*; W. Rip, *Landbouw en publiekrechtelijke bedrijfsorganisatie*.
126. Windmuller, *Labor Relations in the Netherlands*, p. 137, n. 8.
127. Interview with an official of the Christian Employers' Federation, 1976 (Interview 3).
128. Windmuller, *Labor Relations in the Netherlands*, p. 117.
129. R. Singh, *Policy Development: A Study of the Social and Economic Council of the Netherlands*, p. 120.
130. The name of the coordinating committee is "Stichting Katholiek Maatschappelijk Beraad." See *Pius Almanak: Adresboek Katholiek Nederland 1971*.
131. *Statuten van de Katholieke radio omroep*, pp. 18–20; *Omroep ABC*, p. 58.
132. *Pius Almanak 1971*, pp. 265, 352.
133. Ibid., passim.
134. Joel Mokyr, *Industrialization in the Low Countries, 1795–1850*, pp. 83–102.
135. See Peter Hall, "A Polycentric Metropolis: Randstad Holland," *Delta* 10, nos. 1 and 2 (Spring/Summer 1967): 5–32.
136. William Petersen, *Planned Migration: The Social Determinants of the Dutch-Canadian Movement*, p. 20.
137. I. J. Brugmans, "Koning Willem I als neo-mercantilist," cited in Petersen, *Planned Migration*, p. 59.
138. H. Hoefnagels, *Een eeuw sociale problematiek: De Nederlandse sociale ontwikkeling van 1850 tot 1940*, p. 10.
139. Ibid., p. 7.
140. Ibid., p. 11.
141. Ibid., p. 71.
142. L. G. Verberne, *De Nederlandse arbeidersbeweging in de 19^e eeuw*, p. 179.
143. CBS, *De ontwikkeling van het onderwijs in Nederland* Deel I, pp. 306–7; M.M.J. van Hemert, *Kerkelijke gezindten*, pp. 58–69.
144. M. Matthijsen, *Katholiek middelbaar onderwijs en intellectuele emancipatie*, p. 42.
145. CBS, *De ontwikkeling van het onderwijs in Nederland*, p. 148.
146. Thurlings, *De wankele zuil*, p. 62.

147. A. E. Diels, "Opvattingen van ondertrouwde vrouwen omtrent de grootte van haar toekomstig gezin," cited in Van Heek, *Het geboorteniveau*, p. 171.
148. Ibid., pp. 172-73.
149. Conversely, if socialist, neutral, or Protestant organizations were lacking in a given area, Catholic organizations would also frequently be lacking. Particularly in the north Catholic organizations were more likely to develop if there was competition. For treatment of this theme, see Frans van Waarden, "Corporatisme als probleemoplossing," in *Corporatisme in Nederland: Belangengroepen en democratie*, ed. H. J. G. Verhallen et al., esp pp. 49-50.
150. Th. Wöltgens, "Mislukte doorbraak: Geschiedenis van de socialistische mijnwerkersbond 1909-1965," M.A. thesis, Volkshogeschool Valkenburg, 1966, p. 13.
151. Petersen, *Planned Migration*, p. 183.
152. Thurlings, *De wankele zuil*, pp. 25-26.
153. KASKI, "Godsdienstig-sociale aspekten van de industrielisatie in Nederland," Report No. 85, 1952.
154. J. van Tulder, *Sociale stijging en daling in Nederland*, 3:219.
155. A. Chorus, *De Nederlander*, p. 79.
156. KASKI did not begin gathering mass attendance data until 1965 when it became evident that attendance was beginning to decline. Some individual parishes and deaneries collected data, but their means of measuring mass attendance varied considerably, making the data unreliable.
157. KASKI, "Katholicisme in West-Europa en de wereldkerk," Memorandum No. 113, 1960, pp. 21-22.
158. Cited in Van Heek, *Het geboorte-niveau*, p. 167. There are further examples. The mineworkers had received dispensation from the bishops in 1906 concerning the "Catholics only" rule, but in 1918 they were asked to become members of "Catholics only" unions. They duly complied. During the 1930s most Dutch Catholics who had joined the National Socialist League (NSB) did give up their membership when asked to do so by the church. Thus in the vast majority of cases the edicts of the bishops met with a positive response. Windmuller, *Labor Relations in the Netherlands*, referring specifically to the Unitas case, notes: "It is indicative of the relationship between Catholic workers and the Church, indeed of the entire relationship between Dutch Catholics in general and their Church, that in this and similar issues the ultimate decisions were made by the highest dignitaries of the Church and were obediently accepted by the faithful" (p. 23). In the case of Catholics and the NSB, see Stokman, *Het verzet van de Nederlandse bisschoppen*, passim; Velenga, *Katholiek Zuid-Limburg*, passim.

CHAPTER THREE
1. According to Maurice Duverger, Catholic parties tend to be disciplined and centralized. M. Duverger, *Political Parties: Their Organization and Activity in the Modern State*, pp. 58-59.
2. J. de Jong, *Politieke organisatie na 1800 in West Europa*, p. 279.
3. Hans Daalder, "Extreme Proportional Representation—the Dutch Experience," in *Adversary Politics and Electoral Reform*, ed. S. E. Finer, p. 224; Th. van Tijn, "De wording van de moderne politieke-partij-orga-

nisaties in Nederland," in *Vaderlands verleden in veelhoud*, ed. G. Beekelaar, p. 591; see also chap. 2, n. 3.
4. De Jong, *Politieke organisatie*, p. 279.
5. Ibid.
6. Th. van Tijn, "The Party Structure of Holland and the Outer Provinces in the Nineteenth Century," in *Vaderlands verleden*, ed. G. Beekelaar, p. 566.
7. Ibid.
8. Ibid.
9. Quoted in J. Bornewasser, "De Katholieke partijvorming tot de eerste wereldoorlog," in *De confessionelen: Onstaan en ontwikkeling van hun politieke partijen*, ed. L. Scholten et al., p. 30.
10. L. J. Rogier and N. de Rooy, *In vrijheid herboren: Katholiek Nederland 1853–1953*, p. 144.
11. P. Steenhoff, *Erfgoed: Bijdrage tot geschiedenis der Katholieke Staatspartij, haar stichting en voltooing*, p. 19.
12. Van Tijn, "Party Structure of Holland," p. 574.
13. De Jong, *Politieke organisatie*, p. 295.
14. *Een kleine eeuw kleine luyden: Grepen uit de geschiedenis van de ARP*, p. 21.
15. Steenhoff, *Erfgoed*, p. 12.
16. De Jong, *Politieke organisatie*, p. 309.
17. Daalder, "Extreme Proportional Representation," p. 225; Jan Verhoef, "Kiesstelsels en politieke samenwerking in Nederland, 1888–1917," *Acta Politica* 6, no. 3 (July 1971): 261–68.
18. Steenhoff, *Erfgoed*, p. 14.
19. De Jong, *Politieke organisatie*, p. 308.
20. Ibid., p. 310.
21. Bornewasser, "De Katholieke partijvorming tot de eerste wereldoorlog," pp. 32–37; De Jong, *Politieke organisatie*, pp. 308–14.
22. Daalder, "The Netherlands: Opposition in a Segmented Society," in *Political Oppositions in Western Democracies*, ed. Robert A. Dahl, pp. 201–2; Arend Lijphart, *The Politics of Accommodation: Pluralism and Democracy in the Netherlands*, pp. 111–12; Steenhoff, *Erfgoed*, p. 44; Rogier and De Rooy, *In vrijheid herboren*, p. 448.
23. The system is still in use (1981). Most parties present a similar, though not necessarily identical, list in each of the eighteen national electoral districts. The first fifteen or so names on the list, and their order, are usually the same, but there may be different names lower on the list in different districts to take into account candidates with special local appeal. The Dutch P.R. system is a little more complex than it at first appears. For details, see Daalder, "Extreme Proportional Representation," esp. pp. 228–32.
24. Steenhoff, *Erfgoed*, p. 44.
25. De Jong, *Politieke organisatie*, p. 357.
26. Murray Edelman, *The Symbolic Uses of Politics*.
27. Steenhoff, *Erfgoed*, p. 118; J. P. Gribling, *Willem Hubert Nolens 1860–1931: Uit het leven van een priester-staatsman*, p. 138.
28. J. P. Gribling, *P. J. M. Aalberse, 1871–1948*, p. 206.
29. Steenhoff, *Erfgoed*, pp. 66–85.
30. H. Ruitenbeek, *Het onstaan van de Partij van de Arbeid*, pp. 137–67.

31. A. F. Manning, "Geen doorbraak van de oude structuren," in *De confessionelen*, ed. L. Scholten et al., pp. 61–72.
32. Ibid., p. 83.
33. See H. Schaafsma, "Mirror of a Pillarized Society: Broadcasting in the Netherlands," *Delta* 9, no. 4 (Winter 1966): 57–69.
34. The RKSP was highly ambivalent about these fiscal policies which were based mainly on adherence to the gold standard and maintaining the value of the guilder. In two instances during the 1930s governments fell directly as a result of withdrawal of Catholic party support. In 1935 support was withdrawn a few months after the RKSP minister of economic affairs, Steenberghe, resigned when his proposals for devaluation were rejected by the cabinet under the leadership of Colijn (ARP). However, the new cabinet, again with Colijn as prime minister and including the RKSP, continued to adhere to the gold standard until 1936 when, after virtually all other Western nations had abandoned this standard, the Netherlands finally decided to do the same. From 1937 to 1939 the RKSP, under the leadership of Romme, continually pressed the Colijn government, which included the RKSP, for increased expenditures to deal with the high levels of unemployment. Colijn, who by 1939 was not only prime minister but also minister of finance, indicated that he was going to cut rather than increase expenditures. In view of this and other factors, the RKSP withdrew its support and the government was forced to resign. Shortly thereafter Colijn formed a new government which for the first time excluded the RKSP, but it lasted only fifteen days. The next government excluded the ARP but included the RKSP and, for the first time, the SDAP. It lasted until the German invasion of 1940. P. J. Oud, *Honderd jaren. Een eeuw van staatkundige vormgeving in Nederland*, pp. 283–93; E. Janssen, "De Rooms Katholiek Staatspartij en de krisis, 1930–1940," *Jaarboek van het Katholiek Documentatie Centrum* 5 (1975): 39–79.
35. W. van Eekeren, "The Catholic People's Party in the Netherlands: A Study of the Party's Origin, Unity, Organization and Policies" (Ph.D. diss., Georgetown University, 1956), p. 141.
36. I. Schöffer, "De Nederlandse confessionelen partijen 1918–1939," in *De confessionelen*, ed. L. Scholten et al., p. 46.
37. Ibid., p. 59.
38. Gribling, *P. J. M. Aalberse*, p. 289.
39. Daalder, "The Netherlands," p. 224. See also n. 34 above.
40. For a further description of Romme's role and personality, see Robbert Ammerlaan, *Het verschijnsel Schmelzer. Uit het dagboek van een politieke teckel*, pp. 53–74. On Nolens, see Gribling, *Willem Hubert Nolens*, p. 135.
41. Daalder, "The Netherlands," p. 224, n. 60.
42. For example, one prominent Catholic politician, when asked for an interview, refused, explaining that, "On account of my responsibility as minister of . . . and as . . . I always bore in mind as a ruling principle to abstain from any direct activity in a political party." Letter to the author, June 20, 1976. See also Daalder, "The Netherlands," p. 221.
43. Daalder, *Politisering en lijdelijkheid in de Nederlandse politiek*; see also Lijphart, *The Politics of Accommodation*, esp. pp. 122–38.

44. Daalder, "The Netherlands," p. 222.
45. Schöffer, "De Nederlandse confessionelen partijen," p. 45.
46. Unfortunately there is no systematic study of the socio-economic origins of the leaders and parliamentarians of the Catholic party. Most sources seem to indicate that members of the upper echelons were largely of middle-class origins. Evidence of this can be found by looking at the brief biographical sketches of the members of the Second Chamber in the parliamentary guide published annually. Thus in 1963 of the forty-eight KVP members in the Second Chamber, two appear to have had no secondary school education. Both were from the Catholic trade union movement. The remainder had either a classical secondary school education (usually an indicator of a middle-class upbringing) or a post-secondary school technical training (e.g., engineering). Twenty-three had at least six or more years of education at a university; eight of them had doctorates. P. Goossen, *Parlement en kiezer*.
47. I. Lipschits, "De politieke partij en de selectie van candidaten," *Sociologische Gids* 10, no. 3 (1963): 276.
48. Organizational membership in the case of the forty-eight KVP members of the Second Chamber in 1963 was as follows: labour (including white-collar unions and the Catholic Women's Labour Federation), five; employers, three; social culture-education (including hospital insurance associations, White-Yellow Cross, etc.), eleven; agriculture, six; retailers, five; academia, five; military, two; journalism, two; miscellaneous (includes chairman of Catholic Mayoralty Association, two high-ranking executives of Philips Electronics, lawyers, and government bureaucrats), eight. All the organizations were Catholic with the exception of certain international organizations. Source: Goossen, *Parlement en kiezer*, passim. See also Hans Daalder and Sonja Hubée-Boonzaaijer, "Sociale herkomst en politieke recrutering van Nederlandse kamerleden in 1968-I," *Acta Politica* 5, no. 3 (April 1970): 292–333.
49. Jean Beaufays, *Les partis Catholiques en Belgique et aux Pays-Bas 1918–1958*, p. 584.
50. Van Eekeren, "The Catholic People's Party in the Netherlands," p. 241.
51. J. de Vries, "Spiral and Miracle: The Dutch Economy since 1920," *Delta* 13, no. 3 (Autumn 1970): 15–28.
52. Ammerlaan, *Het verschijnsel Schmelzer*, p. 75.
53. In part this was due to the fact that the largest corporations like Shell, Unilever, and Hoogovens steel mills were not members of any of the confessional employer associations. This enabled the Catholic Association to be closer to the Retailers' and Farmers' organizations on a number of issues as a result of not having to defend the interests of the large corporations (Interview 41).
54. Schöffer, "De Nederlandse confessionelen partijen," p. 48.
55. Beaufays, *Les partis Catholiques*, p. 583.
56. Ibid.
57. Manning, "Geen doorbraak van de oude structuren," pp. 62–70.
58. See Arend Lijphart, *The Trauma of Decolonization: The Dutch and West New Guinea*.
59. A. F. Manning, "Uit de voorgeschiedenis van het Mandement van 1954," *Jaarboek van het Katholiek Documentatie Centrum* 1 (1971): 143.

60. Commissie van Grinten, *Staatkundige eenheid der Katholieken*.
61. Beaufays, *Les partis Catholiques*, pp. 602–3.
62. I. Lipschits, *Politieke stromingen in Nederland. Inleiding tot de geschiedenis van de Nederlandse politieke partijen*, pp. 47–48.
63. S. Vellenga, *Katholiek Zuid-Limburg en het fascisme*, p. 44.
64. Ibid., p. 45.
65. Van Eekeren, "The Catholic People's Party in the Netherlands," p. 83.
66. Ibid. The appeals by the bishops were stronger in 1948 than in 1946, and were made during the election campaign, not before as in 1946.
67. The *Mandement* stated that since the Netherlands was a democracy the hierarchy could not order its flock to vote for the KVP. Nevertheless, the bishops did note that it was their sincerest wish that Catholics would indeed support the KVP. *De Katholiek in het openbare leven van deze tijd. Bisschoplijk mandement van 1954*, pp. 35–36.
68. It should be noted that people were rarely prosecuted for not voting, and if they were, the fines were minimal. See Galen Irwin, "Compulsory Voting Legislation: Impact on Voter Turnout in the Netherlands," *Comparative Political Studies* 7, no. 3 (October 1974): 292–315.
69. Michel van der Plas, *Uit het rijke Roomsche leven: Een documentaire over de jaren 1925–1935*, pp. 248–49.
70. Communication from KRO to the author, April 2, 1976.
71. Beaufays, *Les partis Catholiques*, p. 420.
72. *De Opmars*, 24 September 1954.
73. Ibid., 18 April 1952.
74. R. Andeweg et al., "Aan de deur geen politiek," *Acta Politica* 10, no. 3 (July 1975): pp. 237–54.
75. *De Opmars*, 7 November 1947.
76. Ibid., 28 May 1948.
77. Ibid., July 1957.
78. Ibid., 18 May 1956.
79. J. Th. J. van den Berg and H. A. A. Molleman, *Crisis in de Nederlandse politiek*, p. 73.
80. Cited in C. Ruygers, "De Katholiek in de PvdA," *Socialisme en Democratie* 11, no. 5 (August 1954): 447.
81. Beaufays, *Les partis Catholiques*, p. 420.
82. One full-time KVP worker was sent from The Hague to the province of North Brabant in 1955 to do organizational work in communities, setting up committees to study economic problems, sending back reports to The Hague, and so on (Interview 43).
83. Centraal Bureau voor Statistiek (CBS), *Vrije-tijdsbesteding in Nederland winter 1955/56* Deel 9, p. 46.
84. KASKI, "De pastorale funktie van het katholiek verenigingsleven: Een godsdienst-sociologisch onderzoek in een middelgrote stad van N.O. Nederland," Report No. 227, 1959, p. 9.
85. Steven B. Wolinetz, "Party Re-alignment in the Netherlands" (Ph.D. diss., Yale University, 1973), p. 97.
86. Ibid.
87. E.g., KASKI, "De politieke structuur van Utrecht in vergelijking met de religieuze en maatschappelijke structuur," Report No. 90b.1, 1953.
88. I. Gadourek, *A Dutch Community: Social and Cultural Structure and Process*

in a Bulb-growing Region in the Netherlands, p. 435.
89. KASKI, "De katholieke arbeider en zijn politieke houding," Report No. 192, 1958, p. 23.
90. Gadourek, *A Dutch Community*, p. 392.
91. See Schöffer, "De Nederlands confessionelen partijen," p. 59.
92. See J. Colton, *Léon Blum, Humanist in Politics.* For the problems faced by social democratic governments generally, see Ralph Miliband, *The State in Capitalist Society.*
93. Even if all Catholic workers had voted for the SDAP this would have given the socialists only 42 per cent of the total popular vote.
94. KASKI, Report No. 192, p. 25.
95. Ibid., pp. 25-27.
96. This is due almost entirely to the fact that the Catholic party was the only party which was represented in virtually all coalition governments in the period 1918-72. All the other parties had been left out in the cold, so to speak, for significant periods of time, particularly the Liberals and the Socialists. One way of examining the amount of leverage enjoyed by the Catholic party in coalition cabinets is to look at the extent to which it was able to initiate and/or affect the outcome of decisions. Rogowski, drawing on the literature on coalition behaviour and welfare economics, has calculated the "probabilities of unique determination" for factions or blocs (i.e., Catholics, Socialists) in a number of countries including the Netherlands. The "probability of unique determination" is defined as the odds that a given faction will either be able to introduce and pass a proposal, or will be decisive in defeating a proposal that it opposes (and presumably has not introduced). Ronald Rogowski, *Rational Legitimacy: A Theory of Political Support,* p. 138. His calculations for the Netherlands are presented below. For details on how the probabilities of unique determination are calculated see Rogowski, pp. 138-41. Note the difference between the Catholic bloc and the other blocs. The amount of leverage enjoyed by the Catholic party in parliament may well have enhanced the credibility of the party in the eyes of its electorate.

Bloc	Probabilities of Unique Determination	Percentage of Popular Vote	Ratio
Catholic	.354	30+	~1.18
Socialist	.276	30−	~ .89
Protestant (ARP & CHU)	.193	~20	~ .97
Liberal	.082	~10	~ .82

Source: Adapted from Ronald Rogowski, *Rational Legitimacy: A Theory of Political Support* (Princeton, N.J.: Princeton University Press, 1974), table 3.1, p. 109.

97. De Vries, "Spiral and Miracle," pp. 15-28.
98. W. J. Kusters, "Stembusgedrag en maatschappijstructuur," *Sociologische Gids* 10, no. 3 (1963): 233.
99. CBS, *Historical Statistics of the Netherlands,* p. 37.

100. Contextual variables such as these have not been much discussed in the literature. The best single work is Herbert Tingsten, *Political Behaviour: Studies in Election Statistics*. See also David J. Elkins, "Regional Contexts of Political Participation: Some Illustrations from South India," *Canadian Journal of Political Science* 5, no. 2 (June 1972): 167–89.
101. See Appendix 2 for details on these ecological data.
102. See W. Goddijn, "Catholic minorities and social integration," *Social Compass* 7, no. 2 (1960): 161–76; W. Goddijn, *Katholieke minderheid en Protestantse dominant. Sociologische nawerking van de historische relatie tussen Katholieken en Protestanten in Nederland en in het bijzonder in de provincie Friesland*.
103. Peter Hall, "A Polycentric Metropolis: Randstad Holland," *Delta* 10, no. 1 (Spring 1967): 15–16.
104. P. Bouman, *Anton Philips: De mens, de ondernemer*, pp. 187, 243.
105. There are *no* northern *urban* districts where Catholics constitute more than 60 per cent of the population.

CHAPTER FOUR
1. Erwin Kleine, *Kerk van Nederland contra Rome? Een buitenlandse visie op de Nederlandse Katholieken van vandaag*, trans. M. Weetink, p. 158.
2. L. J. Rogier and N. de Rooy, *In vrijheid herboren: Katholiek Nederland 1853–1953*, p. 492.
3. John A. Coleman, *The Evolution of Dutch Catholicism, 1958–1974*, p. 53.
4. Ibid., pp. 99–100.
5. W. Goddijn, *De beheerste kerk: Uitgestelde revolutie in Rooms-Katholiek Nederland*, p. 82.
6. John A. Coleman, "Strategy, Coalition and Conflict: The Evolution of Dutch Catholicism, 1958–1973" (Ph.D. diss., Pro Maniscripto, University of California, Berkeley, 1973), p. 45.
7. Coleman, *Evolution of Dutch Catholicism*, p. 95. See Y. M. Congar, *Lay People in the Church*, trans. D. Attwater; H. de Lubac, *Corpus mysticum: l'eucharistie et l'Eglise au moyen âge*.
8. Coleman, *Evolution of Dutch Catholicism*, pp. 94–95.
9. Ibid., p. 96. This commission became the Pastoral Institute of the Dutch Church Province (PINK) in 1963, charged with carrying out research on pastoral care and advising the bishops. By the late 1960s it had become a de facto executive secretariat for the ecclesiastical hierarchy. In 1972 the PINK was phased out and its advisory functions were taken over by a formal secretariat.
10. *Katholiek Archief* 14, no. 7 (February 1959): col. 152, cited in Coleman, "Strategy, Coalition and Conflict," p. 206.
11. Ibid.
12. Goddijn, *De beheerste kerk*, pp. 108–9.
13. *Bisschop Bekkers: Negen jaar met Gods volk onderweg*, p. 206.
14. Nico van Hees, "Everyone's Bishop," in *Those Dutch Catholics*, ed. Michel van der Plas and Henk Suèr, p. 63.
15. *Bisschop Bekkers*, pp. 148–65.
16. Coleman, *Evolution of Dutch Catholicism*, pp. 207–8.
17. Kleine, *Kerk van Nederland contra Rome?*, pp. 58–60.
18. Van Hees, "Everyone's Bishop," p. 85.

19. Michel van der Plas, "What is going on in the Dutch Church?" in *Those Dutch Catholics*, ed. Van der Plas and Suèr, p. 17.
20. Henk Suèr, "The Dutch Pastoral Council," in ibid., p. 129.
21. Ibid., p. 135.
22. Coleman, *Evolution of Dutch Catholicism*, pp. 204–10.
23. J. M. G. Thurlings, *De wankele zuil: Nederlandse Katholieken tussen assimilatie en pluralisme*, p. 158.
24. Katholiek Sociaal-Kerkelijk Instituut (KASKI), "De kerk van vandaag; een verkenning van Katholiek Nederland anno 1966," Memorandum No. 167, 1966, p. 11.
25. KASKI, "Rapport over de priesterroepingen van sekulieren en regulieren in Nederland," Report No. 72, 1952, p. 15.
26. Van der Plas, "Vatican II and the Dutch Catholics," in *Those Dutch Catholics*, ed. Van der Plas and Suèr, p. 56; for a general theoretical discussion of the possible reactions of individuals to the decline of organizations and their efforts in changing these organizations, see A. O. Hirschman, *Exit, Voice and Loyalty: Resposes to Decline in Firms, Organizations and States*; Hirschman argues that organizations are much more likely to respond to people who use "voice," that is, people who make their concerns known, either within the organization or upon leaving it, than to people who "exit" quietly. People who neither voice concern nor exit, but instead continue working away, remaining loyal to the firm, are least likely to have an impact on improving the behaviour of the organization.
27. KASKI, *Vijf jaar kerkontwikkeling in Nederland: 1967–1971*, p. 45.
28. Van der Plas, "Vatican II and the Dutch Catholics," p. 57.
29. ibid., p. 58.
30. Van Hees, "Everyone's Bishop," p. 78.
31. Coleman, *Evolution of Dutch Catholicism*, pp. 141–43.
32. Ibid., pp. 237, 239–47; KASKI, *Vijf jaar kerkontwikkeling*, pp. 27–28. For a history of the progressive organizations which followed *Septuagint*, see Gerard Dierick, "Basisgroepen in Nederland," *Jaarboek van het Katholiek Documentatie Centrum* 9 (1979).
33. Instituut voor Toegepaste Sociologie (ITS), *Ambtscelibaat in een veranderende kerk: Resultaten van een onderzoek onder alle priesters, diakens en subdiakens in Nederland*.
34. Ibid., p. 32.
35. Ibid., p. 43.
36. Ibid., p. 40.
37. Coleman, *Evolution of Dutch Catholicism*, p. 235.
38. M. M. J. van Hemert, *Kerkelijke gezindten: Een analyse op basis van de volkstelling 1971*, p. 8.
39. KASKI, *Vijf jaar kerkontwikkeling*, p. 34.
40. CBS, *De ontwikkeling van het onderwijs in Nederland*, p. 148; CBS, *14e Algemene volkstelling 28 Februari 1971*, "Totale bevolking naar kerkelijke gezindte en onderwijs niveau," table 5/4.
41. KASKI did not start to collect systematic data on mass attendance until 1966 when the church sensed that attendance had begun dropping off.
42. CBS, *Historical statistics of the Netherlands, 1899–1974*, p. 50.
43. Ibid., pp. 50, 101.
44. Dutch priests generally do not watch television; hence they tend to be unaware of its impact. In recent years the KRO has held seminars for

Notes to pages 112–21 | 207

priests to inform them of the effects and uses of television.
45. Peter Hall, "A Polycentric Metropolis: Randstad Holland," *Delta* 10, nos. 1 and 2 (Spring/Summer 1967): 15.
46. Ibid., p. 19.
47. Ibid.
48. The migration index is calculated by adding the percentage of the population leaving their abode to the percentage of those newly arrived. Thus if in a given province 20 per cent of the population left their abode and resettled within the province the index would be 40. H. ter Heide and Ch. L. Eichperger, "De Interne migratie," in *Van nu tot nul: Bevolkingsgroei en bevolkingspolitiek in Nederland*, ed. H. J. Heeren and Ph. van Praag, p. 226.
49. Ibid., p. 227.
50. Coleman, *Evolution of Dutch Catholicism*, pp. 232–37. Coleman suggests that in the late 1960s and early Seventies there were strong links between *Confrontatie* and the Roman Curia.
51. Ibid., p. 231–32.
52. Ibid., p. 238–39.
53. Ibid., p. 239; Richard Auwerda, *Johannes Gijsen: Omstreden bisschop*, pp. 82–99. Many of the participants in the Open Church group were from the Pastoral Institute of the Dutch church province (PINK).
54. *Elseviers Magazine*, 5 April 1969, p. 207.
55. Ibid., p. 208.
56. Thurlings, *De wankele zuil*, pp. 160–61.
57. Ibid., p. 152.
58. KASKI, "De ontwikkeling van het misbezoekcijfer, 1966–1979," Memorandum No. 213, 1980, p. 7.
59. KASKI, "Het weekendmisbezoek in Januari 1974," Memorandum No. 198, 1975, p. 24.
60. Van Hemert, *Kerkelijke gezindten*, p. 8.
61. KASKI, "De ontwikkeling van het misbezoekcijfer," p. 20. Two of the surveys in question are W. Goddijn et al., *Opnieuw: God in Nederland (1979)* (31 per cent of sample were Catholic), and Galen Irwin et al., *Nationaal kiezersonderzoek 1977* (33.9 per cent were Catholic). See also J. Peters, "Cijferportret van kerkelijk en onkerkelijk Nederland," *Jaarboek van het Katholiek Documentatie Centrum* 9 (1979) in print. Peters notes that approximately one-half of former Catholics have no contact whatsoever with the church; the remainder may attend mass at Easter and may have been married in the church, but few of these bother even to have their children baptized.
62. Thurlings, "The Case of Dutch Catholicism," *Sociologica Neerlandica* 7, no. 2 (Spring 1971): p. 134.
63. Suèr, "The Dutch Pastoral Council," p. 134.
64. Van der Plas, "What is going on in the Dutch Church," p. 16.
65. Jill Uris and Leon Uris, *Ireland: A Terrible Beauty*, p. 35.
66. A. F. Manning, "Uit de voorgeschiedenis van het Mandement van 1954," *Jaarboek van het Katholiek Documentatie Centrum* 1 (1971): 140–42.
67. Thurlings, "The Case of Dutch Catholicism," p. 136.
68. J. Th. van den Berg and H. A. A. Molleman, *Crisis in de Nederlandse politiek*, p. 79.
69. Broadcasting organizations receive government subsidies and broadcast-

ing time according to a classification based on membership figures. Those having more than 400,000 members (paid subscribers) receive "A" status which entitles them to the maximum subsidy and broadcast time; those having less than 400,000 but more than 250,000 members are entitled to "B" status with proportionally less financial support and broadcast time; "C" status organizations are those having more than 100,000 but fewer than 250,000. The annual membership fee is at least five guilders (three Canadian dollars). In most cases people become members by subscribing to the TV and radio program guide (which usually lists the programs of all the organizations) of their particular organization, in which case they have to pay at least 12.5 guilders (eight Canadian dollars) annually. The neutral AVRO doubled its membership in 1968 (see table 4.6) by acquiring a popular entertainment magazine and using it as its official program guide. *Omroep ABC*, pp. 60, 74, 127–50.
70. A. Querido, *De wit-gele vlam: Gedenkboek ter gelegenheid van het 50-jarig bestaan van de nationale federatie het Wit-Gele Kruis 1923–1973*, p. 270.
71. G. W. Marsman, 'Massa-communicatie en ontzuiling," in *Verzuiling en ontzuiling*, p. 32.
72. J. A. van Kemenade, "Verzuiling en ontzuiling in het katholiek onderwijs," in *Verzuiling en ontzuiling*, p. 47.
73. Katholieke nederlandse boeren-en tuindersbond (KNBTB), "Antwoorden van de KNBTB op vrageniijst van de NCR" (The Hague, 1976), p. 1.
74. Thurlings, "The Case of Dutch Catholicism," p. 133.
75. *Pius Almanac: Adresboek Katholiek Nederland*, p. 358.
76. Querido, *De wit-gele vlam*, p. 251.
77. Interview with an executive officer of the Catholic Retailers' Organization (Interview 37).
78. *Dit is het NCW*, p. 3.
79. K.L.L.M. Dittrich, "De federatieproblematiek: De vakbeweging en haar streven naar eenheid" (report, Leiden University, 1975), p. 8.
80. Ibid., p. 8.
81. Ibid., p. 9.
82. Ibid., p. 10.
83. Ibid., pp. 25–26.
84. Ibid., p. 22.
85. *NRC-Handelsblad*, 6 November 1975. Since 1975 a number of Catholic and neutral trade unions within the federation of NKV-NVV have merged (e.g., those in the transportation and construction industries). In 1978 the acronym NKV-NVV became simply FNV—Federation of Dutch Trade Unions. Although formally still a federation, the FNV has become a de facto merger. John P. Windmuller and C. de Galan, *Arbeidsverhouding in Nederland*, 2:144–58.
86. In 1974 the KNBTB set up a special committee to study the need for the organization to maintain its Catholic identity. It came to the firm conclusion that the Catholic identity of the KNBTB should be maintained. KNBTB, "Rapport van de kommissie struktuur en werkwijze van de KNBTB," pp. 7 ff.
87. Marsman, "Massa-communicatie en ontzuiling," p. 32.
88. Ibid., p. 33.
89. J. A. van Kemenade, *De Katholieken en hun onderwijs*, pp. 126–27.
90. Ibid., p. 123.

priests to inform them of the effects and uses of television.
45. Peter Hall, "A Polycentric Metropolis: Randstad Holland," *Delta* 10, nos. 1 and 2 (Spring/Summer 1967): 15.
46. Ibid., p. 19.
47. Ibid.
48. The migration index is calculated by adding the percentage of the population leaving their abode to the percentage of those newly arrived. Thus if in a given province 20 per cent of the population left their abode and resettled within the province the index would be 40. H. ter Heide and Ch. L. Eichperger, "De Interne migratie," in *Van nu tot nul: Bevolkingsgroei en bevolkingspolitiek in Nederland*, ed. H. J. Heeren and Ph. van Praag, p. 226.
49. Ibid., p. 227.
50. Coleman, *Evolution of Dutch Catholicism*, pp. 232–37. Coleman suggests that in the late 1960s and early Seventies there were strong links between *Confrontatie* and the Roman Curia.
51. Ibid., p. 231–32.
52. Ibid., p. 238–39.
53. Ibid., p. 239; Richard Auwerda, *Johannes Gijsen: Omstreden bisschop*, pp. 82–99. Many of the participants in the Open Church group were from the Pastoral Institute of the Dutch church province (PINK).
54. *Elseviers Magazine*, 5 April 1969, p. 207.
55. Ibid., p. 208.
56. Thurlings, *De wankele zuil*, pp. 160–61.
57. Ibid., p. 152.
58. KASKI, "De ontwikkeling van het misbezoekcijfer, 1966– 1979," Memorandum No. 213, 1980, p. 7.
59. KASKI, "Het weekendmisbezoek in Januari 1974," Memorandum No. 198, 1975, p. 24.
60. Van Hemert, *Kerkelijke gezindten*, p. 8.
61. KASKI, "De ontwikkeling van het misbezoekcijfer," p. 20. Two of the surveys in question are W. Goddijn et al., *Opnieuw: God in Nederland (1979)* (31 per cent of sample were Catholic), and Galen Irwin et al., *Nationaal kiezersonderzoek 1977* (33.9 per cent were Catholic). See also J. Peters, "Cijferportret van kerkelijk en onkerkelijk Nederland," *Jaarboek van het Katholiek Documentatie Centrum* 9 (1979) in print. Peters notes that approximately one-half of former Catholics have no contact whatsoever with the church; the remainder may attend mass at Easter and may have been married in the church, but few of these bother even to have their children baptized.
62. Thurlings, "The Case of Dutch Catholicism," *Sociologica Neerlandica* 7, no. 2 (Spring 1971): p. 134.
63. Suèr, "The Dutch Pastoral Council," p. 134.
64. Van der Plas, "What is going on in the Dutch Church," p. 16.
65. Jill Uris and Leon Uris, *Ireland: A Terrible Beauty*, p. 35.
66. A. F. Manning, "Uit de voorgeschiedenis van het Mandement van 1954," *Jaarboek van het Katholiek Documentatie Centrum* 1 (1971): 140–42.
67. Thurlings, "The Case of Dutch Catholicism," p. 136.
68. J. Th. van den Berg and H. A. A. Molleman, *Crisis in de Nederlandse politiek*, p. 79.
69. Broadcasting organizations receive government subsidies and broadcast-

ing time according to a classification based on membership figures. Those having more than 400,000 members (paid subscribers) receive "A" status which entitles them to the maximum subsidy and broadcast time; those having less than 400,000 but more than 250,000 members are entitled to "B" status with proportionally less financial support and broadcast time; "C" status organizations are those having more than 100,000 but fewer than 250,000. The annual membership fee is at least five guilders (three Canadian dollars). In most cases people become members by subscribing to the TV and radio program guide (which usually lists the programs of all the organizations) of their particular organization, in which case they have to pay at least 12.5 guilders (eight Canadian dollars) annually. The neutral AVRO doubled its membership in 1968 (see table 4.6) by acquiring a popular entertainment magazine and using it as its official program guide. *Omroep ABC*, pp. 60, 74, 127–50.
70. A. Querido, *De wit-gele vlam: Gedenkboek ter gelegenheid van het 50-jarig bestaan van de nationale federatie het Wit-Gele Kruis 1923–1973*, p. 270.
71. G. W. Marsman, 'Massa-communicatie en ontzuiling," in *Verzuiling en ontzuiling*, p. 32.
72. J. A. van Kemenade, "Verzuiling en ontzuiling in het katholiek onderwijs," in *Verzuiling en ontzuiling*, p. 47.
73. Katholieke nederlandse boeren-en tuindersbond (KNBTB), "Antwoorden van de KNBTB op vragenlijst van de NCR" (The Hague, 1976), p. 1.
74. Thurlings, "The Case of Dutch Catholicism," p. 133.
75. *Pius Almanac: Adresboek Katholiek Nederland*, p. 358.
76. Querido, *De wit-gele vlam*, p. 251.
77. Interview with an executive officer of the Catholic Retailers' Organization (Interview 37).
78. *Dit is het NCW*, p. 3.
79. K.L.L.M. Dittrich, "De federatieproblematiek: De vakbeweging en haar streven naar eenheid" (report, Leiden University, 1975), p. 8.
80. Ibid., p. 8.
81. Ibid., p. 9.
82. Ibid., p. 10.
83. Ibid., pp. 25–26.
84. Ibid., p. 22.
85. *NRC-Handelsblad*, 6 November 1975. Since 1975 a number of Catholic and neutral trade unions within the federation of NKV-NVV have merged (e.g., those in the transportation and construction industries). In 1978 the acronym NKV-NVV became simply FNV—Federation of Dutch Trade Unions. Although formally still a federation, the FNV has become a de facto merger. John P. Windmuller and C. de Galan, *Arbeidsverhouding in Nederland*, 2:144–58.
86. In 1974 the KNBTB set up a special committee to study the need for the organization to maintain its Catholic identity. It came to the firm conclusion that the Catholic identity of the KNBTB should be maintained. KNBTB, "Rapport van de kommissie struktuur en werkwijze van de KNBTB," pp. 7 ff.
87. Marsman, "Massa-communicatie en ontzuiling," p. 32.
88. Ibid., p. 33.
89. J. A. van Kemenade, *De Katholieken en hun onderwijs*, pp. 126–27.
90. Ibid., p. 123.

91. See Annalen van het Thijmgenootschap, *Katholieke universiteit?*, 2 vols.
92. KNBTB, "Rapport van de kommissie struktuur," pp. 7–12.
93. Interview 41. See also the resolutions of the Dutch Pastoral Council in W. Goddijn, *De beheerste kerk*, pp. 173–210.
94. Interview 51. The name of the committee is "Katholieke raad voor kerk en samenleving."
95. See R. J. Cornelissen, "Heeft de confessionele organisatie nog een toekomst," *Politiek Perspectief* 2, no. 2 (March/April): 34–43.

CHAPTER FIVE

1. J. P. Kruijt in the late 1950s suggested that if depillarization were to occur (i.e., organizations losing their confessional identity), it would begin in those areas most remote from religious life, such as sports, recreation, and economic life. In fact it appears that deconfessionalization has had the greatest impact on religious life itself (e.g., decline in mass attendance); secondly, on politics; and thirdly, on economic life. Contrary to expectations, Catholic organizations dealing with sports and recreation have remained relatively intact. J. P. Kruijt, "The Netherlands: The Influence of Denominationalism on Social Life and Organizational Patterns," in *Consociational Democracy: Political Accommodation in Segmented Societies*, ed. Kenneth D. McRae, p. 136.
2. David Butler and Donald Stokes, *Political Change in Britain: Forces Shaping Electoral Choice*, p. 503.
3. "Grondslag en karakter van de KVP" (The Hague: KVP, 1966).
4. I. Lipschits, *Politieke stromingen in Nederland: Inleiding tot de geschiedenis van de Nederlandse politieke partijen*, pp. 49–52. See also I. Lipschits, "Fuseren en splintering in de Nederlandse partijpolitiek sinds 1945," paper presented at the "Nederlands Historisch Genootschap," Utrecht, 1971.
5. Lipschits, "Fuseren en splintering," p. 5.
6. Ibid., p. 4.
7. Steven Wolinetz has noted that of the thirteen KVP politicians he interviewed in 1969 not one favoured the continuation of the KVP as a Catholic party. S. B. Wolinetz, "Party Re-alignment in the Netherlands" (Ph.D. diss., Yale University, 1973), p. 121.
8. J. Th. van den Berg and H. A. A. Molleman, *Crisis in de Nederlands politiek*, p. 86.
9. Ibid., p. 86.
10. H. Schaafsma, "Mirror of a Pillarized Society: Broadcasting in the Netherlands," *Delta* 9, no. 4 (Winter 1966–67): 64.
11. Robbert Ammerlaan, *Het verschijnsel Schmelzer: Uit het dagboek van een politieke teckel*, p. 199.
12. Wolinetz, "Party Re-alignment in the Netherlands," p. 117.
13. Ammerlaan, *Het verschijnsel Schmelzer*, p. 197.
14. For a discussion of the changes in the style and quality of political leadership in the Netherlands during the 1960s, see A. Lijphart, *The Politics of Accommodation: Pluralism and Democracy in the Netherlands*, esp. chap. 10; Wolinetz, "Party Re-alignment in the Netherlands," p. 178; Hans Daalder, *Politisering en lijdelijkheid in de Nederlandse politiek*, passim; M. P. van Schendelen, "Groei en achtergronden van parlementair aktivisme," *Beleid en Maatschappij* 1, no. 4 (April 1974): 309–20. On the role of the

KVP leader Schmelzer, see Ammerlaan, *Het verschijnsel Schmelzer*, pp. 121–44, and Van den Berg and Molleman, *Crisis in de Nederlandse politiek*, pp. 145 ff.
15. Van den Berg and Molleman, *Crisis in de Nederlandse politiek*, pp. 89–90.
16. Lipschits, "Fuseren en splintering," p. 5.
17. H. C. Rottier, "Mijnsluitingen en de illusie van de herstructuring," *ESB* no. 3042 (1976): 229–31.
18. Ibid., p. 231.
19. See "Eerste communique christen-radicale werkgroep," 22 March 1967. Reprinted in *Denken over partijvernieuwing: Een bundeling van documenten en beschouwingen over de partij-vernieuwing; in het bijzonder over de gedachten in de KVP en de andere Christelijke partijen*, ed. H. G. Cloudt and Th. Westerwoudt, p. 8.
20. "Communique KVP-Radicalen," 16 August 1967; reprinted in *Denken over partijvernieuwing*, ed. Cloudt and Westerwoudt, p. 25.
21. Communique Hoofdbestuur KVPJG, 22 August 1967; reprinted in *Denken over partijvernieuwing*, ed. Cloudt and Westerwoudt, p. 26.
22. Lipschits, *Politieke stromingen in Nederland*, p. 52.
23. Ibid.
24. Jean Beaufays, *Les partis Catholiques en Belgique et aux Pays-Bas, 1918–1958*, p. 584.
25. Ammerlaan, *Het verschijnsel Schmelzer*, p. 272. The former prime minister Cals and the head of the NKV, both of whom were highly critical of the KVP, nevertheless remained within the party, though maintaining a low profile.
26. For example, the vice-chairman of the Catholic Transport Workers' Union and a senior research officer of the Catholic Construction Workers' Union both became members of the PvdA parliamentary party in the early 1970s.
27. "Verkiezingsprogram 1967 van de KVP" (The Hague: KVP, 1967), p. 1.
28. Van den Berg and Molleman, *Crisis in de Nederlandse politiek*, p. 89.
29. Ibid., p. 87.
30. "Vergelijking per kring van aantal stemmers en betalers van de KVP in 1972" (The Hague: KVP, 15 January 1973).
31. Interview 28.
32. K.L.L.M. Dittrich, "De gevolgen van de veranderingen in partijvoorkeur van de Nederlandse kiezers sinds 1966 voor KVP en PvdA" (M.A. thesis, Leiden University, 1975). p. 9.
33. Ibid.
34. *Politiek Nieuws*, January 1976.
35. Dittrich, "De gevolgen van de veranderingen in partijvoorkeur," p. 12.
36. *De KVP*, July 1965.
37. Erwin Kleine, *Kerk van Nederland contra Rome? Een buitenlandse visie op de Nederlandse Katholieken van vandaag*, trans. M. Weetink, p. 158.
38. Michel van der Plas, "What is going on in the Dutch Church," in *Those Dutch Catholics*, ed. Michel van der Plas and Henk Suèr, p. 16.
39. Van den Berg and Molleman, *Crisis in de Nederlandse politiek*, pp. 77–78.
40. Ibid., p. 79.
41. Ammerlaan, *Het verschijnsel Schmelzer*, p. 336.
42. For a further discussion of deconfessionalization in the Netherlands, see

W. E. Miller and Ph. C. Stouthard, "Confessional Attachment and Electoral Behaviour in the Netherlands," *European Journal of Political Research* 3, no. 3 (September 1975): 219–58. Unfortunately their analysis is not a time series one.

43. Katholiek-Sociaal Kerkelijk Instituut (KASKI), "Het weekendmisbezoek in January 1974: Gegevens, kanttekeningen en enige achtergronden," Memorandum No. 198, 1974, p. 1.
44. For a discussion as to how context can help accelerate change, see William McPhee and J. Ferguson, "Political Immunization," in *Public Opinion and Congressional Elections*, ed. W. McPhee and W. Glaser, pp. 155–79.
45. Richard F. Hamilton, *Affluence and the French Worker in the Fourth Republic*, pp. 40–67; Lawrence Hazelrigg, "Religious and Class Bases of Political Conflict in Italy," *American Journal of Sociology* 75, no. 2 (January 1970): 498–512; Juan Linz, "The Social Bases of West German Politics" (Ph.D. diss., Columbia University, 1959), pp. 373 ff; Klaus Liepelt, "The Infra-structure of Party Support in Germany and Austria," in *European Politics*, ed. Mattei Dogan and Richard Rose, pp. 183–201; Herbert Tingsten, *Political Behavior: Studies in Election Statistics*, passim.
46. See Hamilton, *Affluence and the French Worker*, pp. 311–14.
47. For example, in terms of the social bases of the KVP, 12 per cent of the KVP electorate were businessmen, 23 per cent white collar workers, 34 per cent blue collar workers and 8 per cent farmers, to give a partial listing, while of the entire electorate 11 per cent were businessmen, 24 per cent white collar workers, 34 per cent blue collar workers and 4 per cent farmers (N of sample equals 1,595). Lijphart, *The Politics of Accommodation*, pp. 28–29, 34.
48. The survey was carried out shortly before the provincial elections in the spring of 1970. A stratified random sample was used resulting in a final sample of 1,838 cases. Principal investigators were Ph. Stouthard, F. Heunks, W. Miller, and J. Rusk. The data set was made available through the Inter-university Consortium for Political Research (ICPR), Ann Arbor, Mich. The dependent variable used in this table, and in all subsequent tables for the year 1970, is the question: "If there was a national election tomorrow for which party would you vote?" Tables for the year 1967 are based on the following question: "Which party did you vote for in the 1967 national election?" In all tables the designation Catholic is based on responses to the question: "Do you belong to a certain religion? (If yes) Which?"
49. For a discussion of intergenerational mobility and its effects on political behaviour, see S. M. Lipset and Reinhard Bendix, *Social Mobility in Industrial Society*; Kenneth Thompson, "A Cross-National Analysis of Intergenerational Social Mobility and Political Orientations," *Comparative Political Studies* 4, no. 1 (April 1971): 3–34. Unfortunately the literature on the effects of geographical mobility is much sparser. For an interesting analysis of the phenomenon in Italy, see Robert Fried, "Urbanization and Italian Politics," *Journal of Politics* 29, no. 3 (August 1967): 505–34.
50. A comparison was done between the vote in 1967 and voting choice in 1970. The relationships between KVP support and geographical mobility are substantially the same for 1967 and 1970.

51. There was no significant change in the relationship over time (1967 to 1970). Analyses for both years yielded similar results. For a more detailed and technical examination of these movements, using analysis of variance and multiple regression, see Herman Bakvis, "Electoral Stability and Electoral Change: The Case of Dutch Catholics," paper presented at the European Politics Group Workshop, Canadian Political Science Association, London, Ont., December 1979.
52. Butler and Stokes, *Political Change in Britain*, pp. 65–89.
53. Ronald Inglehart, "The Silent Revolution in Europe: Intergenerational Change in Post-Industrial Societies," *American Political Science Review* 65, no. 4 (December 1971): 991–1017.
54. Ibid., p. 996.
55. The survey was carried out shortly before the election in 1971. A stratified random sample was used with a final sample size of 2,495 cases. Principal investigators were H. Daalder, H. Daudt, A. Hoogerwerf, G. Kuypers, R. Mokken, and Ph. Stouthard. The data set was made available through the Inter-university Consortium for Political Research (ICPR), Michigan.
56. Several variables which were shown to be related to differences in the Catholic vote for the KVP—age, urbanization, geographical, and occupational mobility, organizational membership, and region—were entered into a multiple regression equation. The total variance explained was only a little over 15 per cent. See Bakvis, "Electoral Stability and Electoral Change," p. 24.
57. This does not mean that these variables are unimportant in other respects. As shown in chapter 6, variables such as class are important in explaining which parties Catholics supported after leaving the KVP.
58. The categories used are the same as in table 5.12. Total N of all switchers equals 116. Total N of constant KVP voters equals 301. Not a single switcher was found in the "Don't know" category. This finding is interesting in that it differs from findings elsewhere. Butler and Stokes imply that voters interested in and exposed to political information are less likely to switch their vote than those less interested in politics (see pp. 217–39, *Political Change in Britain*). This suggests that the nature of political change with regard to the KVP vote in the Netherlands is different from that in Britain and perhaps elsewhere.
59. G. H. Zeegers, *God in Nederland*, pp. 216–17.
60. R. de Rooi, "Statenverkiezingen 1966," *Socialisme en Democratie* 25, no. 5 (May 1966): 322, 329.
61. J. A. van Kemenade, *De Katholieken en hun onderwijs*, p. 123.
62. Dittrich, "De gevolgen van de verandering in partijvoorkeur," p. 8.
63. V. O. Key, "A Theory of Critical Elections," *Journal of Politics* 17, no. 1 (March 1955): 3–18.
64. Wolinetz, "Party Re-alignment in the Netherlands," pp. 1–14.
65. See table 1.1.
66. For a discussion of the impact of the removal of compulsory voting laws, see Galen Irwin, "Compulsory Voting Legislation: Impact on Voter Turnout in the Netherlands," *Comparative Political Studies* 7, no. 3 (October 1974): 292–315. Data for 1966 and 1967 indicate that Catholics were somewhat less likely to show up at the polls than other groups even

W. E. Miller and Ph. C. Stouthard, "Confessional Attachment and Electoral Behaviour in the Netherlands," *European Journal of Political Research* 3, no. 3 (September 1975): 219–58. Unfortunately their analysis is not a time series one.
43. Katholiek-Sociaal Kerkelijk Instituut (KASKI), "Het weekendmisbezoek in January 1974: Gegevens, kanttekeningen en enige achtergronden," Memorandum No. 198, 1974, p. 1.
44. For a discussion as to how context can help accelerate change, see William McPhee and J. Ferguson, "Political Immunization," in *Public Opinion and Congressional Elections*, ed. W. McPhee and W. Glaser, pp. 155–79.
45. Richard F. Hamilton, *Affluence and the French Worker in the Fourth Republic*, pp. 40–67; Lawrence Hazelrigg, "Religious and Class Bases of Political Conflict in Italy," *American Journal of Sociology* 75, no. 2 (January 1970): 498–512; Juan Linz, "The Social Bases of West German Politics" (Ph.D. diss., Columbia University, 1959), pp. 373 ff; Klaus Liepelt, "The Infra-structure of Party Support in Germany and Austria," in *European Politics*, ed. Mattei Dogan and Richard Rose, pp. 183–201; Herbert Tingsten, *Political Behavior: Studies in Election Statistics*, passim.
46. See Hamilton, *Affluence and the French Worker*, pp. 311–14.
47. For example, in terms of the social bases of the KVP, 12 per cent of the KVP electorate were businessmen, 23 per cent white collar workers, 34 per cent blue collar workers and 8 per cent farmers, to give a partial listing, while of the entire electorate 11 per cent were businessmen, 24 per cent white collar workers, 34 per cent blue collar workers and 4 per cent farmers (N of sample equals 1,595). Lijphart, *The Politics of Accommodation*, pp. 28–29, 34.
48. The survey was carried out shortly before the provincial elections in the spring of 1970. A stratified random sample was used resulting in a final sample of 1,838 cases. Principal investigators were Ph. Stouthard, F. Heunks, W. Miller, and J. Rusk. The data set was made available through the Inter-university Consortium for Political Research (ICPR), Ann Arbor, Mich. The dependent variable used in this table, and in all subsequent tables for the year 1970, is the question: "If there was a national election tomorrow for which party would you vote?" Tables for the year 1967 are based on the following question: "Which party did you vote for in the 1967 national election?" In all tables the designation Catholic is based on responses to the question: "Do you belong to a certain religion? (If yes) Which?"
49. For a discussion of intergenerational mobility and its effects on political behaviour, see S. M. Lipset and Reinhard Bendix, *Social Mobility in Industrial Society*; Kenneth Thompson, "A Cross-National Analysis of Intergenerational Social Mobility and Political Orientations," *Comparative Political Studies* 4, no. 1 (April 1971): 3–34. Unfortunately the literature on the effects of geographical mobility is much sparser. For an interesting analysis of the phenomenon in Italy, see Robert Fried, "Urbanization and Italian Politics," *Journal of Politics* 29, no. 3 (August 1967): 505–34.
50. A comparison was done between the vote in 1967 and voting choice in 1970. The relationships between KVP support and geographical mobility are substantially the same for 1967 and 1970.

51. There was no significant change in the relationship over time (1967 to 1970). Analyses for both years yielded similar results. For a more detailed and technical examination of these movements, using analysis of variance and multiple regression, see Herman Bakvis, "Electoral Stability and Electoral Change: The Case of Dutch Catholics," paper presented at the European Politics Group Workshop, Canadian Political Science Association, London, Ont., December 1979.
52. Butler and Stokes, *Political Change in Britain*, pp. 65–89.
53. Ronald Inglehart, "The Silent Revolution in Europe: Intergenerational Change in Post-Industrial Societies," *American Political Science Review* 65, no. 4 (December 1971): 991–1017.
54. Ibid., p. 996.
55. The survey was carried out shortly before the election in 1971. A stratified random sample was used with a final sample size of 2,495 cases. Principal investigators were H. Daalder, H. Daudt, A. Hoogerwerf, G. Kuypers, R. Mokken, and Ph. Stouthard. The data set was made available through the Inter-university Consortium for Political Research (ICPR), Michigan.
56. Several variables which were shown to be related to differences in the Catholic vote for the KVP—age, urbanization, geographical, and occupational mobility, organizational membership, and region—were entered into a multiple regression equation. The total variance explained was only a little over 15 per cent. See Bakvis, "Electoral Stability and Electoral Change," p. 24.
57. This does not mean that these variables are unimportant in other respects. As shown in chapter 6, variables such as class are important in explaining which parties Catholics supported after leaving the KVP.
58. The categories used are the same as in table 5.12. Total N of all switchers equals 116. Total N of constant KVP voters equals 301. Not a single switcher was found in the "Don't know" category. This finding is interesting in that it differs from findings elsewhere. Butler and Stokes imply that voters interested in and exposed to political information are less likely to switch their vote than those less interested in politics (see pp. 217–39, *Political Change in Britain*). This suggests that the nature of political change with regard to the KVP vote in the Netherlands is different from that in Britain and perhaps elsewhere.
59. G. H. Zeegers, *God in Nederland*, pp. 216–17.
60. R. de Rooi, "Statenverkiezingen 1966," *Socialisme en Democratie* 25, no. 5 (May 1966): 322, 329.
61. J. A. van Kemenade, *De Katholieken en hun onderwijs*, p. 123.
62. Dittrich, "De gevolgen van de verandering in partijvoorkeur," p. 8.
63. V. O. Key, "A Theory of Critical Elections," *Journal of Politics* 17, no. 1 (March 1955): 3–18.
64. Wolinetz, "Party Re-alignment in the Netherlands," pp. 1–14.
65. See table 1.1.
66. For a discussion of the impact of the removal of compulsory voting laws, see Galen Irwin, "Compulsory Voting Legislation: Impact on Voter Turnout in the Netherlands," *Comparative Political Studies* 7, no. 3 (October 1974): 292–315. Data for 1966 and 1967 indicate that Catholics were somewhat less likely to show up at the polls than other groups even

before the repeal of the compulsory voting law. After the repeal, voting decreased considerably among Catholics and those with no religion. Only among Calvinists and, to a lesser extent, moderate Protestants did turnout remain fairly high, though even among these groups there was a decline. Repeal of the law was made on the initiative of the PvdA and D'66 and supported by the KVP and the other confessional parties. The Communists, most of the VVD, and two members of the CHU were opposed.
67. Dittrich, "De gevolgen van de verandering in partijvoorkeur," p. 15.
68. Werkgroep Nationaal Verkiezingsonderzoek, *De Nederlandse kiezer '72*, p. 34.
69. Dittrich, "De gevolgen van de veranderingen in partijvoorkeur," p. 18.
70. *NRC-Handelsblad*, 5 February 1973.
71. In 1977, 5.5 per cent of 1972 PvdA voters cast their ballots for the CDA (5 per cent of the total vote for the CDA) and these were virtually all Catholics; 16.5 per cent of 1972 VVD voters voted CDA in 1977 (6 per cent of the total vote for the CDA) and of these two-thirds were Catholic. Source: 1977 National Election Survey. The survey was carried out shortly before and after the national election of May 1977. A stratified random sample was used with a total sample size of 1,856. Principal investigators were G. Irwin, J. Verhoef, and C. Wiebrens. The data were made available by the Steinmetz Archives, Amsterdam.
72. A poll taken in May 1980, in which respondents were asked how they would vote if an election were held, showed the following (1977 election results in brackets): the CDA gaining slightly, 33.2 per cent (31.9); the D'66 gaining substantially, 13.3 per cent (5.4); the PvdA and VVD losing, 28.7 per cent (33.8) and 14.7 per cent (17.9) respectively. Dutch National Institute of Public Opinion (NIPO). Cited in *NRC-Handelsblad*, 19 May 1980. Sample size was not given.

CHAPTER SIX
1. W. P. Shively, "Party Identification, Party Choice, and Voting Stability: The Weimar Case," *American Political Science Review* 66, no. 4 (December 1972): 1222. See also Shively, "The Development of Party Identification among Adults: Exploration of a Functional Model," *American Political Science Review* 73, no. 4 (December 1979): 1049–50.
2. See, for example, S. M. Lipset and Stein Rokkan, "Cleavage Structures, Party Systems, and Voter Alignments," in *Party Systems and Voter Alignments*, ed. Lipset and Rokkan, pp. 1–64; Giovanni Sartori, *Parties and Party Systems: A Framework for Analysis*.
3. Klaus Liepelt, "The Infra-Structure of Party Support in Germany and Austria," in *European Politics*, ed. Mattei Dogan and Richard Rose, pp. 183–202.
4. I. Gadourek, *A Dutch Community: Social and Cultural Structure and Process in a Bulb-growing Region in the Netherlands*, pp. 133–35.
5. Jean Laponce, *The Protection of Minorities*, p. 139.
6. It is worth stressing that in Western countries religion is still the major source of social cohesion for political parties. Even in North America, where well-defined subcultures of the European variety are generally lacking, religion still has an enormous impact on political life. For exam-

ple, in Canada religion is the single most important predictor of how individuals will vote. See Richard Rose and Derek Urwin, "Social Cohesion, Political Parties and Strains in Regimes," *Comparative Political Studies* 2, no. 1 (April 1969); 7–67; Arend Lijphart, "Religious vs. Linguistic vs. Class Voting: The 'Crucial Experiment' of Comparing Belgium, Canada, South Africa, and Switzerland," *American Political Science Review* 73, no. 2 (June 1979): 442–58; William Irvine, "Explaining the Religious Basis of the Canadian Partisan Identity: Success on the Third Try," *Canadian Journal of Political Science* 7, no. 3 (September 1974): 560–63. John Meisel, *Working Papers on Canadian Politics*, esp. chap. 6; Mary Hanna, *Catholics and American Politics*.

7. Guenther Roth, *The Social Democrats in Imperial Germany*, esp. chaps. 9 and 10.
8. The German Social Democrats after World War I had to compete with the Communist Party, among others, for the working-class vote. The SPD's support fluctuated considerably and near the end of the Weimar Republic the party lost considerable ground to the Communist and National Socialist parties. See W. D. Burnham, "Political Immunization and Political Confessionalism," *Journal of Interdisciplinary History* 3, no. 1 (Summer 1972): 1–30.
9. Shively, "Party Identification," pp. 1220–22.
10. Laponce, *Protection of Minorities*, pp. 154–55.
11. Shively, "Party Identification," p. 1222.
12. Angus Campbell et al., *The American Voter*; David Butler and Donald Stokes, *Political Change in Britain: Forces Shaping Electoral Choice*; Jack Dennis and Donald McCrone, "Pre-adult Development of Political Party Identification in Western Democracies," *Comparative Political Studies* 3, no. 3 (July 1970): 243–63.
13. Dennis and McCrone, "Pre-adult Development of Political Party Identification," p. 247. This generalization concerning the lack of party identification among Catholics is not necessarily true for non-Catholics, although some students of Dutch voting behaviour have argued that party identification is generally lacking. For example, Jacques Thomassen has argued that the concept of party identification is not applicable to the Netherlands. He demonstrates, among other things, that party identification for all Dutch voters is less stable than vote preference; that is, respondents were more likely to change their party preference than their actual vote. Nevertheless, one can ask whether party identification is really absent in the non-Catholic sectors of the Dutch population. Historically, certain of the blocs in Dutch society have been organized on a more political plane. For example, the party supported by Calvinists, the Anti-Revolutionary Party (ARP), was the focal point around which other Calvinist organizations revolved. Over the years the ARP was in the forefront of Dutch politics, dominating the Catholics during their years of coalition, constantly propounding its evangelical message. In contrast the Catholic party had a much weaker profile and was much more reticent about entering the public limelight. The differences between the ARP and the Catholic party were such that followers of the ARP probably had a much stronger attachment to their party.

The data used by Thomassen were collected in the period 1970 to

1972, when Catholics began leaving the KVP for other parties on a massive scale. A substantial proportion of both PvdA and VVD support during this period consisted of newly arrived Catholics who had travelled either directly from the KVP or via the smaller, newer parties. Given the lack of any definite party identification among many Catholics, both those remaining with the KVP and those leaving, the presence of Catholics in the sample may well have confounded his findings. Moreover, the timing of the arrival of new parties meant that voters may well have indicated a switch in allegiance to a new party without ever having had the opportunity to vote for that party. This might explain Thomassen's unusual finding of voters switching their allegiance more quickly than their actual vote. Analysing the socio-religious groupings separately and taking into account the timing of the appearance of new parties might alter the results and make the notion of party identification plausible for at least some groups in the Netherlands. Jacques Thomassen, "Party Identification as a Cross-National Concept: Its Meaning in the Netherlands," in *Party Identification and Beyond*, ed., Ian Budge et al., pp. 63–80. See also M. K. Jennings, "Partisan Commitment and Electoral Behavior in the Netherlands," *Acta Politica* 7, no. 4 (October 1972): 445–70.

14. Source: 1977 National Election Survey. The survey was carried out shortly before and after the election of May 1977. A stratified random sampling was used with a final sample of 1,956 respondents. Of these 1,434 were reinterviewed after the election. Principal investigators were G. Irwin, J. Verhoef, and C. Wiebrens. The data set was made available by the Steinmetz Archives, Amsterdam. In my analysis of the data I have used the post-election sample of 1,434 people. The survey shows that 66 per cent of Catholics over fifty years of age voted CDA, constituting 46 per cent of Catholic support for the CDA; only 40 per cent of those fifty years of age and under voted CDA; 43 per cent of all CDA voters (Catholic and non-Catholic) were over fifty years of age while the comparable figures for the PvdA and VVD were 37 and 31 per cent respectively.

15. Source: 1977 National Election Survey. Of the 1,856 respondents 40.2 per cent said they were brought up Catholic but only 33.9 per cent said they were Catholic when asked their religion. The remainder said they had no religion. Only 14.7 per cent of these "former" Catholics voted CDA in 1977. Of this group (N = 109), drawn from the post-election sample, 51.4 per cent were self-assigned to the middle class; 38.5 per cent to the working class; and 10.1 per cent "did not know." See also chap. 5, n. 61.

16. Shively, "The Development of Party Identification among Adults," pp. 1039–54. See also Arthur Goldberg, "Discerning a Causal Pattern among Data on Voting Behavior," *American Political Science Review* 60, no. 4 (December 1966): 913–22; Goldberg, "Social Determinism and Rationality as Bases of Party Identification," *American Political Science Review* 63, no. 1 (March 1969): 5–25. See Philip Converse, "Of Time and Partisan Stability," *Comparative Political Studies* 2, no. 2 (July 1969): 139–71.

17. The PvdA and VVD originally favoured abortion on demand while the CDA, though not unalterably opposed to it, argued that there had to be additional criteria such as possible harm to the physical or mental well-

being of the woman as judged by physicians. In the fall of 1980 the three parties and the Dutch parliament as a whole, after extensive debate, arrived at a compromise solution, and in December new legislation governing abortions was passed. The new law essentially leaves the decision to the woman and her doctor; it also requires a five-day waiting period after the initial decision is made to give the woman an opportunity to change her mind. As a result the debate surrounding the abortion question has eased considerably. Nonetheless the issue will continue to play a role in election campaigns and political life generally as a number of political leaders and groups, both pro- and anti-abortion, have indicated that they are unhappy with the new legislation.

18. Most of the dissidents tended to be in the progressive wing of the ARP and were concerned with social welfare issues and the placement of nuclear weapons on Dutch soil by NATO. One of the key dissidents, who resigned in May 1980, was Professor Goudzwaard, a member of the CDA program committee and author of the 1977 CDA election program, "Niet bij brood alleen." *De Volkskrant* 20 May 1980. Many were also unhappy with the fact that in 1977 the CDA opted to form a coalition government with the VVD rather than the PVDA.

19. The details of the procedures and timetable of the merger between the three parties, including the fate of municipal and provincial organizations, party newspapers, research institutes, etc., are outlined in a merger protocol that was signed by the executives of the three parties in 1979. At that time the KVP had 50,000 members, the ARP 52,000, the CHU 23,000, and the CDA 25,000 (prior to the merger it was possible to obtain a direct membership in the CDA alone rather than through one of the parties). Representation in the CDA executive and the 1981 election list will reflect the parliamentary strength of the three parties rather than membership figures. Of the forty-nine CDA members in the 1977–81 parliament, twenty-six were from the KVP, thirteen ARP, and ten CHU. A complicated formula has been developed to weigh representation depending on who becomes the list leader. See "Ontwerp—regelingen fusie CDA" (The Hague: CDA, 1979).

20. See Emil Deutsch et al., *Les familles politiques aujourd'hui en France*, pp. 12–14.

21. Some analysts have detected a tendency on the part of certain institutions in areas like broadcasting and education to return to traditional practices. See, for example, S. Piët, "Omroepen willen oude nestgeur weer ruiken," *NRC-Handelsblad*, 8 November 1975; J. M. G. Thurlings, "Pluralism and Assimilation in the Netherlands, with Special Reference to Dutch Catholicism," *International Journal of Comparative Sociology* 20, no. 1–2 (March–June 1979): 82–100.

22. For details on the synod, see *NRC-Handelsblad*, 1 February 1980; *L'Osservatore Romano* (English weekly edition), 21 and 28 January, 4 February 1980. The agreement also stated that theological centres in the Netherlands, which provide training for the priesthood, should become more like seminaries with suitably qualified teachers. A special commission will examine each school for conformity to the rules by September 1981. Another commission will examine the role of laymen in pastoral work and attempt to draw clear boundaries between the duties of priests and

laymen. The synod also affirmed the celibacy rule for priests. In spite of the shortage of clerical manpower and the lack of candidates for the priesthood, the synod nevertheless expressed the hope that the future will bring a new harvest of workers for the church. Another commission will investigate the possibility of creating new dioceses by dividing existing ones. Among other things this would provide the Roman authorities with the opportunity of appointing additional bishops with views more to their liking.
23. *NRC-Handelsblad*, 11 April 1980.
24. *Ibid.*, 1 February 1980.

APPENDIX TWO
1. For further details on these data, see Joseph J. Houska, "The Organizational Connection: Elites, Masses and Elections in Austria and the Netherlands" (Ph.D. diss., Yale University, 1979).
2. Lijphart finds that in a 1964 survey less than 1 per cent of KVP voters were non-Catholic. Arend Lijphart, *The Politics of Accommodation: Pluralism and Democracy in the Netherlands*, p. 31.
3. For a discussion of these problems, see Juan Linz, "Ecological Analysis and Survey Research," in *Quantitative Ecological Analysis in the Social Sciences*, ed. Mattei Dogan and Stein Rokkan, p. 92; W. P. Shively, "Ecological Inference: The Use of Aggregate Data to Study Individuals," *American Political Science Review* 58, no. 4 (December 1969): 1183–96.
4. W. J. Kusters, "Stembusgedrag en maatschappijstructuur," *Sociologische Gids* 10, no. 3 (1963): 233. Kusters notes that he used election returns and census data in his calculations but does not indicate the criteria used in arriving at the actual number of voting-age Catholics.

Bibliography

MATERIAL IN ENGLISH, FRENCH, AND GERMAN

Abramson, Paul R. "Social Class and Political Change in Western Europe: A Cross-National Longitudinal Analysis." *Comparative Political Studies* 4, no. 2 (July 1971): 131–56.
——— and Books, John W. "Social Mobility and Political Attitudes." *Comparative Politics* 3, no. 3 (April 1971): 403–28.
Apter, David, ed. *Ideology and Discontent*. New York: The Free Press, 1964.
Bakvis, Herman. "Electoral Stability and Electoral Change: The Case of Dutch Catholics." Paper presented at the European Politics Group Workshop, Canadian Political Science Association, London, Ontario, 1979.
Barry, Brian. "Political Accommodation and Consociational Democracy." *British Journal of Political Science* 5, pt. 4 (October 1975): 477–505.
Beaufays, Jean. *Les Partis Catholiques en Belgique et aux Pays-Bas 1918–1958*. Brussels: Bruylant, 1973.
Blake, Donald E. "The Measurement of Regionalism in Canadian Voting Patterns." *Canadian Journal of Political Science* 5, no. 1 (March 1972): 55–81.
Bochel, J. M. and Denver, D. J. "Religion and Voting: A Critical Review and a New Analysis." *Political Studies* 18, no. 2 (June 1970): 205–19.
Burnham, W. D. "Political Immunization and Political Confessionalism." *Journal of Interdisciplinary History* 3, no. 1 (Summer 1972): 1–30.
Butler, David E. and Stokes, Donald E. *Political Change in Britain: Forces Shaping Electoral Choice*. Harmondsworth: Penguin, 1971.
Campbell, Angus et al. *The American Voter*. New York: Wiley, 1960.
——— and Valen, Henry. "Party Identification in Norway and the U.S." *Public Opinion Quarterly* 25, no. 4 (March 1961): 505–25.
Central Bureau of Statistics. *Historical Statistics of the Netherlands, 1899–1974*. The Hague: Staatsuitgeverij, 1975.
Coleman, John A. *The Evolution of Dutch Catholicism, 1958–1974*. Berkeley: University of California Press, 1978.
———. "Strategy, Coalition and Conflict: The Evolution of Dutch Catholi-

cism, 1958–1973. Ph.D. dissertation, *Pro Maniscripto*, University of California, Berkeley, 1973.

Colton, J. *Léon Blum, Humanist in Politics*. New York: Knopf, 1966.

Congar, Y. M. *Lay People in the Church*. Translated by D. Attwater. Westminster: Newman, 1957.

Converse, Philip E. "Of Time and Partisan Stability." *Comparative Political Studies* 2, no. 2 (July 1969): 139–71.

——— and Dupeux, Georges. "Politicization of the Electorate in France and the United States." *Public Opinion Quarterly* 26, no. 1 (1962): 1–23.

Crewe, Ivor. "Do Butler and Stokes Really Explain Political Change in Britain?" *European Journal of Political Research* 2, no. 1 (March 1974): 47–92.

Daalder, Hans. "Extreme Proportional Representation—The Dutch Experience." In *Adversary Politics and Electoral Reform*, pp. 223–48. Edited by S. E. Finer. London: Wigram, 1975.

———. "The Netherlands." In *Political Parties in the European Community*, pp. 175–208. Edited by Stanley Henig. London: Allen and Unwin, 1979.

———. "The Netherlands: Opposition in a Segmented Society." In *Political Oppositions in Western Democracies*, pp. 188–236. Edited by Robert A. Dahl. New Haven: Yale University Press, 1966.

———. "Parties, Elites, and Political Developments in Western Europe." In *Political Parties and Political Development*. Edited by Joseph LaPolombara and Myron Weiner. Princeton: Princeton University Press, 1966.

——— and Rusk, Jerold G. "Perceptions of Party in the Dutch Parliament." In *Comparative Legislative Behavior*, pp. 143–97. Edited by Samuel C. Patterson and John C. Wahlke. New York: Wiley, 1972.

Daudt, H. *Floating Voters and the Floating Vote*. Leiden: Stenfert Kroese, 1961.

Dennis, Jack and McCrone, Donald. "Pre-Adult Development of Political Party Identification in Western Democracies." *Comparative Political Studies* 3, no. 2 (July 1970): 243–63.

Deutsch, E., Lindon, D., and Weill, P. *Les familles politiques aujourd'hui en France*. Paris: Minuit, 1966.

Di Palma, Giuseppe. *Apathy and Participation: Mass Politics in Western Societies*. New York: The Free Press, 1970.

Duverger, Maurice. *Political Parties: Their Organization and Activities in the Modern State*. London: Methuen, 1954.

Edelman, Murray. "Sources of Popular Support for the Italian Christian Democratic Party in the Post-War Decade." *Midwest Journal of Political Science* 2, no. 2 (May 1958): 151–63.

———. *The Symbolic Uses of Politics*. Urbana: University of Illinois Press, 1964.

Eekeren, W. van. "The Catholic People's Party in the Netherlands: A Study of the Party's Origin, Unity, Organization and Policies." Ph.D. dissertation, Georgetown University, 1956.

Einaudi, M. and Goguel, F. *Christian Democracy in France and Italy*. Notre Dame: University of Notre Dame Press, 1952.

Elkins, David J. "The Measurement of Party Competition." *American Political Science Review* 68, no. 2 (June 1974): 682–700.

———. "Regional Contexts of Political Participation: Some Illustrations from South India." *Canadian Journal of Political Science* 5, no. 2 (June 1972): 167–89.

Ellemers, J. "The Revolt of the Netherlands: The Part Played by Religion." *Social Compass* 14, no. 2 (1967): 93–103.
Fogarty, Michael P. *Christian Democracy in Western Europe*. London: Routledge and Kegan Paul, 1957.
Fried, Robert C. "Urbanization and Italian Politics." *Journal of Politics* 29, no. 3 (August 1967): 505–34.
Furnivall, J. S. *Netherlands India: A Study of Plural Economy*. Cambridge: University Press, 1939.
Gadourek, I. *A Dutch Community: Social and Cultural Structure and Process in a Bulb-growing Region in the Netherlands*. Leiden: Stenfert Kroese, 1956.
Glenn, Norval D. *Cohort Analysis*. Beverly Hills: Sage, 1977.
Glock, Charles Y. and Stark, Rodney. *Religion and Society in Tension*. Chicago: Rand McNally, 1965.
Goddijn, W. "Catholic Minorities and Social Integration." *Social Compass* 7, no. 2 (1960): 161–76.
Goldberg, Arthur. "Discerning a Causal Pattern Among Data on Voting Behavior." *American Political Science Review* 60, no. 4 (December 1966): 913–22.
———. "Social Determinism and Rationality as Bases of Party Identification." *American Political Science Review* 63, no. 1 (March 1969): 5–25.
Goudsblom, Johan. *Dutch Society*. New York: Random House, 1967.
Graubard, Stephen R., ed. *A New Europe? A Timely Appraisal*. Boston: Beacon, 1967.
Greenstein, Fred and Tarrow, Sydney. "The Study of French Political Socialization: Toward the Revocation of a Paradox." *World Politics* 22, no. 1 (October 1969): 95–138.
Hall, Peter. "A Polycentric Metropolis: Randstad Holland." *Delta* 10, no. 1 (Spring 1967): 5–32.
Hamilton, Richard F. *Affluence and the French Worker in the Fourth Republic*. Princeton: Princeton University Press, 1967.
———. "Affluence and the Worker: The West German Case." *American Journal of Sociology* 71, no. 2 (September 1965): 144–52.
Hanna, Mary. *Catholics and American Politics*. Cambridge: Harvard University Press, 1979.
Hazelrigg, Lawrence R. "Religious and Class Bases of Political Conflict in Italy." *American Journal of Sociology* 75, no. 4, pt. 1 (January 1970): 498–512.
Hees, Nice van. "Everyone's Bishop." In *Those Dutch Catholics*, pp. 63–86. Edited by Michel van der Plas and Henk Suèr. London: Chapman, 1967.
Helm, R. P. van den and Verhoef, Jan. "Dutch Politics in Historical Perspective: A Research Note." Paper for the Workshop on Indicators of Social and Political Change, Mannheim, April 1973.
Henig, Stanley, ed. *Political Parties in the European Community*. London: Allen and Unwin, 1979.
——— and Pinder, J., eds. *European Political Parties*. London: Allen and Unwin, 1969.
Hirschman, A. O. *Exit, Voice and Loyalty: Responses to decline in Firms, Organizations and States*. Cambridge: Harvard University Press, 1970.
Hoggart, Richard. *The Uses of Literacy: Aspects of Working-Class Life with special reference to Publications and Entertainments*. Harmondsworth: Penguin, 1965.

Houska, Joseph J. "The Organizational Connection: Elites, Masses and Elections in Austria and the Netherlands." Ph.D. dissertation, Yale University, 1979.
Inglehart, Ronald. *The Silent Revolution: Changing Values and Political Styles among Western Publics.* Princeton: Princeton University Press, 1977.
―――. "The Silent Revolution in Europe: Intergenerational Change in Post-Industrial Societies." *American Political Science Review* 65, no. 4 (December 1971): 991–1017.
Irvine, William. "Explaining the Religious Basis of the Canadian Partisan Identity: Success on the Third Try." *Canadian Journal of Political Science* 7, no. 3 (September 1974): 560–63.
Irving, R. E. M. *The Christian Democratic Parties of Western Europe.* London: Allen and Unwin, 1979.
Irwin, Galen. "Compulsory Voting Legislation: Impact on Voter Turnout in the Netherlands." *Comparative Political Studies* 7, no. 3 (October 1974): 292–315.
Janowitz, M. and Segal, D. "Social Cleavage and Party Affiliation, Germany, Great Britain and the U.S." *American Journal of Sociology* 72, no. 6 (May 1967): 601–18.
Key, V. O. "A Theory of Critical Elections." *Journal of Politics* 17, no. 1 (March 1955): 3–18.
Knox, R. A. *The Belief of Catholics.* New York: Harper, 1927.
Kruijt, J. P. "The Netherlands: The Influence of Denominationalism on Social Life and Organizational Patterns." In *Consociational Democracy: Political Accommodation in Segmented Societies*, pp. 128–36. Edited by Kenneth D. McRae. Toronto: McClelland and Stewart, 1974.
Lange, D. de. "Dutch Catholicism." *Delta* 9, no. 4 (Winter 1966): 17–30.
Laponce, Jean. *The Protection of Minorities.* Berkeley: University of California Press, 1960.
Lazarsfeld, Paul et al. *The People's Choice.* New York: Columbia University Press, 1944.
Liepelt, Klaus. "The Infra-Structure of Party Support in Germany and Austria." In *European Politics*, pp. 183–202. Edited by Mattei Dogan and Richard Rose. Boston: Little, Brown, 1971.
Lijphart, Arend. "Class Voting and Religious Voting in the European Democracies: A Preliminary Report." *Acta Politica* 6, no. 2 (April 1971): 158–71.
―――. "Comparative Politics and the Comparative Method." *American Political Science Review* 65, no. 3 (September 1971): 682–93.
―――. "The Netherlands: Continuity and Change in Voting Behavior." In *Electoral Behavior: A Comparative Handbook*, pp. 227–68. Edited by Richard Rose. New York: The Free Press, 1974.
―――. *The Politics of Accommodation: Pluralism and Democracy in the Netherlands.* 3rd ed. Berkeley: University of California Press, 1979.
―――. "Religious vs. Linguistic vs. Class Voting: The "Crucial Experiment" of Comparing Belgium, Canada, South Africa, and Switzerland." *American Political Science Review* 73, no. 2 (June 1979): 442–58.
―――. *The Trauma of Decolonization: The Dutch and West New Guinea.* New Haven: Yale University Press, 1966.
Linz, Juan. "Ecological Analysis and Survey Research." In *Quantitative Ecological Analysis in the Social Sciences*, pp. 91–131. Edited by Mattei Dogan and Stein Rokkan. Cambridge: M.I.T. Press, 1969.

———. "The Social Bases of West German Politics." Ph.D. dissertation, Columbia University, 1959.
Lipset, S. M. *Political Man: The Social Bases of Politics*. Garden City: Anchor, 1963.
——— and Bendix, Reinhard. *Social Mobility in Industrial Society*. Berkeley: University of California Press, 1959.
——— and Rokkan, Stein. "Cleavage Structures, Party Systems, and Voter Alignments." In *Party Systems and Voter Alignments: Cross-National Perspectives*, pp. 1–64. Edited by S. M. Lipset and Stein Rokkan. New York: The Free Press, 1967.
Lorwin, Val R. "Segmented Pluralism: Ideological Cleavages and Political Cohesion in the Small European Democracies." *Comparative Politics* 3, no. 2 (January 1971): 141–75.
Lubac, H. de. *Corpus Mysticum: l'eucharistie et l'Eglise au moyen âge*. Paris: Aubier, 1949.
Lyon, Margot. "Christian Democratic Parties and Politics." *Journal of Contemporary History* 2, no. 4 (October 1967): 69–88.
McClosky, Herbert and Dahlgren, Harold. "Primary Group Influence on Party Loyalty." *American Political Science Review* 53, no. 3 (September 1959): 757–76.
MacCorquodale, K. and Meehl, P. "On a Distinction between Hypothetical Constructs and Intervening Variables." *Psychological Review* 55, no. 1 (March 1948): 95–107.
Mackie, Thomas and Rose, Richard. *The International Almanac of Electoral History*. London: Macmillan, 1974.
McPhee, William N. and Ferguson, Jack. "Political Immunization." In *Public Opinion and Congressional Elections*, pp. 155–79. Edited by William N. McPhee and William Glaser. New York: The Free Press, 1962.
McRae, Kenneth D., ed. *Consociational Democracy: Political Accommodation in Segmented Societies*. Toronto: McClelland and Stewart, 1974.
Meisel, John. *Working Papers on Canadian Politics*. 2nd ed. Montreal: McGill-Queen's University Press, 1975.
Michelat, Guy and Simon, Michel. "Religion, Class, and Politics." *Comparative Politics* 10, no. 1 (October 1977): 159–86.
Miliband, Ralph. *The State in Capitalist Society*. London: Weidenfeld and Nicolson, 1969.
Miller, W. E. and Stouthard, Ph. "Confessional Attachment and Electoral Behaviour in the Netherlands." *European Journal of Political Research* 3, no. 3 (September 1975): 219–58.
Mokyr, Joel. *Industrialization in the Low Countries, 1795–1850*. New Haven: Yale University Press, 1976.
Morsey, R. *Die Deutsche Zentrumspartei 1917–1923*. Dusseldorf: Droste Verlag, 1966.
Myers, Frank E. "Social Class and Political Change in Western Industrial Systems." *Comparative Politics* 2, no. 3 (April 1970): 389–412.
Olson, Mancur. *The Logic of Collective Action: Public Goods and the Theory of Groups*. Cambridge: Harvard University Press, 1965.
L'Osservatore Romano (Rome).
Parkin, Frank. *Class Inequality and Political Order*. London: MacGibbon and Kee, 1971.
Petersen, William. "Fertility Trends and Population Policy: Some Comments

on the Van Heek-Hofstee Debate." *Sociologica Neerlandica* 3, no. 1 (1967): 2-16.

———. *Planned Migration: The Social Determinants of the Dutch-Canadian Movement*. Berkeley: University of California Press, 1955.

Plas, Michel van der. "What is going on in the Dutch Church?" In *Those Dutch Catholics*, pp. 13-28. Edited by Michel van der Plas and Henk Suèr. London: Chapman, 1967.

Poeisz, J. "Déterminants sociaux des inscriptions dans les seminaires et des ordinations de nouveaux prêtres aux Pays-Bas." *Social Compass* 10, no. 4 (1963): 491-524.

———. "God's People on the Way." In *Those Dutch Catholics*, pp. 87-109. Edited by Michel van der Plas and Henk Suèr. London: Chapman, 1967.

Popitz, H. et al. *Das Gesellschaftbild des Arbeiters*. Tubingen: Mohr, 1957.

Przeworski, Adam and Teune, Henry. *The Logic of Comparative Social Inquiry*. New York: Wiley, 1970.

Raalte, E. van. *The Parliament of the Kingdom of the Netherlands*. London: Hansard Society, 1959.

Rabushka, Alvin and Shepsle, Kenneth A. *Politics in Plural Societies: A Theory of Democratic Instability*. Columbus: Merrill, 1972.

Robertson, David. "Surrogates for Party Identification in the Rational Choice Framework." In *Party Identification and Beyond: Representations of Voting and Party Competition*, pp. 365-81. Edited by Ian Budge, Ivor Crewe, and Dennis Farlie. London: Wiley, 1976.

Rogowski, Ronald. *Rational Legitimacy: A Theory of Political Support*. Princeton: Princeton University Press, 1974.

Rose, Richard and Urwin, Derek. "Social Cohesion, Political Parties and Strains in Regimes." *Comparative Political Studies* 2, no. 1 (April 1969): 7-67.

Roth, Guenther. *The Social Democrats in Imperial Germany: A Study in Working-Class Isolation and National Integration*. Totowa: Bedminster Press, 1963.

Sartori, Giovanni. *Parties and Party Systems: A Framework for Analysis*. Cambridge: Cambridge University Press, 1976.

Schaafsma, H. "Mirror of a Pillarized Society: Broadcasting in the Netherlands." *Delta* 9, no. 4 (Winter 1966): 57-69.

Schurmann, Franz. *Ideology and Organization in Communist China*. Berkeley: University of California Press, 1966.

Shively, W. Phillips. "The Development of Party Identification among Adults: Exploration of a Functional Model." *American Political Science Review* 73, no. 4 (December 1979): 1039-54.

———. "Ecological Inference: The Use of Aggregate Data to Study Individuals." *American Political Science Review* 58, no. 4 (December 1969): 1183-96.

———. "Party Identification, Party Choice, and Voting Stability: The Weimar Case." *American Political Science Review* 66, no. 4 (December 1972): 1203-25.

Singh, R. *Policy Development: A Study of the Social and Economic Council of the Netherlands*. Rotterdam: Rotterdam University Press, 1972.

Smith, M. G. *The Plural Society in the British West Indies*. Berkeley: University of California Press, 1965.

Suèr, Henk. "The Dutch Pastoral Council." In *Those Dutch Catholics*, pp. 127-42. Edited by Michel van der Plas and Henk Suèr. London: Chapman, 1967.

Thomassen, Jacques. "Party Identification as a Cross-National Concept: Its Meaning in the Netherlands." In *Party Identification and Beyond: Representations of Voting and Party Competition*, pp. 63-79. Edited by Ian Budge, Ivor Crewe, and Dennis Farlie. London: Wiley, 1976.
Thompson, Kenneth. "A Cross-National Analysis of Intergenerational Social Mobility and Political Orientations." *Comparative Political Studies* 4, no. 1 (April 1971): 3-34.
Thurlings, J. M. G. "The Case of Dutch Catholicism." *Sociologica Neerlandica* 7, no. 1 (Spring 1971): 118-36.
―――. "Pluralism and Assimilation in the Netherlands, with Special Reference to Dutch Catholicism." *International Journal of Comparative Sociology* 20, no. 1-2 (March-June 1979): 82-100.
Tijn, Th. van. "The Party Structure of Holland and the Outer Provinces in the Nineteenth Century." In *Vaderlands verleden in veelhoud*, pp. 560-79. Edited by G. Beekelaar. The Hague: Nijhoff, 1975.
Tingsten, Herbert. *Political Behavior: Studies in Election Statistics*. Totowa: Bedminster Press, 1963.
Troelsch, Ernst. *The Social Teaching of the Christian Churches*. Translated by O. Wyon. 2 vols. New York: Macmillan, 1950.
Uris, Jill and Uris, Leon. *Ireland: A Terrible Beauty*. New York: Doubleday, 1975.
Vries, J. de. "Spiral and Miracle: The Dutch Economy since 1920." *Delta* 13, no. 3 (Autumn 1970): 15-28.
Weil, Gordon. *The Benelux Nations: The Politics of Small-Country Democracies*. New York: Holt, Rinehart and Winston, 1970.
Williams, M. *The Catholic Church in Action*. New York: Macmillan, 1934.
Windmuller, John P. *Labor Relations in the Netherlands*. Ithaca: Cornell University Press, 1969.
Wolinetz, Steven B. "The Dutch Labour Party: A Social Democratic Party in Transition." In *Social Democratic Parties in Western Europe*, pp. 342-87. Edited by William E. Paterson and Alastair Thomas. London: Croom Helm, 1977.
―――. "Dutch Politics in the 1970's: Re-alignment at a Standstill?" *Current History* 70, no. 415 (April 1976): 163-82.
―――. "Electoral Change and Attempts to Build Catch-All Parties in the Netherlands." Paper presented at the Canadian Political Science Association Annual Meeting, 1973.
―――. "Party Re-alignment in the Netherlands." Ph.D. dissertation, Yale University, 1973.

MATERIAL IN DUTCH

Alfrink en de kerk, 1951-1976. Baarn: Ambo, n.d.
Ammerlaan, Robbert. *Het verschijnsel Schmelzer: Uit het dagboek van een politiek teckel*. Leiden: Sijthoff, 1974.
Andeweg, R., Dittrich, K., and Haeften, M. van. "Aan de deur geen politiek." *Acta Politica* 10, no. 3 (July 1975): 237-54.
Andeweg, R., Dittrich, K., and Tak, T. van der. *Kabinetsformatie, 1977*. Leiden: 1978.
Annalen van het Thijmgenootschap. *Katholieke universiteit?* 2 vols. Bussum: Brand, 1971.

Auwerda, Richard. *Johannes Gijsen: Omstreden bisschop.* Amsterdam: Becht, 1973.
Berg, J. Th. J. van den, and Molleman, H. A. A. *Crisis in de Nederlandse politiek.* Alphen aan den Rijn: Samsom, 1975.
Bisschop Bekkers: Negen jaar met Gods volk onderweg. Utrecht: Ambo, 1966.
Bornewasser, J. "De katholieke partijvorming tot de eerste wereldoorlog." In *De confessionelen: Onstaan en ontwikkeling van hun politieke partijen,* pp. 23–40. Edited by Scholten et al. Utrecht: Ambo, 1968.
Bouman, P. *Anton Philips: De mens, de ondernemer.* Utrecht: Prisma, 1966.
Bruyn, L. P. J. de. "Groen licht voor een christen-democratische partij, of een valse start?" *Politiek Perspectief* 2, no. 4 (August 1973): 3–9.
―――. "KVP-koers op empirische basis." *Politiek Perspectief* 1, no. 1 (October 1971): 16–25.
―――. "Omvang van partij-aanhang." *Acta Politica* 5, no. 3 (April 1970): 269–91.
―――. "Statenverkiezingen 1978—CDA winst ontleed." *Politiek Perspectief* 7, no. 2 (March 1978): 3–17.
CD/Aktueel (The Hague).
Centraal Bureau voor de Statistiek (CBS). *1899–1979: Tachtig jaren statistiek in tijdreeksen.* The Hague: Staatsuitgeverij, 1979.
―――. *De ontwikkeling van het onderwijs in Nederland,* Deel I. The Hague: Centraal Bureau Statistiek, 1966.
―――. *Statistiek Zakboek 1974.* The Hague: Staatsuitgeverij, 1974.
―――. *Vrije-tijdsbesteding in Nederland Winter 1955/56,* Deel 9. Zeist: W. de Haan, 1959.
Chorus, A. *De Nederlander innerlijk en uiterlijk: Een characteristiek.* Leiden: Sijthoff, 1964.
Colsen, J. P. *Poels.* Roermond: Romen en Zonen, 1955.
Commissie van Grinten. *Staatkundige eenheid der Katholieken.* The Hague: Centrum voor Staatkundige Vorming, 1953.
"Communique Hoofdbestuur KVPJG." In *Denken over partijvernieuwing: Een bundeling van documenten en beschouwingen over partijvernieuwing,* p. 26. Edited by H. G. Cloudt and Th. Westerwoudt. The Hague: KVP, 1967.
"Communique KVP-Radicalen." In *Denken over partijvernieuwing: Een bundeling van documenten en beschouwingen over de partijvernieuwing,* p. 25. Edited by H. G. Cloudt and Th. Westerwoudt. The Hague: KVP, 1967.
Cornelissen, R. "Heeft de confessionele organisatie nog een toekomst." *Politiek Perspectief* 2, no. 2 (March/April 1973): 34–43.
Daalder, Hans. *Politisering en lijdelijkheid in de Nederlandse politiek.* Assen: Van Gorcum, 1974.
―――― and Hubée-Boonzaaijer, Sonja. "Sociale herkomst en politieke recruitering van Nederlandse kamerleden in 1968-I." *Acta Politica* 5, no. 3 (April 1970): 292–333.
Daudt, H. "Constante kiezers, wisselaars en thuisblijvers." *Acta Politica* 7, no. 1 (January 1972): 30–41.
Dekker, G. *Het kerkelijk gemengde huwelijk in Nederland.* Meppel: J. A. Boom, 1962.
Dierick, Gerard. "Basisgroepen in Nederland." *Jaarboek van het Katholiek Documentatie Centrum* 9 (1979) in print.
Dieteren, R. *De migratie in de mijnstreek 1900–1935.* Nijmegen: Centrale Drukkerij, 1962.

Bibliography | 227

Dit is het NCW. The Hague: NCW, 1975.
Dittrich, K. L. L. M. "De Federatieproblematiek: De vakbeweging en haar streven naar eenheid." Report, Leiden University, 1975.
———. "De gevolgen van de veranderingen in partijvoorkeur van de Nederlandse kiezers sinds 1966 voor KVP en PvdA." M.A. thesis, Leiden University, 1975.
———. "Partij-politieke verhoudingen in Nederlandse gemeenten: Een analyse van de gemeenteraadverkiezingen 1962–1974." Ph.D. dissertation, Leiden University, 1978.
Doornik, N. van. *Het Katholiek geloof in hedendaagse gestalte.* Utrecht: Spectrum, 1965.
Een kleine eeuw kleine luyden: Grepen uit de geschiedenis van de ARP. The Hague: Stichting kader-en vormingswerk ARP, 1975.
"Erste communique christen-radicale werkgroep." In *Denken over partijvernieuwing: Een bundeling van documenten en beschouwingen over de partijvernieuwing,* p. 8. Edited by H. G. Cloudt and Th. Westerwoudt. The Hague: KVP, 1967.
Elsevier (Amsterdam).
Geyl, P. "De Protestantisering van Noord-Nederland." In *Vaderlands verleden in veelhoud,* pp. 209–21. Edited by G. Beekelaar. The Hague: Nijhoff, 1975.
Goddijn, W. *De beheerste kerk: Uitgestelde revolutie in Rooms-Katholiek Nederland.* Amsterdam: Elsevier, 1973.
———. *Katholieke minderheid en Protestantse dominant. Sociologische nawerking van de historische relatie tussen Katholieken en Protestanten in Nederland en in het bijzonder in de provincie Friesland.* Assen: Van Gorcum, 1957.
Goddijn, W., Smets, H., and Tillo, G. van. *Opnieuw: God in Nederland (1979).* Amsterdam: De Tijd, 1979.
Goossen, P. *Parlement en kiezer.* The Hague: M. Nijhoff, 1964.
Gribling, J. P. *P. J. M. Aalberse, 1871–1948.* Utrecht: De Lanteern, 1961.
———. *Willem Hubert Nolens, 1860–1931: Uit het leven van een priester-staatsman.* Assen: Van Gorcum, 1978.
Heek, F. van. *Het geboorte-niveau der Nederlandse Rooms-Katholieken.* Leiden: Stenfert Kroese, 1954.
Hees, N. van. *Bisschop Bekkers: Vriend van ons allen.* Amsterdam: Becht, n.d.
Heide, H. ter, and Eichperger, Ch. "De interne migratie." In *Van nu tot nul: Bevolkingsgroei en bevolkingspolitiek in Nederland,* pp. 222–43. Edited by H. J. Heeren and Ph. van Praag. Utrecht: Spectrum, 1974.
Hemert, M. M. J. van. *Kerkelijke gezindten: Een analyse op basis van de volkstelling 1971.* The Hague: Centraal Bureau Statistiek, 1979.
Hoefnagels, H. J. M. *Een eeuw sociale problematiek: De Nederlandse sociale ontwikkeling van 1850 tot 1940.* Alphen aan den Rijn: Samsom, 1974.
Hoogerwerf, A. "Sociaal-politiek strijdpunten: Smeulend vuur." *Sociologische Gids* 10, no. 3 (1963): 249–63.
Hooijdonk, P. van. "Intellectuele emancipatie van de Nederlandse Katholieken in de laatste jaren." *Sociale Wetenschappen* 8, no. 3 (1965): 217–29.
Instituut voor Toegepaste Sociologie. *Ambtscelibaat in een veranderende kerk: Resultaten van een onderzoek onder alle priesters, diakens en subdiakens in Nederland.* Amersfoort: Pastoraal Instituut van de Nederlandse Kerkprovincie, 1969.
Irwin, G., Verhoef, J., and Wiebrens, C. J. *De Nederlandse kiezer '77.* Voorschoten: VAM, 1977.

Janssen, E. "De Rooms Katholiek Staatspartij en de krisis, 1930-1949." *Jaarboek van het Katholiek Documentatie Centrum* 5 (1975): 39-79.
Jong, J. de. *Politieke organisatie na 1800 in West Europa*. The Hague: Nijhoff, 1951.
De Katholiek in het openbare leven van deze tijd. Bisschoplijk mandement van 1954. Zeist, 1954.
Katholiek Nederlandse boeren-en tuindersbond (KNBTB). "Antwoorden van de KNBTB op vragenlijst van de NCR." The Hague, 1976.
―――. "Rapport van de kommissie struktuur en werkwijze van de KNBTB." The Hague, 1975.
Katholiek Sociaal-Kerkelijk Instituut (KASKI). "Het beeld van en de waardering voor het geestelijk beroep; probleem-stelling voor een sociologisch onderzoek naar het roepingen-vraagstuk in Nederland." Memorandum No. 155, 1964.
―――. "Enige aspekten van de religieuze en sociale achtergrond van het mandement van de Nederlandse bisschoppen betreffende de katholiek in het openbare leven van deze tijd." Memorandum No. 7, 1954.
―――. "Godsdienstig-sociale aspekten van de industrialisatie in Nederland." Report No. 85, 1952.
―――. "Jeugd in Amsterdam-Noord." Report No. 293, 1963.
―――. "Katholicisme in West-Europa en de wereldkerk." Memorandum No. 113, 1960.
―――. "De katholieke arbeider en zijn politieke houding." Report No. 192, 1958.
―――. "De kerk van vandaag; een verkenning van Katholiek Nederland anno 1966." Memorandum No. 167, 1966.
―――. "Memorandum betreffende de priester-roepingen uit de boerenstand in het gebied van de noordbrabantse christelijke boerenbond." Memorandum No. 67, 1958.
―――. "De ontwikkeling van het misbezoekcijfer, 1966-1979." Memorandum No. 213, 1980.
―――. "De pastorale funktie van het katholiek verenigingsleven. Een godsdienst-sociologisch onderzoek in een middelgrote stad van N. O. Nederland." Report No. 227, 1959.
―――. "De politieke keuze der Nederlandse Katholieken." Report No. 171, 1957.
―――. "De politieke structuur van Utrecht in vergelijking met de religieuze en maatschappelijke structuur." Report No. 90b.1, 1953.
―――. "Rapport over de priesterroepingen van sekulieren en regulieren in Nederland." Report No. 72, n.d.
―――. "Het weekendmisbezoek in January 1974: Gegevens, kanttekeningen en enige achtergronden." Memorandum No. 198, 1974.
Kemenade, J. A. van. *De Katholieken en hun onderwijs*. Meppel: Boom, 1968.
―――. "Verzuiling en ontzuiling in het Katholiek onderwijs." In *Verzuiling en ontzuiling*, pp. 47-51. Hilversum: KRO, 1969.
Kleine, Erwin. *Kerk van Nederland contra Rome? Een buitenlandse visie op de Nederlandse Katholieken van vandaag*. Translated from the German by M. Weetink. Bilthoven: Nelissen, 1968.
Kok, J. de. *Nederland op de breuklijn Rome-Reformatie*. Assen: Van Gorcum, 1964.
Kruijt, J. P. *De onkerkelijkheid in Nederland: Haar verbreiding en oorzaken; proeve ener sociografiese verklaring*. Groningen: Noordhoff, 1933.

――― and Goddijn, W. "Verzuiling en ontzuiling als sociologisch proces." In *Drift en koers: Een halve eeuw sociale verandering in Nederland*, pp. 231–53. Edited by A. den Hollander et al. Assen: Van Gorcum, 1962.
Kusters, W. "Stembusgedrag en maatschappijstructuur." *Sociologische Gids* 10, no. 3 (1963): 226–38.
De KVP (The Hague).
Laan, H. *De Rooms-Katholieke kerkorganisatie in Nederland: Een sociologisch structuur analyse van het bisschoppelijk bestuur.* Utrecht: Bijleveld, 1967.
Lipschits, I. "Fuseren en splintering in de Nederlandse partijpolitiek sinds 1945." Paper presented at the "Nederlands Historisch Genootschap." Utrecht, 1971.
―――. "De politieke partij en de selectie van candidaten." *Sociologische Gids* 10, no. 3 (1963): 273–81.
―――. *Politieke stromingen in Nederland: Inleiding tot de geschiedenis van de Nederlandse politieke partijen.* Deventer: Kluwer, 1978.
Manders, H. "Objectief en subjectief norm en mondigheid. Analyse van de besluiten van de Nederlandse bisschoppensynode." *Praktische Theologie* 20, no. 2 (1980): 67–77.
Manning, A. F. "Geen doorbraak van de oude structuren." In *De confessionelen: Onstaan en ontwikkeling van hun politieke partijen.* pp. 61–88. Edited by L. Scholten et al. Utrecht: Ambo, 1968.
―――. "De Nederlandse Katholieken in de eerste jaren van de Duitse bezetting." *Jaarboek van het Katholiek Documentatie Centrum* 8 (1978): 105–29.
―――. "Uit de voorgeschiedenis van het Mandement van 1954." *Jaarboek van het Katholiek Documentatie Centrum* 1 (1971): 138–48.
Marsman, G. "Massa-communicatie en ontzuiling." In *Verzuiling en ontzuiling*, pp. 32–35. Hilversum: KRO, 1969.
Matthijsen, M. *Katholiek middelbaar onderwijs en intellectuele emancipatie.* Assen: Van Gorcum, 1958.
Middendorp, Cees P. *Ontzuiling, politisering en restauratie in Nederland.* Amsterdam: Boom en Meppel, 1979.
Niet bij brood alleen: CDA-verkiezingsprogram '77–'81. The Hague: CDA, 1977.
NRC-Handelsblad (Rotterdam).
Omroep ABC. Hilversum: Uitgave van het college van perschefs van AVRO, KRO, NCRV, NOS, TROS, VARA, VPRO, 1971.
Op weg naar een verantwoordelijke maatschappij. The Hague: CDA, n.d.
De Opmars (The Hague).
Oud, P. J. *Honderd jaren: Een eeuw van staatkundige vormgeving in Nederland.* 7th ed. Revised by J. Bosmans. Assen: Van Gorcum, 1979.
Peters, J. "Cijferportret van kerkelijk en onkerkelijk Nederland." *Jaarboek van het Katholiek Documentatie Centrum* 9 (1979) in print.
Piët, S. "Omroepen willen oude nestgeur weer ruiken." *NRC-Handelsblad*, 8 November 1975.
Pius Almanak: Adresboek Katholiek Nederland 1971. The Hague, 1971.
Plas, Michel van der. *Uit het rijke Roomsche leven: Een documentaire over de jaren 1925–1935.* Utrecht: Ambo, n.d.
Politiek Nieuws (The Hague).
Querido. A. *De wit-gele vlam: Gedenkbloek ter gelegenheid van het 50-jarig bestaan van de Nationale Federatie het Wit-Gele Kruis 1923–1973.* Tilburg: Bergmans, 1973.

Rip, W. *Landbouw en publiekrechtelijke bedrijfsorganisatie.* Wageningen: Veenman, 1952.
Roes, Jan. *R.K. Kerk Nederland 1958–1973: Een encyclopedisch overzicht.* Nijmegen: Dekker en Van de Vegt, 1974.
Rogier, L. J. *Geschiedenis van het Katholicisme in Noord-Nederland in de zestiende en zeventiende eeuw.* Vols. 4 and 5. Amsterdam: Elsevier, n.d.
———. *Het verschijnsel der culturele inertie bij de Nederlandse Katholieken.* Amsterdam: Urbi et Orbi, 1958.
——— and Rooy, N. de. *In vrijheid herboren: Katholiek Nederland, 1853–1953.* The Hague: Pax, 1953.
Romme, C. P. M. *Katholieke politiek.* Utrecht: Spectrum, 1953.
Rooi, R. de. "Statenverkiezingen 1966." *Socialisme en Democratie* 25, no. 5 (1966): 321–36.
Rottier, H. C. "Mijnsluitingen en de illusie van de herstructuring." *ESB,* no. 3042 (1976), pp. 229–31.
Ruitenbeek, H. *Het onstaan van de Partij van de Arbeid.* Amsterdam: Arbeiderspers, 1955.
Ruygers, C. "De Katholiek in de PvdA." *Socialisme en Democratie* 11, no. 5 (1954): 443–51.
Schendelen, M. P. van. "Groei en achtergronden van parlementair aktivisme." *Beleid en Maatschappij* 1, no. 4 (April 1974): 309–20.
Schöffer, I. "De Nederlandse confessionele partijen 1918–1939." In *De confessionelen: Onstaan en ontwikkeling van hun politieke partijen,* pp. 41–60. Edited by L. Scholten et al. Utrecht: Ambo, 1968.
Scholten, Harry. *Aspecten van het tijdschrift De Gemeenschap.* Baarn: Ambo, 1978.
Sociaal-Wetenschappelijk Instituut van de Vrije Universiteit Afdeling Politicologie. *De Nederlandse kiezers in 1967.* Amsterdam: Elsevier, 1967.
Statuten van de Katholiek Radio Omroep. Hilversum, 1973.
Steenhoff, P. *Erfgoed: Bijdrage tot geschiedenis der Katholieke Staatspartij, haar stichting en voltooing.* The Hague: Roomsch-Katholieke Staatspartij, 1939.
Stokman, S. *Het verzet van de Nederlandse bisschoppen tegen Nationaal-Socialisme.* Utrecht: Spectrum, 1945.
Thijn, Ed van. *Dagboek van een onderhandelaar, 25 mei–11 november 1977.* Amsterdam: Van Gennep, 1978.
———. "Kritische kanttekeningen bij een trek naar rechts." *Sociologische Gids* 10, no. 3 (1963): 239–48.
Thung, Mady A. *Naar een publiek ethos? Goddienstsociologische kanttekeningen bij de jaren '60 en '70.* Leiden: Leiden University Press, 1980.
Thurlings, J. M. G. *De wankele zuil: Nederlandse Katholieken tussen assimilatie en pluralisme.* 2nd ed. Deventer: Van Loghum Slaterus, 1978.
Tijn, Th. van. "De wording van de moderne politieke-partij-organisaties in Nederland." In *Vaderlands verleden in veelhoud,* pp. 590–601. Edited by G. Beekelaar. The Hague: Nijhoff, 1975.
Tulder, J. van. *Sociale stijging en daling in Nederland.* Vol. 3. Leiden: Stenfert Kroese, 1962.
Vellenga, S. *Katholiek Zuid-Limburg en het fascisme.* Assen: Van Gorcum, 1975.
Veraart, J. *Beginselen der publiekrechtelijke bedrijfsorganisatie.* Bussum: Brand, 1947.
Verberne, L. G. *De Nederlandse arbeidersbeweging in de 19^e eeuw.* Utrecht: Spectrum, 1959.

"Vergelijking per kring van aantal stemmers en betalers van de KVP in 1972." The Hague: KVP, 1973.
Verhoef, Jan. "Kiesstels en politieke samenwerking in Nederland, 1888–1917." *Acta Politica* 6, no. 3 (July 1971): 261–68.
"Verkiezingsprogram 1967 van de KVP." The Hague: KVP, 1967.
Versluis, W. G. *Beknopte geschiedenis van de Katholieke arbeidersbeweging in Nederland*. Utrecht: Dekker en Van de Vegt, 1949.
Vijf jaar kerkontwikkeling in Nederland 1967–1971. The Hague: KASKI/De Horstink, 1973.
De Volkskrant (Amsterdam).
Waarden, Frans van. "Corporatisme als probleemoplossing." In *Corporatisme in Nederland: Belangen groepen en democratie*, pp. 18–69. Edited by H. J. G. Verhallen et al. Alphen aan den Rijn: Samsom, 1980.
Werkgroep Nationaal Verkiezingsonderzoek. *De Nederlandse kiezer '72*. Alphen aan den Rijn: Samsom, 1973.
Windmuller, John P. and Galan, C. de. *Arbeidersverhoudingen in Nederland*. Vols. 1 and 2. 3rd ed. Utrecht: Spectrum, 1979.
Wöltgens, Th. "Mislukte doorbraak: Geschiedenis van de socialistische mijnwerkersbond 1909–1965." M.A. thesis, Volkshogeschool Valkenburg, 1966.
Zeegers, G. H. *God in Nederland*. Amsterdam: Van Ditmar, 1967.

Index

Aalberse, P. J. M., 41, 65, 69
Abortion, 146, 182; new legislation, 215n17
Action Group Open Church, 114
Action Group World Church, 113
Advanced Institute for Catechetics, 100
Age structure, 109, 190. *See also* Generational change
Aggiornamento, 102
Agriculture, changes in, 112
Agt, Andries van, 184
Alfrink, Cardinal Bernard, 119, 183; role in *Mandement*, 34, 120; and Pastoral Council, 102
Algemeen Handelsblad, Het, 128
Anti-Revolutionary Party (ARP), 2, 3, 65, 67, 69, 139, 140; origins, 61; program of 1878, 62; alliance with Catholics, 62–63; coalition with RKSP, 68–69; attachment to, 166; and formation of CDA, 135, 168, 182
Anti-School Law League, 61
Ariens, Father, 49, 56
Austria, 11, 56

Bahlmann, B., 62
Batavian Republic, 24
Bazuin, De, 98, 99
Beaufays, Jean, 85
Beerenbrouck, Ruys de, 69

Bekkers, Mgr. Wilhelmus, 100, 101, 102, 104, 119, 159; on television, 101, 118, 127
Belgium, 3, 4, 28, 30, 34, 35, 42, 56, 116
Berg, J. Th. J. van den, 136
Birth control, 101, 114–15
Birth rate, 44, 50–51, 88–89
Bishops: in Belgium, 30; in Germany, 109, 119; in Ireland, 119
Bishops in Netherlands: and subcultural cohesion, 30–34; number, 30; and collegiality, 30, 118; and Unitas conflict, 31; council formed, 32; and ban on Rotary International, 34; and Catholic party, 75–77; and electoral mobilization, 78–80; and changes in orientation, 99–103, 119–21; and Pastoral Council, 102; public confidence in, 114; role in Vatican II, 121; attitudes towards socio-economic organizations, 31–32, 129–31; and political cohesion, 140; withdraw support for KVP, 144–45; and John Paul II, 183–84. *See Mandement*
Blum, Leon, 90
Bluyssen, Mgr., 145
Bogaers, P., 140
"Brabant" faction, 135, 139
Brandpunt, 53, 127
Britain, political change in, 7

Broadcasting law, 137
Broek, Le Sage ten, 60
Brugmans, J., 48
Bruyn, de, A. C., 77
Butler, David, 7, 133, 159

Cabinet, role of, 70–71
Callier, Mgr., 76
Cals, J. M. L. Th., 137, 138, 153, 167
Calvinism, 21, 26–28, 120
Calvinists, 16–17, 50, 166, 182
Campen, J. van der, 47
Canada, 2, 213n6
Canon law, 39
Capucin order, 31
Carnival celebrations, 27–28
Catechesis, 99, 100, 128
Campbell, Angus, 6, 180
Catholic Action, 36, 44, 197n119
Catholic Broadcasting Organization (KRO), 16, 65, 121, 133, 187–88; founding, 26, 27; directors, 47; viewer recognition, 52–53; and electoral mobilization, 83, 144; role in change, 118; membership figures, 121–22; criticism of, 127; and deconfessionalization, 127
Catholic Bureau for Internal Migration, 47
Catholic businessmen, 54
Catholic Civil Service Union, 126
Catholic Conservative party (Switzerland), 4, 5
Catholic Council of Discussion, 46, 131
Catholic Council for Social Welfare, 47, 130
Catholic educational system, 25, 49–50, 128, 130. *See also* Catholic University; Schools issue
Catholic Emigration Bureau, 47
Catholic Employers' Federation, 124
Catholic farmers, voting behaviour of, 155–56
Catholic Farmers' Association (KNBTV), 36, 44, 45, 123, 188; relations with Catholic party, 74; and deconfessionalization, 127
Catholic Goat Breeders' Association, 41

Catholic Health Care Organization (White-Yellow Cross), 29, 44, 123, 124, 173
Catholic Higher School of Economics, 129
Catholic Illustrated, 15
Catholic Life, 105
Catholic Marriage Bureau, 123
Catholic Miners' Union, 42, 52
Catholic National Party (KNP), 76–77, 96
Catholic newspapers, 16–17, 123; and deconfessionalization, 127–28
Catholic party (Belgium), 4, 5
Catholic party (Netherlands), 1–5, 10, 23, 47, 58 ff.; origins, 60–64; and schools issue, 62–63; instrumentality of, 64–67; representation in cabinet, 69; policy and programs, 68–69; leadership, 69–70; relations between cabinet and parliamentary party, 70–71; personnel, 72–73; and *kieskring, statenkring* organizations, 72–73, 80, 81, 139, 143; and electoral lists, 73; and pressure groups, 73–75; and trade unions, 74–75; and relations with church, 75–78; and electoral mobilization, 78–86; selling of party memberships, 81; propaganda council, 81–82. *See also* Catholic People's Party; League of Roman Catholic Electoral Associations; Roman Catholic State Party
Catholic People's Party (KVP), 1–5; vote for, 1–3, 86–95, 146 ff., 176; compared with other European Catholic parties, 4–5; founding, 66–67; coalitions with Labour party, 67–68, 137, 141; policies and programs, 68–69, 138–39, 141; and primaries, 72; decolonization policy, 76; membership, 85, 142; factions within, 76–77, 135, 137, 139; defections from, 135, 139; and Pastoral Council, 137; and intraparty conflict, 137; youth movement, 140; fundraising, 142; and public opinion polls, 144, 176; and withdrawal of

church support, 144–45; voters' attachment to, 165–66; composition of parliamentary party, 202nn46, 48
Catholic population: as minority, 4, 13–14; in cities, regions, 13, 92–94; and ethnicity, 13–19; and race, 13–14; and language, 14; and culture, 15; life-style, 16–17, 110–12; civil rights of, 21, 24–25; decline in, 22, 91, 116; educational level, 49–51, 110; increase in, 91, 92, 109; defections from, 91–92. *See also* Age structure; Birth rate
Catholic Policemen's Union, 126
Catholic Retailers' Organization (KNOB), 45, 132, 188; representation in Catholic party, 74–75; role in fund-raising, 82; decline in membership, 124; merger with Protestant Retailers, 124; merger with neutral retailers, 124; voting behaviour, 155; and collapse of Cals cabinet, 155
Catholic Social Action, 41, 42
Catholic Social Research Institute (KASKI), 82, 88, 104
Catholic socio-economic organizations, 41 ff.; service function, 51–52; and deconfessionalization, 131
Catholic Textile Workers' Union, 56
Catholic trade unions: origins, 29; and clergy, 41; membership, 122–23; voting behaviour, 155–56
Catholic Trade Union Federation (NKV), 42, 45, 74; survey of membership, 125; and proposed trade union merger, 125–26; merger with NVV, 126; relations with KVP
Catholic Transport Workers' Union, 141
Catholic University, 32, 43; founding, 26, 29; theological faculty, 105; and deconfessionalization, 129
Catholic vote: in Belgium, 4, 5; in Germany, 4, 179; in Italy, 4, 5; in Switzerland, 4, 5
Catholic vote in Netherlands: for Catholic party, 1–4; for KVP, 86 ff., 146 ff., 176; and religiosity, 86–89; and birth rate, 88–89; and rationality, 89–91; and context, 91–95, 148–53; and rural-urban cleavage, 92–93, 148–53; and deconfessionalization, 147; and class, 153–56, 180–81; and organizational membership, 155; and geographical mobility, 157; and generational change, 7, 159–62; dispersion of, 167–72; for smaller parties, 167–72; for PVdA and VVD, 168–72, 180–81; for CDA, 180–82
Catholic Workers' Movement, 74–75
Celibacy rule, 104, 106–8
Central Bureau of Statistics survey (1956), 16–17
Centre Party (Germany), 4, 179
Christian Democratic Appeal (CDA), 2–3, 125, 144, 169, 172, 177, 180–82
Christian Democratic faction, 135
Christian Democratic Party (CDU) (Germany), 154
Christian Democratic Party (DC) (Italy), 4, 5, 154
Christian Employers' Federation (NCW), 125, 131, 188
Christian Historical Union (CHU), 2, 3, 67, 68, 182
Church authority, 19 ff.; in politics, 75–80, 145; recession of, 97 ff., 184
Church doctrine, 18, 99 ff.
"Church and Everyday Life," 130
Clergy: in post-Reformation period, 23; and church organization, 34; as authority figures, 35; numbers, 35, 109; training, 39–40; recruitment, 39–40, 103, 109; and electoral mobilization, 78–80; and pressures for change, 103; views on celibacy, 106–8; age structure, 109; reaction to change, 119–20; and generational change, 120; political preferences, 146; feuds with Gijsen, 183
Cock, Theodore de, 22
Codde, Peter, 22
Coleman, John A., 99, 100

Colijn, H., 69
Collegiality: among bishops, 30-31, 183; at parish level, 103, 108
Compulsory voting law, 80, 170, 212n66
Confessional, 37-38, 101
Confrontatie (Confrontation), 109, 116, 184
Congar, Y., 99
Conservative party, 62
Consociational democracy. *See* Elite accommodation
Context: and voting behaviour, 91-95, 148-53; and generational change, 161
Corporatism, 45-47
Counter-Reformation, 23

Daalder, Hans, 69, 71, 189
Deaneries, 28-29
Deconfessionalization, 97 ff. *See also* Catholic socio-economic organizations; Catholic vote
Democratic Centre faction, 135
Democratic Socialists '70 (DS'70), 3, 170, 173
Democrats '66 (D'66), 3, 142, 167-69, 173
Dennis, Jack, 6, 180
Depillarization, 9, 209n1
Diels, A. E., 50, 51
Diocesan autonomy, 30
Dioceses, 28, 55, 57, 101
Discrimination against Catholics, 21, 26, 84
Dittrich, Karl, 171-73
Dodewaart, Mgr. van, 101, 104
Duinkerken, Anton van, 15
Dutch Society for Sexual Reform, 102
Dutch State Mines (DSM), 52
Dutch Trade Union Federation (NVV), 122-26, 141, 156
Duverger, Maurice, 199n1

Easter observance, 55-56
Ecclesiastical hierarchy, 12, 25, 33, 97. *See also* Bishops in Netherlands
Economy: in sixteenth century, 20; in eighteenth and nineteenth centuries, 48-49; in interwar period, 89-90; in postwar period, 40-41, 110-13, 123
Education. *See* Catholic educational system; Catholic population; Catholic University; Schools issue
Education Act, 25
Eiberger, Van, 125
Eighty Years' War, 20, 22
Eindhoven, 92
Electoral districts, 72-74, 143
Electoral franchise, 62-63
Electoral system, 191n3, 200n23; effect on Catholic party, 62-63, 65
Elite accommodation, 1, 25, 62-65, 67-71, 90. *See also* Interbloc cooperation; Pacification; Pillarization; Schools issue
Emancipation ideology, 24-26
Erasmus, 20
Ethnicity, and subcultures, 11-12

Farmers' Party (BP), 168-69, 173
Fasting, 34
Federation of Dutch Unions (FNV), 208n85
First Chamber, 74
"Foundation and Character of the KVP," 134, 137
Foundation for Cooperating Cross Associations, 124
France, 27, 42, 56, 182, 191n6
Furnivall, J. S., 11

G-3, 98
Gadourek, I., 15, 16, 88, 89, 177
Generational change, 110, 119-20, 159-62
Geographical mobility, 31-32, 42, 157-58
German occupation (1940-45): effect on Catholic organizations, 32-33; role of bishops, 32-33; effect on interbloc cooperation, 66
Germany, 4, 8, 9, 11, 12, 35, 42, 44, 55, 119, 154-55, 179
Gielen, J., 85
Gijsen, Mgr. Johannes, 114, 183
Goddijn, W., 92, 166

Hamilton, Richard F., 12
Hanssen, Mgr., 84
Heek, F. van, 27
Hees, Nico van, 102
Hoggart, Richard, 15
Houska, Joseph, 189
Humanae Vitae, 106, 115

Ideology of Dutch Catholicism, 19 ff.
Industrialization: in Limburg, 42; in late nineteenth century, 49; in postwar period, 112
Inglehart, Ronald, 159
Interbloc cooperation, 66, 178
Interfaith marriages, 10, 123
Intergenerational mobility, 157–59
Isolationist mentality, 20–24

Jansen, Fons, 115
Jansenism, 22, 27, 50, 175
Jansenius, Cornelius, 27
Jesuit order, 23, 105
John XXIII, 102
John Paul II, 117, 183–84
Jong, Cardinal de, 32, 33, 34, 40, 66, 103

KAB. *See* Catholic Workers' Movement
KASKI. *See* Catholic Social Research Institute
Katholieke Volkspartij (KVP). *See* Catholic People's Party
Kemenade, J. A. van, 128, 166
Key, V. O., 167
Kieskringen, 72–74, 80–81, 139, 143
Kilsdonk, Jan van, 104
Klarenbeekse Club, 23–24, 98
Klompé, Marga, 136
Kloos, A. H., 125
KRO. *See* Catholic Broadcasting Organization
Kruijt, J. P., 209n1
Kulturkampf (Germany), 40, 54
Kusters, W. J. J., 81, 190
Kuyper, Abraham, 61
KVP. *See* Catholic People's Party
KVP, De, 143
KVP-Radicals, 135

Labour party (PVDA), 2, 3, 75, 141, 146, 164, 167–72, 180–82; coalition with KVP, 74, 90–91; and electoral mobilization, 83; Catholic caucus in, 33, 60, 76–77; links with NVV, 141
Lay councils, 100–101, 108
League of Roman Catholic Electoral Associations (BRKKV), 1, 26, 63, 64
Leo XIII, 41
Liberal party (VVD), 2, 3, 68, 91, 167–71, 180; coalition with KVP, 67–68, 91, 137
Liberals, 25, 60, 63
Lijphart, Arend, 1, 87, 154
Linie, De, 105
Lipschits, I., 135
Lorwin, Val, 11
Lubac, H. de, 99
Lubbers, Ruud, 184

McCrone, Donald, 6, 180
Mackie, T., 5
Mandement (1954), 24, 26, 33, 98, 102, 119, 134, 140, 188; and trade unions, 45; effect on KVP, 77, 85; and electoral mobilization, 79; defended by Catholic politicians, 84–85; repeal of, 97
Mass, changes in, 108, 116
Mass attendance, 55–56, 87, 110, 116–17, 147
Matthijsen, M., 49
Merger of confessional parties, 2, 182–83
Mertens, 125
Migration, 31, 42, 112–13
Modernist movement, 18
Molleman, H. A. A., 136
Mutsaers, Father, 41

National Socialism (Germany), 8, 179
National Socialist party (NSB) (Netherlands), 32, 78, 121
Natural gas, discovery of, 75
Neerkassel, J. van, 22
Neo-Malthusian Society, 102
Neutral Trade Union Federation. *See* Dutch Trade Union Federation

New Catholic Party, 81
Newspapers, 16–17, 123, 127–28
Nieuwe Linie, De, 105
Nieuwe Rotterdamsche Courant, 128
"Night of Schmelzer," 137–38, 147, 153–55, 164–65
NKV. *See* Catholic Trade Union Federation
Nolens, W., 70, 76, 138
Noort, Father van der, 41
Norway, 8
Nuclear weapons, 216n18
Nuyens, W., 60
NVV. *See* Dutch Trade Union Federation

Old Catholic Church, 22
Olson, Mancur, 36
Opmars, De, 82–85, 87, 143
Overlapping memberships, 47

Pacification (1917), 25, 26, 63, 67–68
Pacification of Ghent (1576), 20
Pacifist Socialist Party (PSP), 145–46
Papal infallibility, 18
Papo-Thorbecke coalition, 25, 60–61
Parishes, 29, 100–101, 108
Parliament of the Netherlands, 58–59, 70–71, 74
Party identification, theory of, 6–8, 180, 192n18
Party identification in Netherlands, 7–9, 166, 179–80, 214n13; among Catholics, 7–9, 88–89, 181–82
Pastoral Council (1966–70), 102, 108, 118, 130; and KVP, 136; apolitical character of, 136–37
Pastoral Institute of Dutch Church Province (PINK), 205n9
Perquin, W., 47, 74
Petersen, William, 44, 48
Philips Electronics, 92
Pillar, 9, 193n25
Pluralism, 11
Poeisz, J., 18–19
Poels, H. A., 42–43, 49, 52; role in Catholic Miners' Union, 42; and electoral mobilization, 79

Poland, 42
Poldersveldt, Dommer van, 60
Political change: in Netherlands, 1–9, 185; theories of, 6–9; in Britain, 7; in Weimar Germany, 8–9, 179–80
Politiek Nieuws, 144
Prinsterer, Groen van, 25, 61
Proportional representation. *See* Electoral system
Protestantism. *See* Anti-Revolutionary Party; Calvinism
Publicly Ordered Enterprises (PBO), 46
PVDA. *See* Labour party

Quadragesimo Anno, 43
Quanta Cura, 25, 61
Quay, J. E. de, 96

Radio and television organizations, 15, 52, 121, 122, 127, 207n69. *See also* Catholic Broadcasting Organization
Radio program guide, 16–17
Railway strike (1903), 49
Recreational activities, 18
Reformed Church, 21. *See also* Calvinism
Repillarization, 183
Rerum Novarum, 41, 42, 62–63, 98
Revolt of the Netherlands (1566), 20
"Rich Roman Life" (*Rijke Roomsche Leven*), 15, 16, 26
Rogier, L. J., 21, 24, 27, 31
Rogowski, Ronald, 193n25, 204n96
Roman Catholic Central Council of Corporate Organization, 45
Roman Catholic Electoral Association of North Brabant, 61, 63
Roman Catholic Party of the Netherlands (RKPN), 170, 193n26
Roman Catholic People's Party, 81
Roman Catholic State Party (RKSP), 1, 26, 32; founding, 64; role in coalition cabinets, 66, 89; policy and programs, 67–68; and Catholic labour, 69; leadership, 72
Romme, C. P. M., 67, 120, 138; as parliamentary leader, 70; and

coalition with PVDA, 75; and *Mandement*, 77; and *De Volkskrant*, 81
Roomsch-Katholiek Staatspartij. *See* Roman Catholic State Party
Rotary International, 34
Roth, Guenther, 11, 178
Rovenius, Philip, 22
Ruijgers, 77
Rural-urban cleavage, 92–95, 148–53, 161

Saint Michäel League, 63–64
Saint Michäel Legion, 113
Saint Raphaël, 41
Sasbout, 22, 27
Sassenheim, 15, 177
Schaepman, H., 23, 134; elected to Second Chamber, 61; interconfessional cooperation, 64–65; as parliamentary leader, 69–70
Schaveren, J. van, 81
Schillebeeckx, Edward, 98–99, 101
Schism of Utrecht, 22, 27
Schmelzer, Norbert, 137, 164; as parliamentary leader, 138; role in KVP-Radicals split, 141; and abortion issue, 146. *See also* "Night of Schmelzer"
Schöffer, I., 15, 68, 72
Schools issue, 25, 49, 61–63, 67, 84
Schoonenberg, Piet, 99
Second Chamber, 58–59, 70
Second Vatican Council. *See* Vatican II
Segmental pluralism, 11
Seminaries, 40, 102, 105
Septuagint, 105, 116
Shell, Royal Dutch, 125
Shively, W. P., 8–9, 12, 174, 179
Simonis, Mgr. A., 183
Smith, M. G., 11
Social Christian Party (Belgium), 4, 5
Social Democratic Party (SPD) (Germany), 11, 178–79
Social Democratic Party (SDAP) (Netherlands), 26, 63, 66, 69, 78, 90
Social Economic Council (SER), 46
Socialist Broadcasting Organization (VARA), 121–22, 144
Socialist Mineworkers' Union, 52
Socialist Trade Union Federation. *See*

Dutch Trade Union Federation
Son, J. B. van, 61
Spain, 20, 35
Spiritual advisers, 29, 36, 44
Standaard, De, 61
Statenkringen, 72–74
Steenberghe, M. P. L., 77
Steenkamp, Piet, 136, 184
Stigmata, 11–12
Stokes, Donald, 7, 133, 159
Stokman, Father S., 67, 74, 76, 77, 140, 143
Subcultural cohesion, 9, 177–79
Subculture, definition of, 11–12
Sweden, 20
Switzerland, 4, 5, 12, 35
Syllabus of Errors, 25
Synod (1980), 183–84

Tariff law (1862), 61
Te Elfder Ure, 98, 105
Television. *See* Radio and television organizations
Tendance, 182–83
Textile Workers' Union. *See* Unitas
Theology, changes in, 98 ff.
Thomassen, J., 214n13
Thorbecke, J., 25
Thurlings, J. M. G., 27, 103, 116–17, 120, 123
Tijd, De, 60, 128
Trade unions, origins of, 48–49. *See also* Catholic trade unions; Catholic Trade Union Federation; Catholic Workers' Movement; Dutch Trade Union Federation
Troelstra, P. J., 26, 45, 90

Ultramontaan, De, 60
Underground churches, 21, 22, 28
Unilever, 125
Union of Utrecht (1579), 20
Unitas, 31, 56, 199n158
United States, 6, 167
Unity Movement, 33
"Universal Civilized Dutch," 14

Van der Grinten commission, 76–77
VARA. *See* Socialist Broadcasting Organization

Vatican, 23, 100, 114, 183–84
Vatican II, 99, 100, 102, 115, 116, 118, 119, 121, 123, 134, 159
Vellenga, S., 78
Verhoef, J., 189
Veringa, Gerhard, 142
Vet, Mgr. de, 101
Volkskrant, De, 37, 81, 83, 85
Voting behaviour: in Canada, 2, 213n6; in Germany, 2, 4, 5, 8, 9, 153–54, 178–80; in Italy, 4, 5, 153–54; in U.S., 2, 6, 167; in Britain, 7; and mass attendance, 87, 147; and organizational membership, 87, 155; and birth rate, 88–89; and rural-urban cleavage, 92–95, 148–53, 161; in France, 153–54, 182–83, 191n6; and occupation, 153–56; and gender, 155; and generational change, 159–62; and political issues, 164–67
Vrije Volk, Het, 102
VVD. *See* Liberal party

Wage and price controls, 75, 90–91
Weimar Germany, 4, 8, 9, 179
Welter, C., 76, 137
White-Yellow Cross. *See* Catholic Health Care Organization
Willebrands, Cardinal J., 183
William II, 25, 60
Windmuller, J., 199n158
Witteman, 67
Wolinetz, Steven B., 3, 87, 148, 167

Yugoslavia, 42

Zeegers, G., 166

THE LIBRARY
ST. MARY'S COLLEGE OF MARYLAND
ST. MARY'S CITY, MARYLAND 20686